The Newsprint Mask

The Newsprint Mask

The Tradition of the
Fictional Journalist in America

INTRODUCED AND EDITED BY

Welford Dunaway Taylor

Iowa State University Press / Ames

Welford Dunaway Taylor is professor of English
at the University of Richmond, Virginia.

©1991 Iowa State University Press, Ames, Iowa 50010
All rights reserved

Manufactured in the United States of America
⊚ This book is printed on acid-free paper.

First edition, 1991

Library of Congress Cataloging-in-Publication Data

The Newsprint mask : the tradition of the fictional journalist in America / introduced
and edited by Welford Dunaway Taylor.—1st ed.
    p. cm.
    Includes bibliographical references and index.
    ISBN 0-8138-0682-8 (alk. paper)
    1. American newspapers—History. 2. Anonyms and pseudonyms, American.
I. Taylor, Welford Dunaway.
PN4832.N49 1991
071'.3—dc20   90-40072

For D. Tennant Bryan,

a mirror for Lord Chesterfield

I TAKE UP A VOLUME of Doctor Smollett, or a volume of the *Spectator,* and say that fiction carries a greater amount of truth in solution than the volume which purports to be true. Out of the fictitious book I get the expression of the life of the time; of the manners, of the movement, the dress, the pleasures, the laughter, the ridicules of society—the old times live again. . . . Can the heaviest historian do more for me?

—WILLIAM MAKEPEACE THACKERAY, *Steele*

Contents

7. COLYUMNISTS

8. CRACKER-BARREL PHILOSOPHERS

Preface

*T*HESE PAGES trace a design that presently lies disconnected and largely forgotten. For, strangely, the journalistic masks created by American authors have never been recognized as constituting a separate literary tradition. It is true that most such creations have been given piecemeal acknowledgment—as fictional humorists, satirists, political caricatures, commonsense philosophers, or vehicles of light entertainment—but never as members of a single company whose primary function is to provide a device through which a journalistic author may speak with impunity in a frank, and usually engaging, manner.

This patterning of representative examples seems both overdue and timely. During the last fifty years, as journalism has burgeoned as an American enterprise, its chief exponents have ceased to need the subterfuge of a fictional mask. They have moved to syndicated columns (complete with by-lines and photographs), to radio, and finally to the electronic screen that brings them face-to-face with their audience. The fictional mask has all but disappeared from the American newspaper.

In giving this endangered genre the recognition it has long deserved, this volume traces salient patterns of development and presents a selection of primary texts. These two components exist symbiotically: a solitary essay on development would prove frustrating, as it would draw upon many inaccessible sources; yet the texts would have limited meaning were their connections not explained. Nevertheless, at first glance this may seem a gallery of strange bedfellows, juxtaposing authors and genres that are traditionally given identifying labels other than those assigned here.

Nor, given the disarray of American newspaper archives and the voluminous sources, can one ever be certain that all potential examples have been examined. Moreover, while American newspapers feature a wealth of pseudonymous writing, many putative "authors" are characterized little if at all. In the interest of presenting a series of recognizable fictional characters, examples of the latter extreme were rejected. There are, however, considerable gradations between pseudonymous neutrality and fully developed characterization. Editorial discretion has dictated the inclusion or rejection of debatable examples. Questions of inclusion or omission should not obscure the central aim of demonstrating the unifying principle of the journalistic eidolon. This perspective will, it is hoped, invite recognition, reevaluation, and further exploration.

A substantial number of institutions and individuals have aided in the preparation of *The Newsprint Mask.* Grants and fellowships from the John Stewart Bryan Foundation and from the Faculty Research Committee of the University of Richmond provided indispensable assistance. In addition to thanking these generous entities, I owe special debts of gratitude to their prime movers, D. Tennant Bryan and William S. Woolcott.

Research assistance was supplied by librarians at the Alderman Library of the University of Virginia, the Library of Congress, the Boatwright Memorial Library of the University of Richmond, and the Virginia State Library. In particular, I thank Marcia Whitehead, Kate Duvall, Sue Ratchford, Erwin Davis, and the late Milton C. Russell.

I am also indebted to the editors of *American Literature* for advertising for examples of the journalistic mask and to the following individuals who offered advice and assistance in various forms: Walter Blair, Reba Collins, Judith Fernandez, Melvin J. Friedman, David Leary, Steven Nash, Cameron Nickels, George Scheer, Mary Wheatley, Stuart Wheeler, Wendy Thompson, and Norris C. Yates.

As this project occupies the cusp of my typewriting and word-processing phases, I am grateful to the patient and able colleagues who dragged me kicking and swearing into the age of high technology: notably Louise Bickerstaff, Lois Morley, Carolyn Ratcliffe, Rusty von Klein, and various members of the University of Richmond Computer Center.

Finally, I owe various thanks to the following for permissions to reprint certain selections: Charles R. McDowell, Jr. (two "Aunt Gertrude" letters); the Macmillan Publishing Company ("The Country Newspaper," from *Abe Martin's Broadcast* by Frank McKinney Hubbard; copyright 1930, renewed © 1958 by Bobbs-Merrill); the University Press of Virginia ("Buck Fever Says" and "The Three Hens" from *The Buck Fever Papers*); and the Will Rogers Memorial (numerous selections from *The Writings of Will Rogers*). Special thanks go to Professor Richard E. Yates, who supplied texts and permissions for two "Hardscrabble" letters and allowed himself to be disclosed as their author.

In this, as in all other projects, I again thank my wife, Carole. Her support, assistance, understanding, and calm presence provide an irreplaceable sustenance.

The Newsprint Mask

Introduction

DESPITE ITS CLAIM to a long and distinguished history, the modern American newspaper bears only a shallow resemblance to its journalistic ancestors of the colonial period. In addition to obvious changes in size, design, writing styles, editorial policies, and advertising content, the newspaper of today is much less a product of the contemporary literary ferment than was its counterpart of 250 years ago. Journalism became firmly established in the American colonies during the first quarter of the eighteenth century, at the same time that the simple news sheets of England were being supplanted by journals whose staple was the familiar essay. The essay established immediately and irrevocably the principle that news journals need not simply purvey the facts of recent events; they could just as well contain imaginative, polished forms of expression that characterize literature itself. Indeed, among those responsible for establishing the familiar essay were the most prominent names in contemporary English letters—Defoe, Swift, Steele, Addison. But it was Steele who introduced into the genre one of its most enhancing literary elements. This was the fictitious journalist—sometimes called an eidolon, mask, or persona—who was able to speak with an openness impossible for its creator, while maintaining its own credibility and engaging mien.

Steele's first eidolon was Isaac Bickerstaff, Esq. Already known, though only as a pseudonym with which Jonathan Swift had signed a pamphlet series the previous year, Bickerstaff was given a distinctive personality, an easily recognizable mode of dress and manners, a coterie of friends, and a round of weekly activities that fleshed him out as the putative editor-author of the new journal. Beginning with the inaugural issue of the *Tatler* (12 April 1709), Bickerstaff enjoyed, through 271 triweekly issues, a widespread esteem among London readers that was rare for a fictional creation. His immense popularity following the *Tatler*'s demise in 1711 was even more remarkable.

Steele's creation of Isaac Bickerstaff as his narrator was more than a deft stroke of characterization. The presence of this shadowy figure, who assumed the position that an actual author-editor would normally occupy, represented both a culmination and an alteration of existing literary elements. One of the chief reasons why Bickerstaff attracted attention was that he had been endowed with sufficient accoutrements of the contemporary London ambiance to make him recognizable within this context. Portraying character through the use of familiar detail was by no means novel, however. Character sketches, cast in the classical mold of Theophrastus by such English authors as Joseph Hall, John Earle, and Sir Thomas Overbury, had enjoyed considerable vogue in the seventeenth century. These were stereotypes such as Puritans, scholars, or gallants—in other words, an aggregation of specific details adumbrating a generalized type or category.

Toward the end of the seventeenth century, the influence of La Bruyère's *Caractères* became felt in England, and this new strain of character writing was in no small way reflected in the *Tatler.* Concentrating upon topics of current interest such as fashion, customs, the town, and the court, and illustrated by character sketches of individual examples reflecting the author's observations, La Bruyère's *Caractères* were natural paradigms for an eidolon whose musings were to be aimed at manners, morals, virtues, and vices. Thus, in the manner of the French author, Steele's observations were exemplified by characters in Bickerstaff's circle such as the pedant Tom Folio and the poetaster Ned Softly.

While Bickerstaff characterized himself in general terms as a censor, he was in actuality a unique personality, who expressed highly individualized opinions upon the passing London parade. It is true that Jonathan Swift had recently used "Isaac Bickerstaff" as a pseudonym, but there was nothing remarkable about this fact. Swift had employed simply a fictitious name and had the pamphlets themselves not achieved such notoriety, it would have attracted little attention. In an age when periodical writing was characteristically left anonymous or was signed with a pseudonym that might reflect the content of the text to which it was appended, Bickerstaff as editor-author of the *Tatler* stands out in bold relief. For here was a pseudonym become a character; a narrator become a persona; a former generality become unique. Thus the *Tatler* is distinguished as "the first essay journal to use in a subtle and substantial way the device of assumed author-editorship" (Bond 1963, 113).

Nor was Steele's innovative creation a halting start that would look to future authors for development. Rather, the personality of Bickerstaff was so fully realized, and the course upon which he was to guide his journal so clearly charted, that Steele's eidolon, no less than his intended mission, can be said to have been established from the outset. When examples of the fictional journalist are cited, Bickerstaff usually comes first to mind. For example Richmond P. Bond, whose detailed descriptions of the eidolon have established a foundation for definition, has relied heavily upon Bickerstaff for his criteria. In his seminal essay, "Isaac Bickerstaff, Esq.," he offers an assessment of the type:

> Bickerstaff became a person who conducted the *Tatler* and was the writer of all the words on his leaf of letterpress save for some of the epistles and of course the hundreds of advertisements; Steele and Addison and the others were, shall we say his agents or amanuenses, or so we must allow if we are willing to play in the game of fictitious authorship by its most vigorous rules.
>
> The persona as a device in periodical literature has not been so carefully studied as the eidolon in other types or media, and there are special characteristics for the mask in an essay journal. . . . [But] the eidolon of an essay paper, if he would have a long and good life, must be an interesting individual in his own right, with enough personality to attract and preserve his band of followers. He must have admirable traits without ascending to the dull paragon, but he can wander from normality and typicality with quirks and eccentric wiles so long as he does not descend to such disconformities as will forfeit him the confidence and respect and even affection that his audience expects and desires to give him. . . . The effective persona, we see, should establish himself in the minds and also the hearts of his day-to-week-to-month adherents as a man worthy of welcome acceptance, humanly constituted but not sacrosanct or enveloping, a participant in the current circus of mundane things but not its major end. If he can maintain the center road between the definite and the indefinite and wear his character mask to speak his lines with fictive sincerity and

> reasonable authority, he will promote his purpose, be it lit-
> erary, social, political, philosophical. (Bond 1963, 113–14)

These guidelines for the ideal persona, for which Bickerstaff may be seen as an essential paradigm, represented a tall
order for subsequent practitioners and one seldom filled in
every respect. Still, with Bickerstaff as a primary influence,
journalists have continued to embellish their sheets with fictional personalities, even though they have seldom allowed
them to dominate entire journals as Bickerstaff had done.
After the demise of the *Tatler* new journals and eidolons not
only proliferated, but the voices of fictional journalists would
continue to be heard thereafter.

Literary conventions, like certain species of flora, can occasionally be transplanted to a foreign soil and produce a
strain more vigorous than in the country of origin. Of the
numerous literary translocations from England to the American colonies, the fictitious persona in journalism is a solid
example. In the mid-1710s, while the *Tatler*'s popularity remained strong, and while similar creations (e.g., Addison and
Steele's Mr. Spectator and Steele's Nestor Ironside of the
Guardian) were appearing, James Franklin left Boston to
learn the printing trade in London (Cook 1912, 4). The new
periodical fare he encountered was quite different from that
of his native city, where the single newspaper, the *Boston
News-Letter,* was published by a printer named John Camp-
bell, who bragged of never once having sullied his pages with
opinions, ideas, or arguments (Cook 1912, 15).

The *News-Letter*'s editorial posture seemed both appropriate and safe for a newspaper published in Boston at this
time. For, although in its waning years, the long dark shadow
of the Mathers still brooded over public morals and expression. It was against the entrenched Massachusetts theocrats,
no less than against the lackluster *News-Letter,* that James
Franklin introduced his *New England Courant* on 7 August
1721. Like English essay journals of the time the *Courant,*
while not indifferent to current news, was more interested in
opinion for its primary content and in satire (as opposed to
flat reportage) for its tone. It incorporated, in other words,
"the very tricks and manners of Addison and Steele" (Cook
1912, 15), which James had observed firsthand in London
and which discerning American readers were enjoying in im-

ported copies. It was therefore not surprising that Franklin's English borrowings should soon be embellished with a fictional journalist fashioned somewhat after Isaac Bickerstaff, but adorned with the trappings of a contemporary Bostonian. Her name was Silence Dogood, obviously a sobriquet both descriptive and satiric. Silence's verisimilitude, like Bickerstaff's, derived from the native ambiance. Orphaned at an early age, married young to a Puritan divine, widowed, and subsequently the proprietress of a respectable boarding-house, she discourses over such topics as the education of children, female vices and virtues, pride, hypocrisy, and drunkenness. In addition to these topics of current interest, Silence occasionally ventures into more hazardous areas by professing herself "a mortal enemy to arbitrary government and unlimited power." "Jealous for the rights and liberties of [her] country," she declares that the least encroachment is "apt to make [her] blood boil exceedingly" (Franklin 1959, 1:13). Silence Dogood's appearance in the *Courant* was as little expected as that of Bickerstaff in the *Tatler*. The first of her pieces had been mysteriously pushed under James Franklin's door one spring night in 1722. The initial offering promised fortnightly installments, all thirteen of which were enthusiastically carried in the *Courant*. Still, it was not until after the last had appeared on 8 October that James Franklin learned the identity of the author. It was his young half brother and apprentice, Benjamin. Benjamin Franklin's comments on natural rights and representative government, made through this rustic New England mask, represent an incipient assertion of certain Enlightenment ideals which, expressed some half-century later, would resound throughout the colonies.

Within a few years after Silence Dogood's brief career in the *Courant* ended, similar attempts at characterization were made in several other colonies. By early 1729 Benjamin Franklin, well established as a citizen of Philadelphia and the moving force behind the Junto (a social and debating society), was anxious to acquire a newspaper of his own. To accomplish this end, he and his fellow Juntoists enlisted the aid of a journalistic personality whom they created and called "Busy-Body." Though the lineaments of this character were not so sharply defined as those of Silence Dogood, for thirty-two weeks Busy-Body's loquacious opinions appeared in the

American Weekly Mercury of Philadelphia. Busy-Body's remarks on topics ranging from social behavior to actual persons thinly disguised by Latin names, brought unprecedented economic success to the *Mercury*. This windfall was
achieved at the expense of a rival newspaper, the *Pennsylvania Gazette*, whose value became so depressed that Franklin
was able to purchase it on a distress basis.

Franklin was not the only creator of fictional newspaper
personalities in the American colonies. For the 10 December
1728 issue of his *Maryland Gazette*, editor William Parks
had created Plain Dealer, who in some respects resembled
Isaac Bickerstaff as well as Silence Dogood and Busy-Body.
Like these predecessors, Plain Dealer was intended as a censor, but beyond this general trait, he showed little in the way
of distinguishing features. However, Parks was soon to be off
for Williamsburg, where he would found a new journal, the
Virginia Gazette. It was for this Virginia weekly that he
created an eidolon who surpassed the creations of Franklin in
terms of imagination, variety, and artistic flair. The earliest
existing number of the *Virginia Gazette*, that of 10 September 1736, introduces Parks's new character. Called "Monitor," he speaks in the voice of a cultivated, levelheaded
gentleman. As his title would suggest, he is often called upon
to adjudicate the arguments contained in letters from readers
and is frequently appealed to for advice. In the latter capacity,
he suggests the Ann Landers and Abigail Van Burens of a
later period in American journalism. And, like the eidolons of
Addison, Steele, and Benjamin Franklin, he is the central figure in a coterie of characters who frequently make their appearance in his columns. They seem to have been inspired
both by Restoration comedy and by the Fiddle-faddle Club,
which had been an ornament of the *London Magazine* three
years before (Cook 1912, 189). But it was the Monitor, making known his convictions on manners and social behavior as
well as on weightier matters such as poetry, music, aesthetic
theory, and moral questions, who gives the essays the distinction of having been called by one of the most respected
historians of American journalism "pieces of light social
satire, unique in kind, and surpassed by very few colonial
writings up to 1737" (Cook 1912, 213).

As publisher of a newspaper in a colony whose church
and government represented an extension of English author-

ity, Parks not surprisingly drew heavily upon journals then appearing in the mother country, where he had begun his printing career (Cook 1912, 156–213 and passim). The Monitor exhibits far more of an English cast than does Silence Dogood, for instance. Poems, essays, satiric sketches, and other literary pieces that had formerly appeared in English journals were published in the Williamsburg paper in whole or in part. But the source of such offerings is less significant than the fact that by the mid-1730s American journalism had established itself as a medium that was literary as well as factual in character—a commingling that has persisted in varying degrees to the present day.

The majority of essays, letters, and sketches that were signed by pseudonyms in American journals are scarcely deserving of mention in the company of eidolons like Monitor and Silence Dogood. This is because they represent little or no attempt at characterization. For example, the letters that Franklin signed with "Anthony Afterwit," "Celia Single," and "Alice Addertongue" represent only a vague, halfhearted attempt to match a putative author with appropriate subject matter. The list of unknown contributors signing themselves with Latinisms such as "Rusticus," "Ridentius," "Publius," "Cato," "Vindex," etc., and making a single and final appearance in a colonial weekly would probably number in the hundreds. Using Latin as well as English for their noms de plume, both would-be authors and recognized ones followed the practice. Samuel Adams alone is said to have used some twenty-five pseudonyms on various occasions, and his case seems by no means uncharacteristic (Bleyer 1927, 82–83). A modern edition of the prose writings of Philip Freneau, mostly gleaned from newspapers, reveals no fewer than forty-four pen names (Freneau 1955, 23).

What, it may be asked, inspired the widespread adoption of the pseudonym and the more sophisticated eidolon in journals of this period? The question is of particular interest to the present generation in America, whose journalists seek as much public celebrity as possible. Unfortunately no simple answer suffices for all cases. The use of pseudonyms in journalism was certainly a continuation of a practice, followed in several modes of English belles lettres, of naming a character according to a predominant trait or humor. To some extent, however, the pseudonyms reflected a long-standing diffidence on the part of English authors to admit to authorship as a profession. Moreover, authors wishing to emphasize a particular idea or theme in a literary text recognized in the simple pseudonym a means of adding emphasis and of avoiding the distraction that an actual name might cause. Finally, in many cases pseudonyms simply represented an attempt to maintain anonymity and thus guard against reprisal.

But when the fictitious name indicates an actual persona functioning within the text, a different response is elicited. Attention is naturally drawn to the fictional author by the natural curiosity of readers to learn as much as possible about the author of an interesting text. To a person, the creators of journalistic masks seem to have recognized this proclivity and to have exploited it to ultimate ends. One who deplored this exploitation—at least when applied to authors of fiction—was E. M. Forster. In "Anonymity: An Enquiry" he complains that "the demand that literature should express personality is far too insistent in these days" (Forster 1951, 85). Although admitting that "personality does become important after we have read a book and begin to study it," he concludes that "study is only a serious form of gossip" (Forster 1951, 85).

The motivation for creating journalistic masks is often purely practical, however, and many a fictional personage has protected an author while functioning freely as that author's mouthpiece. Since the native press has consistently challenged established authority, this feature has enticed many American authors. For, from its beginnings, the fictional eidolon has taken satire as its province, often saving its creator from censure or more serious consequences.

Still, Forster's objections notwithstanding, the intrigue that surrounds a fictional narrator on a sheet of newsprint has proved sufficient enticement for bringing such creations into being. It was, for example, much more for this reason than fear of reprisal that Richard Steele extended the life span of Bickerstaff to upwards of two years. As a matter of fact, it was the ultimate penetration of Bickerstaff's mask that brought Steele's editorship, and thus the journal, to a close. In the concluding issue Steele, speaking in his own voice, admits that "this work has indeed for some time been disagreeable to me, and the purpose of it wholly lost by my

being so long understood as the author" (*Tatler* 1899, 4:374–
75). In the *Virginia Gazette* the customary letters written to
Monitor are suddenly replaced by missives to "Mr. Parks,"
indicating the strong possibility that the disguise of the Monitor had worn thin.

Whatever their motivation, authors persisted in the practice of inventing fictional personalities for the native press. Of
those employing the device in the later eighteenth century,
none was more prolific than Philip Freneau. Though frequently noted for the pieces he wrote in the guise of "Pilgrim" and "The Philosopher of the Forest," his best-realized
eidolon is Tomo Cheeki, a Creek Indian, who appears in the
Jersey Chronicle beginning 2 May 1795. During the mid-
1790s, while Philadelphia was still the capital of the United
States, this dignified savage and his pagan entourage arrived
in the city for the purpose of negotiating a treaty between his
people and the newly constituted "republican government."

About the same time that Tomo Cheeki was delivering
the satiric thrusts of Philip Freneau to the readers of the
author's *Jersey Chronicle,* a decidedly more moderate and
far more widely broadcast figure was appearing in *The New
Hampshire Journal: Or, The Farmer's Weekly Museum* of
Walpole, New Hampshire. "The Lay Preacher" was the creation of Joseph Dennie, who edited the *Museum.* One reason
for his importance as a representative of the American federal period was his advocacy of the constitutional separation
of church and state. With one foot planted in the religious
world and the other in the secular, the Lay Preacher exhibits
a plentiful measure of the world's knowledge but looks at
secular life with a decidedly moralistic cast.

The Lay Preacher had the distinction of being the first
fictional figure in American journalism to enjoy popularity in
most of the states. The creations of Franklin, Parks, and to a
large measure those of Freneau had been exposed mainly to
local audiences. Though exceptions may be noted, colonial
presses yielded relatively small runs of their journalistic
product, and the majority of these met the same fate as the
read-over newspapers of today. Many and wide are the gaps
in the files of colonial newspapers. Moreover, for much of the
colonial period no effective distribution system existed for
disseminating copies of news journals among the other colonies. But the *Farmer's Weekly Museum* indicated a change

in the scope of distribution. According to Joseph T. Buckingham, who served as Dennie's printer's devil and later distinguished himself as an important historian-anthologist of
early American journalism, the *Museum* had "as a literary
periodical . . . [in 1797] no rival. Its circulation extended from
Maine to Georgia, and large packages, filled, weekly, an extra
mail-bag, to supply the subscribers in New York, Philadelphia, Charleston, and intervening cities" (Buckingham
1850, 2:179). The reason given for such popularity is the sermons of the Lay Preacher which, "called by the best authority the finest group of periodical essays ever produced in
America" (Mott [1941] 1949, 137), appeared in "nearly all the
newspapers in the nation" (Buckingham 1850, 2:175).

Soon to challenge the broad-ranging popularity of the
Lay Preacher were a series of journalistic characters cast in
the mold of the Yankee—an American type well known from
the stage, almanacs, and popular stories. Speaking the Down
East dialect of the Maine–Nova Scotia region, the Yankee traditionally made his livelihood by his wits. His acquisitive-
ness, his slickness in transacting business, and his laconic
manner of speaking embodied much of the humor as well as
the actual nature of the expanding nation. In 1826 George W.
Arnold, a New York entrepreneur, had published sketches in
the *New York Enquirer* signed by a "Varmonter" named Joe
Strickland. Despite shallow characterization and a reliance
upon misspelling rather than authentic dialect, several newspapers freely lifted the Strickland columns from the *Enquirer*
and reprinted them. One of Strickland's readers was surely
Seba Smith, founder and editor of a struggling weekly Maine
newspaper, the *Portland Courier.* Though Smith's paper (the
first to be published north or east of Boston) was nonpartisan,
he recognized in the state legislative session of 1830, a situation that offered promising grist for satire. Arnold had had
Joe Strickland write letters to his editor from the New York
legislature in Albany, and soon Seba Smith developed a
character of his own who, bearing the trappings of a rural
Down-Easter, performed the same function in Maine. The letters that "Jack Downing" wrote from Portland spelled immediate success for the *Portland Courier,* for the literary career
of Smith, and for the future of Jack Downing as a popular
American character.

The collected edition of the letters, *The Life and Writings of Major Jack Downing* (1833), became the first of scores of volumes containing the writings of American fictional journalists. Many of these editions, produced cheaply on pulp paper, enjoyed voluminous sales. The Downing volume alone enjoyed eight editions, not to mention several piracies and continuations, four of which were subsequently published in America and England (Wyman 1927, 139). Once Smith removed Downing from the Portland ambiance and on to the larger political stage of Washington, D.C., and the "kitchen cabinet" of the Jackson administration, virtually the entire country became interested in, and had access to, his political satires. All of which added to his credibility, of course. Walter Blair has given a good account of Downing's popularity and credibility:

> Some Maine legislators cast their good votes to make him speaker pro tem and major general. Some of the people of Portland gave him their votes for mayor. Ballots were counted all over New Hampshire when the state elected a governor, and one town went unanimously for him. Newspapers were always saying he was the man for some office or other. Some put him up for governor and quite a few came out for him as president. More than one considered that a ticket with him for president and Crockett for vice president would be hard to beat. And newspapers everywhere in the East were glad to reprint Downing letters. Sometimes, instead of shouting news, newsboys would yell that their sheet had a new Downing piece that day. (Blair 1942, 64)

Owing doubtlessly to the popularization of the Yankee, especially through the efforts of Smith, several other New England newspapers were soon carrying the work of fictitious Yankee authors. By the mid-1840s a Philadelphia paper, *Neal's Saturday Gazette*, was repeating the success of the New England journalists with their fictional Yankees. Here Frances M. Whitcher, the first female creator of an eidolon, published a series of pieces written in the guise of "Widow Bedott." In a style interlarded with malapropisms ("ridicule" for "reticule"; "swearee" for "soiree"; "reverated" for "revered," etc.), the loquacious matron ranged tirelessly over myriad topics. Mainly, however, she was concerned with finding a suitable and willing candidate to fill the place of the late

Bedott (her cap setting ultimately meets with success). Once collected in the now popular book form, the Bedott columns enjoyed a success approaching that of the Downing volumes (Blair 1960, 49).

There was, however, only one Yankee eidolon who could be said to have achieved a permanent place in American literature equal to that of Jack Downing. Hosea Biglow, created by James Russell Lowell for the *Boston Courier* in 1846, served as a distinctly commonsense Yankee voice expressing Lowell's opposition to the Mexican War. Both the sentiments and the character of the Yankee hayseed, Biglow, aroused immediate and widespread interest.

> Very far from being a popular author under my own name, so far, indeed, as to be almost unread, I found the verses of my pseudonym copied everywhere; I saw them pinned up in workshops; I heard them quoted and their authorship debated; I once even, when rumor had at length caught up my name in one of its eddies, had the satisfaction of hearing it demonstrated, in the pauses of a concert, that I was utterly incompetent to have written anything of the kind. (Lowell 1893, 7:44)

Both this first series of Biglow papers and a second, published in the *Atlantic Monthly* during the Civil War, enjoyed collected editions and sizable sales. Though the Biglow pieces are not necessarily the finest literary representation of the fictional Yankee in the New England press, the facts that they figured in major historical events and that they were the product of a leading literary influence have made them a fixture in anthologies of American literature and thus the most convenient representatives of their genre for the average reader.

Beginning in the 1830s, the Yankee character had a southern counterpart who, untutored and unpolished for the most part, can be identified with the popular conception of Jacksonian democracy. This Southerner was a far cry from the aristocrats who dominated the culture of the coastal South; he hailed from the interior, a territory that bore the trappings of a frontier that as yet had not yielded to the advance of modern civilization. This region, which represented for eastern Americans the southwestern boundaries of the nation, is commonly called the "Old Southwest."

In many of its settlements and developing towns, an incipient culture was given expression in small weekly newspapers. Several endemic voices found a forum in these sheets, with the result that a number of tiny weeklies are remembered today primarily because they once carried the outpourings of such characters.

Of these unlikely but happy combinations, there were few papers more obscure than the *Union and American* of Nashville, Tennessee, and few fictional voices more outlandish or droll than Sut Lovingood, whose extravagant yarns began appearing in its pages in 1854. With the exception of the war years, the sketches continued sporadically until the death of the author, George Washington Harris, in 1869.

It should not be supposed, however, that the audience for George Washington Harris and other frontier humorists was confined to their rural locality. These characters of the southern backwoods quickly became known to American readers at large through two northern periodicals, *The Spirit of the Times* and *The Yankee Blade*. The *Spirit* in particular, which had been founded in 1831 by William Trotter Porter as a "Chronicle of the Turf, Agriculture, Field Sports, Literature and the Stage," was a major purveyor of southwestern material for the thirty years preceding the Civil War (Yates 1957). Thus the character of Sut, like those created by several of Harris's contemporaries for small newspapers in other areas of the Southwest, has long been part of the national literature.

While the popularity of Sut Lovingood was rivalled by few journalistic voices from the southern frontier, several other characters from the region have enjoyed an enduring, if somewhat more restricted appeal. One of these, Major Joseph Jones, the creation of William Tappan Thompson, made his initial appearance in Thompson's *Family Companion and Ladies' Mirror* of Macon, Georgia, in March 1842. Writing from the mythical Pineville, Georgia, the forthright Jones comments in native dialect on things "so monstrous provokin, that I can't help tellin you about [them]" (Thompson 1848, 11). The telling took the form of letters to the short-lived *Family Companion* and thereafter to the *Southern Miscellany*, which Thompson edited after the demise of his former newspaper. It is perhaps their broad human quality that made the sketches popular as separate pamphlets and books.

In the latter form, one collection had enjoyed thirty reprintings by 1900 (Wheeler 1979, 453–54).

Compared to the outlandish rhetoric and deeds of such earlier frontier types as Lovingood and Jones, the sketches of country life in rural Alabama, written by "Rufus Saunders" for the *Montgomery Advertiser*, seem almost solemn. Francis Bartow Lloyd had written numerous feature articles for the *Advertiser*, of which he was city editor, before the "wholesome and manly face" of a local farmer gave him the idea of inventing a fictional mask through which to speak. Thus was born Rufus Saunders, whose homespun philosophy and country mannerisms delighted Southern audiences in the 1890s. The series, cut short by the assassination of Lloyd in 1897, never achieved the national exposure of the Jones or Lovingood pieces. Yet, as a late voice speaking for a native author, they are no less authentic.

By the middle of the nineteenth century, a portion of the frontier character of the rural South had given way to burgeoning towns and cities. But despite the increase of urban population, Southern journalists and their readers retained a fondness for unvarnished rural characters as a literary type—particularly for their featured roles as literary components of regional journalism. The second half of the century, while a period of growth for American newspapers generally, proved a particularly fertile season for the proliferation of weekly journals in small towns. The weeklies already mentioned—of such southwestern towns as Nashville, Macon, and Montgomery—are representative of a trend that followed patterns of expansion throughout the nation. Thus the newspaper became the ornament of the small but growing settlements and villages in the American provinces. It was looked to as the source of news of both local and national consequence (Hinkle and Henry 1952, 6–7), and in a limited way it often stood alone as a conduit for cultural enrichment. Such small journals faced a chronic problem, however: lack of news. It was up to the weekly editor to draw upon his ingenuity and upon certain available filler material such as ready-print sheets, serial articles, and clippings from newspaper exchanges to fill his blank spaces (Hinkle and Henry 1952, 7). Thus, it was often the need for additional copy, combined with a desire to appeal to the local readership in their own endemic terms, that proved the motivation for the creation of fictional personalities.

"Orpheus C. Kerr," "Petroleum V. Nasby," and "Josh Billings"—three popular likenesses of nineteenth-century literary comedians. (from Phunny Phellows, *1889)*

As the nineteenth century progressed, and as American writing as a whole began to cast off the identifying characteristics of particular localities and regions, a new class of fictional journalist emerged. Mention of the major exponents calls forth associations beyond the newspaper, however. Names such as Mark Twain, Orpheus C. Kerr, Artemus Ward, Petroleum V. Nasby, Josh Billings, and Bill Arp bring to mind humorous writings published in pamphlet, magazine, almanac, and book form as well as oral presentations from the lecture platform. They were part of a growing number of professional writers whose livelihood came from both pen and podium. In the words of a perceptive English observer, writing in 1874:

> The newspapers of the Union are always ready to receive pithy paragraphs from clever men, and to attach the authors' names to them. . . . A smart, terse, pungent paragraph inserted with the author's real or assumed name attached, in one of the journals of the United States, soon finds its way from the Atlantic to the Pacific, and from the Gulf of St. Lawrence to the Gulf of Mexico. With comparatively little trouble, except to worry his brains for comic ideas—no slight trouble, nevertheless—the wit of the Western world soon gains notoriety, if not fame. His racy article of a few lines is copied into paper after paper, until his name becomes familiar in all the cities of the Union. This accomplished, a new field of enterprise opens up. Some speculative man in New York or Boston thinks what a good and profitable enterprise it would be to engage the funny man

whose printed jokes circulate everywhere, engage to give him so much per month for a year or two, have some large woodcuts engraved, some showy posters struck off, some smart advertisements written, halls taken throughout the country, and the man of many jokes made to retail them all over the land at an admission fee varying from one dollar down to twenty-five cents. . . . Things change rapidly across the Atlantic, and at the present day the clown in motley and the minstrel in burnt-cork have their vocation superseded by the facetious lecturer, dressed in evening costume, travelling with gaudy show-bills, and having a literary as well as an oratorical reputation. . . . Simply to write is not excitement enough for your ardent American, if he can enjoy the applause of an audience, and make dollars at the same time, merely by being the mouthpiece of his own jokes. (Shaw 1899, xxxi–xxxii)

It should be emphasized that the work that these versatile authors published in American newspapers represented an integral component of their accomplishment, and that their humorous alter egos substantially characterized the tradition of the fictional mask in the second half of the last century.

One of the earliest and most influential of the group—called "Literary Comedians" (Blair 1960, 102–24; 393–464)—was Charles Farrar Browne, creator of Artemus Ward. Although a native of Maine, and by training a journeyman printer, Browne began submitting a series of sayings signed "Artemus Ward" to the Cleveland *Plain Dealer* in 1857. By the time of his untimely death ten years later, Browne's career—or rather that of his eidolon Artemus Ward—may be said to represent the ultimate in fame and reward that such a fictional creation had achieved thus far. Browne was the first humorous personage from America to win acclaim both in his own country and in Europe. He was warmly received by English audiences who heard him on the lecture platform, by reviewers who praised his books, and by cartoonists who caricatured him in *Punch*. It was on a triumphal tour of England that Browne died of consumption in 1867.

In at least two spheres, Browne can be seen as a pioneer. First, his written texts drew upon tricks such as atrocious grammar and equally abysmal style and spelling ("There4" for "therefore," "2poetic" for "too poetic," etc.) Second, to thousands of Americans he was a platform speaker without peer. His wandering lecture tours took him across the continent, and his audiences were captivated. Walter Blair has observed that both Browne and his public regarded Artemus Ward and his creator as indistinguishable from one another (Blair 1960, 113-14). Browne often signed his correspondence with Ward's name, and in one of the collections of Ward pieces there is an illustration showing Ward with the physiognomy of Browne.

At least two young journalists became beneficiaries of Browne's wise counsel and creative techniques. The first was Henry Wheeler Shaw, whose earliest journalistic efforts (mainly contributions to a number of small New England journals) were cast in rather bland prose. Soon, however, this style crystallized into an easily recognizable persona, and a character named Josh Billings became the putative author. Not only did Billings reflect the influence of Artemus Ward, but Charles Farrar Browne arranged for the publication of the first collection of Billingsiana, *Josh Billings, His Sayings* (1865).

It was not Shaw who best exemplified Browne's precepts, however, but rather an unschooled midwestern newspaper reporter with whom Browne spent a memorable three weeks of close camaraderie in December 1863. Samuel Clemens had been working on the *Enterprise* in Virginia City, Nevada, for more than a year when Browne arrived on a western lecture tour. Though certainly a competent journalist for one of his years and training, Clemens's published efforts could not yet be called remarkable for their style or point of view—the characteristics that would distinguish his alter ego Mark Twain within a very few years. But during the three weeks that he was associated with Charles Farrar Browne, Clemens was able to observe at close range the platform artistry of a first-rate performer. According to DeLancey Ferguson, the memory of Browne's mannerisms, his gestures, his timing, and his tone remained unfaded in Samuel Clemens's memory (Ferguson 1943, 88-89). Firsthand accounts of performances by both men indicate that the Mark Twain of the lecture platform closely resembled the stage presence of Artemus Ward. And it was the gradual transference of speaking style—"of infusing into his writing the charm of his drawling speech," in Ferguson's words—that resulted in the persona of Mark Twain reaching full flower some three years later (Ferguson 1943, 113).

Although Samuel Clemens was later to find greener pas-

tures outside the realm of journalism, many of his contemporaries found newspapers a medium for employing their humorous and satiric creations on an ongoing basis. The
subject that many chose to treat was national politics, which,
then as now, offered fertile possibilities for the humorist and
satirist. Central to the subject was Lincoln, who became the
butt of many a comic lampoon before being transformed into
a tragic legend. His presidency somewhat resembled that of
Jackson in that it symbolized the triumph of the common
man in the expanding nation. It also represented the emer-
gence in Washington of political faces formerly unknown in
the halls of government. The many candidates for presidential appointments formed the basis for the name and the initial impetus for Robert Henry Newell's Orpheus C. Kerr (office
seeker). Newell places Kerr in Washington, with "an unscru-
pulous and, therefore, rising politician" (Newell 1862, 29),
where he is able to observe many attempts to trade spurious
Lincoln anecdotes for postmasterships. There was, however,
a more serious side to Newell, as he used Kerr's humorous
perspective to temper some of the tragedies of the early
months of the Civil War, such as the attack on Fort Sumter
and the massacre of federal volunteers in Baltimore.

Petroleum Vesuvius Nasby, an ironic fictional guise
speaking for David Ross Locke in the latter's newspaper, *The
Jeffersonian,* of Findlay, Ohio, in 1861, assumed a posture
very different from that of Orpheus C. Kerr. Outraged by the
local drunk's attempt to rid the town of its respectable black
families, Locke retaliated by inventing a character who,
while supposedly mouthing the drunk's bigotry, would reveal
his sentiments and actions for what they were. Northerners
who sympathized with the South in the Civil War were called
"copperheads," and Nasby (suggesting, perhaps, "nasty")
was a textbook example.

Other voices championed the Confederate cause with
equally zealous sincerity. One was Bill Arp, who spoke for the
Confederacy while attempting to lighten its flagging spirits
and to reinforce the principles for which it was fighting. Even
when the outcome of Sherman's catastrophic march became
obvious, Arp continued to attempt to relieve the suffering by
defying the military victors to subjugate the spirit of the
South.

In contrast to the literary comedians, who tended to reflect a generalized American character, several decidedly ethnic eidolons appeared in the American press during the closing decades of the nineteenth century. They represented such strains as Irish, Negro, and Pennsylvania Dutch—in other words, groups who had figured prominently in American life and who were easily recognizable in caricature by such distinguishing features as dialect and mannerism. Perhaps such a pronounced ethnic cast represented a coming of age of the American sense of identity. As a people cognizant of their hybrid evolution, and still not yet self-conscious about minority concerns, American newspaper readers could empathize with the individual components of their society while often laughing at their words and actions.

One group that perhaps seemed strange to readers in many parts of America were the Southern Negroes. Both the accents that defined their speech and the social structure that shaped their destiny were unique; however, these limitations did not restrict popularity with readers elsewhere. The *Atlanta Constitution* produced two such personalities during the 1870s. Under the editorship of Henry W. Grady, the *Constitution* was striving to become an advocate of "the New South"—a regional attitude that sought reconciliation and ongoing cooperation with the North. Nevertheless, Grady was sensitive to the unique character of his region, and he saw to it that his newspaper reflected the local ambiance. During the mid-1870s, some local flavor was produced in the columns of "Old Si," the fictional voice of Samuel W. Small. But in 1876 Small temporarily left the newspaper, and the column was discontinued.

Joel Chandler Harris, a staff writer for the *Constitution*, was asked to replace the Old Si pieces after Small's departure. Thus began an effort that would culminate in the creation of Uncle Remus who, though resembling Old Si in a certain limited and general way, soon exceeded him in both breadth and depth of characterization.

While Uncle Remus was appearing in the *Constitution*, a somewhat different kind of black persona was appearing in the *Detroit Free Press*. Though Old Si and Uncle Remus had been created by white authors, a conscious attempt at an authentic rendering of the thought, speech, and manner of a black prototype was made. When Charles Bertrand Lewis created Brother Gardner for the *Free Press*, he had in mind an exaggerated parody of the Negro and his way of life, a parody in many ways resembling the Amos 'n Andy of radio (likewise the creation of white artists). Gardner is a rather pretentious Negro who presides over the "Lime-Kiln Club," a black fraternal order whose purpose is civic betterment. Members such as Rev. Punstock, Trustee Pullback, Elder Bacon Jones, Construction White, and Givedam Jones all play a part in Lewis's attempt to evoke good-natured laughter at Negro life.

Further caricaturing was done by Charles Follen Adams, whose Jacob Strauss spoke in dialect verse to readers of the *Detroit Free Press* for the first time in 1876. Exaggerating the "scrapple English" of the Pennsylvania Dutch and the broken English that Adams had heard German immigrants speak, Strauss's verse commentaries concern primarily his son, "Leedle Yawcob Strauss," whose antics leave the father torn between exasperation and tenderness.

Another fictional creation to rely heavily upon dialect was George Wilbur Peck's Terrence McGrant, who spoke in Irish brogue spelled phonetically. McGrant was, however, no mere caricature, but rather a fleshed-out entity who challenged a controversial American president and his administration with his satire. Indeed, what Newell's Kerr and Smith's Downing were to the Lincoln and Jackson administrations, McGrant was to that of Ulysses S. Grant. The basic posture of the satirist is different, however, in that Peck had McGrant (son of Grant) emphasize the flaws and foibles of the president and his administration in unabashed candor. Terrence, an unschooled, rowdy Irish lad, was a "cousin" of the president. The sanguinal association with Terrence was no benefit to Grant, as the two frequently caroused together, thus calling attention to the president's intemperance. By juxtaposing McGrant and his "Cousin Ulisses," however, Peck was employing a time-honored technique of lending credibility to a fictional character by placing it in the company of a widely recognized personality.

The melting pot was further enriched by a distinctly American caricature, though one obviously springing from foreign antecedents. "Chimmie (Jimmy) Fadden" was the brainchild of Edward W. Townsend, who created him for the *New York Sun*. There, Fadden's accounts of butlering for a well-to-do family, the Burtons, were related in Bowery dialect.

The pieces represent the well-proven satiric situation of the innocent outsider delivering profound insights on an alien, sophisticated world. Fadden's writings were generally short narratives. Their chief interest lay in their style and a satiric view of the New York haut monde.

On balance, the voices that represented ethnic strains in the American press were good natured. The principal purpose was not to criticize, not to condescend, not even to point to ethnic peculiarities of the groups represented by the eidolons. It was rather to seize upon the lighter, more colorful aspects of the various types and to use these to establish a fresh, candid, and unvarnished point of view for reporting on the great passing parade that was fin de siècle America. In achieving this end they were certainly successful, and their remarks remain as unique snapshots of moments in our past, the likes of which will not come again.

By 1900 the newsprint mask could boast a lineage of almost two centuries. As already shown, its numerous scions represented various identities and reasons for being, all of which seem plausible for the particular time and circumstances. The brothers Franklin wished to emulate a new vogue from the London essay journals, and to establish a safe vehicle for satire. Struggling editors like Seba Smith, while sharing the satiric urge of earlier journalists such as Franklin and Freneau, needed to sell more newspapers. Hosea Biglow served primarily as a polemicist for James Russell Lowell. The creators of frontier eidolons looked to the rural press as a logical outlet for artistic expression, aimed primarily at a local audience; whereas the literary comedians saw in fictional guises a springboard to larger and better-paying audiences.

That some of the most celebrated of American comic characters—Mark Twain, Artemus Ward, Bill Arp, Sut Lovingood—should have appeared in small newspapers with no pretensions of reaching anything broader than a local audience is a fact worth noting. But equally noteworthy is the fact that the reputations derived from the local news sheet may be seen as forerunners of a journalistic phenomenon that came to distinguish powerful metropolitan newspapers whose readership figured in the hundreds of thousands and much of whose material was broadly syndicated (Mott 1949, 394). This was of course the humorous "colyum," and its practitioners—the "colyumnists"—enjoyed a kind of national stardom. While the term "colyum" is somewhat un-specific as to form and content, certain characteristics are commonly recognizable. Eugene Field, whose "Sharps and Flats" appeared in the *Chicago Daily News* in the 1880s, established the length of a single newsprint column as stand-ard for the genre (Van Doren 1923, 309). Also, the fact that he filled this space with satire and jokes in prose and verse helped to establish paradigms of theme and content for con-temporaries and successors alike. Another defining aspect is what Carl Van Doren labeled "immensely personal" expres-sion (Van Doren 1923, 310). As primary examples of colyum-nists of the mid-1920s (a flourishing period for such authors), Van Doren cites Franklin P. Adams, Don Marquis, Chris-topher Morley, and Heywood Broun and discusses the highly personal traits of each. A journalistic handbook from the same period states that a colyum "does not follow any mood or seek any goal earnestly and invariably, except that it trails rather closely in the wake of the column conductor. Usually the . . . conductor chooses to be unserious. Consequently, the public often considers the column humorous" (Davis 1926, 3).

Two of the most successful colyumnists chose to be both personal and humorous through the agency of well-defined masks. The result was instant popularity and enduring pres-tige. The creations of Finley Peter Dunne and Don Marquis quickly emerged from journalistic colyums into the canon of American literature, and even into the realm of legend. Other authors, while not creating well-wrought characters to speak for them, attained widespread fame by writing imaginative material in various forms. Their names are touchstones in the history of the genre. Bert Leston Taylor's "A Line o' Type or Two," written for the *Chicago Tribune;* Franklin P. Adams's "The Conning Tower," also in the *Tribune;* and George Ade's "Fables in Slang," written for the *Chicago Rec-ord* were all products of newspapers employing authors whose work would gain them prestige and increased sales.

No creation of these writers was more beloved than Fin-ley Peter Dunne's Martin Dooley, whose engaging Irish ac-cents began appearing in the *Chicago Post* on 7 October 1893. As the character evolved, eager acceptance and adula-tion followed. Syndication in newspapers across America was not far behind, and this was soon accompanied by publication in book form. (*Mr. Dooley in Peace and War* [1898] sold ten thousand copies per month during the first year after publication [Ellis 1941, 120].)

The situation in which Dooley, the proprietor of a gin mill on "Archy" (Archer) Road in Chicago, held forth was as simple as it was commonplace: the comedian playing to the straight sideman (in this case, his friend Hennessey). In referring to the Republican President William McKinley, Dooley, an unswervable "dimmycrat," asks incredulously, "Prisidint iv th' United States, says ye? Well, I'm prisidint iv this liquor store, fr'm th' pitcher iv th' Chicago fire above th' wash-stand in th' back room to th' dure step . . . "(Dunne 1898, 100). Dooley is a mouthpiece for sound commonsense values, seasoned by an expansive Celtic imagination and a finished turn of phrase. After Mark Twain, Dooley is the most quotable—and quoted—of his tradition in American journalism.

Several of Don Marquis's characters likewise stand out as masterpieces of journalistic creativity. Two that spring immediately to mind are his cockroach, archy (the reincarnation of a vers libre poet, who writes his material by jumping on the typewriter keys but who cannot work the shift in tandem with another key), and mehitabel (an alley cat reincarnation of Cleopatra).

Before archy and mehitabel began appearing in Marquis's "The Sun Dial" column in the *New York Sun* (they also appeared later in his "Lantern" column at the *New York Tribune*), his best-known journalistic guise was Hermione, a young society belle. With her "little group of serious thinkers" this committed yet misdirected soul undertook all sorts of causes for the improvement of society. ("Aren't you just crazy about prison reform?" [Marquis 1916, 139]) Her monologues brim with dramatic irony, for her description of "causes" reveals a woeful ignorance, naiveté, and lack of empathy.

The characters archy and mehitabel and Clem Hawley, the "Old Soak" (who called the Volstead Act "the eighteenth commandment") were created with more flair and a lighter touch. They display a point of view that is more worldly and more broadly aware of the human situation and basic human nature. By having wisdom and satire expressed by a seemingly ignoble character—albeit one who commands a degree of affection—Marquis was employing a device well rooted in satiric writing.

In many ways, Marquis's accomplishments can be said to represent the pinnacle of the eidolon tradition in American journalism. A professional journalist and columnist, he obviously was aware of what had been done with the device before he undertook his own efforts. He was also well established as a writer in more serious forms of literature such as poetry, drama, and the novel. And whereas Clemens and the literary comedians had created eidolons that became stepping stones to broader audiences and more numerous dollars, Marquis saw the genre not as a novelty or a filler but as an art form to be taken seriously by artist and audience alike.

Both Marquis and Dunne had serious messages to convey. Each looked upon this medium as the ideal means for his expression. Both functioned as American journalists at a time when the influence of the press was burgeoning. Both worked on big city dailies with circulations in the hundreds of thousands. Both recognized that they had found a vehicle that would be understood and appreciated by the various levels within their masses of readers. These authors, along with their satiric masks, became household words in America—quoted, discussed, reprinted, elevated to the level of mythic folk heroes.

Another group of early twentieth-century characters chose the cracker barrel as a podium from which to deliver wit and wisdom. Of this number the unquestioned patriarch is Will Rogers. Though not the earliest of the lot to "break into the writing game" (Rogers 1935, 27–35), as he phrased it, he certainly best characterizes their traits and goals. Rogers was one of the few popular newspaper humorists to make a seemingly easy transition into radio and even into motion pictures. His plain wit and philosophy, which enjoy a vogue even in the present day, seem as well suited to the radio or newsreel as to the newspaper. To refute Marshall McLuhan, it is not Rogers's medium, but rather his message that has survived the years. His columns began appearing in 1922 on a weekly basis, and by the time of his shocking death in 1935 they had become a daily staple of more than four hundred newspapers and were at times read by forty million people.

Where Rogers is most influential among journalistic eidolons is in epitomizing a tone and prototype that was emulated by a number of lesser creations. The characteristic pattern of the cowboy philosopher was to reduce matters of the times to a simple, homespun point of view that, upon close examination, presented a wisdom and sophistication not obvious in the casual language and down-home guise of the speaker.

Like Dooley, the Old Soak, and the cockroach and alley cat before them, Rogers and the other rustic philosophers represented a classic confrontation in American literature—that of the lowly versus the highly placed or, put another way, of the democrat versus the aristocrat. That the lowly character comes off looking by far the better of the two is a common characteristic of this juxtaposition, and of course another instance in the vast process of democratization that has been taking place in America since before the Revolution.

Rogers and the other cracker-barrel philosophers held forth in the initial four decades of the twentieth century—a time when American readers were conditioned to look to the pages of their newspapers for the sayings of characters who, although fictional creations, were forged from the stuff of common American humanity. Such readers might little note nor long remember what a prestigious reporter or feature writer might say, but they were less likely to forget the words of Will Rogers, Abe Martin, or Senator Sorghum.

Abe Martin was one of the earliest of the lot. He sprang from the typewriter of Frank McKinney Hubbard, of the *Indianapolis News,* in 1905. Martin was supposedly a citizen of Brown County, Indiana. His sayings were accompanied by original drawings by Hubbard, often exaggerated in some detail to emphasize a point made in an essay or proverb. The style is that of a rural midwesterner complete with phonetic spelling (a technique reminiscent of the literary comedians), thus emphasizing the incongruity between a lofty subject being discussed and the homey point of view from which it is related. ("One thousan', five thousan', ten thousan', the newspapers allus use round figures in reportin' Chinese casualties" [Hubbard 1930, 68].)

Another of the fraternity who dealt in political wisdom while skirting partisan affiliation is "Senator Sorghum," whom Philander C. Johnson developed for the editorial pages

of the *Washington Star.* Though Johnson created several
other characters (e.g., Farmer Corntassel and Miss Cayenne)
for his "Shooting Stars" column, the two creations that stand
out in popularity and prominence are Senator Sorghum and
Uncle Eben, a black philosopher. Both characters speak in
epigrams, and occasionally Uncle Eben's thoughts are cast in
verse. Johnson, a valued writer on the *Star* for forty-seven
years, sought to be humorous and wise, yet inoffensive and
engaging. A *Star* editorial of 19 May 1939, marking his
death, spoke of his pen as being "sharp, but . . . not unchari-
table," which summarizes fairly well the utterances of Senator Sorghum and Uncle Eben. Titles of their collected statements (e.g., *Senator Sorghum's Primer of Politics* and
Sayings of Uncle Eben) indicate the short, epigrammatic nature of the material emanating from both characters.

The late 1920s and early 1930s proved a watershed for
the persona tradition. Having begun when journalism in the
American colonies was in its infancy, it enjoyed its proudest
moments when the large newspapers of the 1890s and beyond came to represent a major industry and a powerful
cultural influence. But newspapers would not always enjoy
such unchallenged hegemony. The 1920s saw radio come
into its own as a means of news dissemination and entertainment, and the 1930s witnessed the fledgling beginnings of
television. Fictional eidolons on the printed page had to com-
pete for recognition with the new media. Moreover, some of
the most popular creators of newspaper characters met their
final deadlines during the 1930s. Rogers died in 1935; Dunne
in 1936; Marquis in 1937; Johnson in 1939; and no generation of apprentices was waiting to take their places. Perhaps,
too, the war clouds gathering in Europe produced a sobriety
that was alien to the characteristic satire of fictional journalists. Creating a mask with which to veil one's personal sentiments indicates a certain acknowledgment of propriety,
taste, and innocence. But with the rigors of an economic depression facing American readers at home and a blatantly
perverse side of human nature revealing itself in Europe,
such amenities seemed rather anachronistic.

These factors did not spell the end of the tradition, however. Just two weeks after becoming editor of the *Marion
Democrat* and *Smyth County News* in 1927, Sherwood Anderson had introduced a fictional reporter named Buck

Fever. Speaking in the accent of the mountains of southwestern Virginia, Buck served Anderson in several capacities in the columns of both papers. He covered local news, and he wrote a column of satirical commentary called "Buck Fever Says." He campaigned for various civic causes and, perhaps foremost, he won untold new friends and subscribers for Anderson's venture into journalism.

In reality, Anderson's fictional reporter, instead of representing a step forward in development, offered a nostalgic glance to the past. Like many weekly newspapers of the Old Southwest, which had carried the scribblings of such characters as Sut Lovingood and Rufus Saunders, Anderson's newspapers served a small town and its rural environs. In an engaging, usually teasing, ingenuous vein Buck Fever spoke to a small-town readership that had all but faded from the American consciousness, and he represented one of the last literary characters to be created by a major American man of letters for a small newspaper.

Another voice that trailed from the past was a former soldier named Bill, an American doughboy of World War I who had written a series of letters to his girlfriend Mable. The actual author was a New York businessman named Edward Streeter, who had originally written the pieces in 1917 for a tiny regimental newspaper, the *Gas Attack.* Republished in 1918 as *Dere Mable,* they had sold over 750,000 copies. Following the nostalgic trend of Anderson, Streeter once again republished the collection in 1941, prefaced with a letter by a now middle-aged Bill to his son, a recent recruit into the new Defense Army. Part of this missive refers to the differences between the new army and the one in which the father had served: "Yes son, these [new] fellos is the same as we was—all the way through. An when they get put up against something tough whatll they do? Theyll go right on complainin. Only theyll stand up an take it just about the way we did" (Streeter 1941, xvii). In other words, in the midst of present difficulty and uncertainty, we shall be well served by recalling the past and respecting what we learned from it. Multitudes of readers eagerly shared this retrospective view.

The appearance of new personae since World War II has been sporadic, however. Perhaps the very idea of creating an alter ego to speak for the modern journalist is less attractive than the ambition to establish a "name" and a reputation in one's own right, as large numbers of modern journalists—particularly those working in television—have so successfully done.

Exceptions do exist, nevertheless. One is Horace P. Hardscrabble who, with his friend Timothy Peckworthy, enlivened the pages of the *Arkansas Gazette* with political conversations in the 1950s, 1960s, and 1970s. These writings covered a chronological spectrum from the Little Rock desegregation days to the Watergate era. Written anonymously by Richard E. Yates, a history professor, and often pointedly partisan, the pieces offered a folksy commentary on political matters of major import.

Less partisan, though no less timely in message, are the "Aunt Gertrude" columns, written mainly in the form of epistles to her "nephew" Charles R. McDowell, Jr., a syndicated columnist and Washington correspondent for the *Richmond Times-Dispatch.* The ambiance is rural Virginia, where the general store is still a political forum; where a once-strong Democratic Byrd organization frequently joins forces with the Republican party under the banner of solid conservatism; and where people take their politics more seriously than they do farming, hunting, or shad planking. Once again, the provincial savant has her say in the halls of the mighty. And though the touch is light and ever so slightly wry, the result is anything but comfortable for the exalted.

It seems, however, that McDowell and Yates, no less than Anderson and Streeter, have looked in tender retrospect at the cracker-barrel kings of a bygone era in American journalism—at figures such as Will Rogers, Uncle Henry, Abe Martin, and Senator Sorghum. Theirs is a nostalgic attempt to use older characters who trail clouds of a rural past when the eyes of the common people were sharp, and their wit able to penetrate the bombastic puffery of the mighty. The last two decades in American government have been times of unrest, discord, high-handedness, political skulduggery, and inefficiency. The treatment of this rich vein of journalistic ore has fallen to the "investigative reporters" who, deadly serious in their intent to censure and reform, have usurped the position that might have been served by clever satirists and humorists through their fictional counterparts. Yet the upheaval of the Johnson years, the crisis of the Nixon years, the confusion and despair of the Carter years, and the uneasy "prosperity'' of the Reagan presidency have found few journalists who will speak in any but straightforward, serious, and even moralistic terms.

Thus the Hardscrabbles and the Aunt Gertrudes sound as voices crying in a wilderness of high moral outrage and righteous indignation. We may pray for the increase of their tribe, but we must realistically conclude that as a species they are endangered. It can be hoped, however, that an awareness of earlier journalists and their fictive voices may inspire present and future counterparts. It is certain that they will never lack for promising material.

1

COLONIALS

Benjamin Franklin (1706–1790)

Silence Dogood

Busy-Body

ALTHOUGH NOTED for inventions and innovations, Benjamin Franklin made some significant contributions to colonial journalism by borrowing from English models—especially the *Spectator*. These appropriations included the use of a group or club of fictional contributors; letters from and replies to fictitious correspondents; and most importantly, the introduction of recognizable personalities, or masks, who served as surrogates. Franklin's most successful mask was Silence Dogood, whom he introduced into the *New England Courant* when he was seventeen and serving as a printer's apprentice to his half brother, James.

Silence is perhaps Franklin's most effective fictional character, in that she discourses in a distinctive voice that characterizes her as a candid, agile-tongued New Englander. Having "a natural Inclination to observe and reprove the Faults of others," and warning that she never intended "to wrap [her] Talent in a Napkin," Silence delivered herself freely of opinions on morals, manners, institutions, and ideas.

Like many authors of his time, both English and American, Franklin held that the primary purpose of literature is to instruct. Thus, by making Silence the widow of a preacher, and by having her hammer away in an unabashedly pedantic manner, he left little doubt as to his own sympathies. Still, for all her preachiness and loquacity, Silence's charm keeps her pronouncements from being overbearing. She is at times hu-

---

The Franklin selections are from *The Writings of Benjamin Franklin,* edited by Albert Henry Smith, vol. 2, 1722–1750 (New York: Macmillan Company, 1907).

morous (as in her pursuit of a husband), and she occasionally writes on such relatively noncontroversial subjects as poetry and literary style.

Silence is not so celebrated as Richard Saunders of *Poor Richard's Almanac*, but within the journalistic context she is far more vivid and carefully wrought than such Franklin surrogates as Busy-Body (of *The American Weekly Mercury*), who expresses opinions with little of Silence's keenness or charm.

According to James A. Sappenfield, "Franklin transferred the [mask] device to real life. His greatest achievement in real-life masquerade was the image of fur-hatted American rusticity which he projected in the glittering French court during the American Revolution" (Sappenfield 1973, 14).

SILENCE DOGOOD NO. 4

On the Education of Children

May 14, 1722

An sum etiam nunc vel Graece loqui vel Latine docendus?*
—CICERO

To the Author of the *New-England Courant*.

Sir,

Discoursing the other Day at Dinner with my Reverend Boarder, formerly mention'd, (whom for Distinction sake we will call by the Name of *Clericus*,) concerning the Education of Children, I ask'd his Advice about my young Son *William*, whether or no I had best bestow upon him Academical Learning, or (as our Phrase is) *bring him up at our College:* He perswaded me to do it by all Means, using many weighty Arguments with me, and answering all the Objections that I could form against it; telling me withal, that he did not doubt but that the Lad would take his Learning very well, and not idle away his Time as too many there now-a-days do. These Words of *Clericus* gave me a Curiosity to inquire a little more strictly into

*Must I even now be taught to speak in Latin and in Greek?

the present Circumstances of that famous Seminary of Learning; but the Information which he gave me, was neither pleasant, nor such as I expected.

As soon as Dinner was over, I took a solitary Walk into my Orchard, still ruminating on *Clericus's* Discourse with much Consideration, until I came to my usual Place of Retirement under the *Great Apple-Tree;* where having seated my self, and carelessly laid my Head on a verdant Bank, I fell by Degrees into a soft and undisturbed Slumber. My waking Thoughts remained with me in my Sleep, and before I awak'd again, I dreamt the following DREAM.

I fancy'd I was travelling over pleasant and delightful Fields and Meadows, and thro' many small Country Towns and Villages; and as I pass'd along, all Places resounded with the Fame of the Temple of LEARNING: Every Peasant, who had wherewithal, was preparing to send one of his Children at least to this famous Place; and in this Case most of them consulted their own Purses instead of their Childrens Capacities: So that I observed, a great many, yea, the most part of those who were travelling thither, were little better than Dunces and Blockheads. Alas! Alas!

At length I entred upon a spacious Plain, in the Midst of which was erected a large and stately Edifice: It was to this that a great Company of Youths from all Parts of the Country were going; so stepping in among the Crowd, I passed on with them, and presently arrived at the Gate.

The Passage was kept by two sturdy Porters named *Riches* and *Poverty,* and the latter obstinately refused to give Entrance to any who had not first gain'd the Favour of the former; so that I observed, many who came even to the very Gate, were obliged to travel back again as ignorant as they came, for want of this necessary Qualification. However, as a Spectator I gain'd Admittance, and with the rest entred directly into the Temple.

In the Middle of the great Hall stood a stately and magnificent Throne, which was ascended to by two high and difficult Steps. On the Top of it sat LEARNING in awful State; she was apparelled wholly in Black, and surrounded almost on every Side with innumerable Volumes in all Languages. She seem'd very busily employ'd in writing something on half a Sheet of Paper, and upon Enquiry, I understood she was preparing a Paper, call'd, *The New-England Courant.* On her Right Hand sat *English,* with a pleasant smiling Countenance, and handsomely attir'd; and on her left were seated several *Antique Figures* with their Faces vail'd. I was considerably puzzl'd to guess who they were, until one informed me, (who stood beside me,) that those Figures on her left Hand were *Latin, Greek, Hebrew,* &c. and that they were very much reserv'd, and seldom or never unvail'd their Faces here, and then to few or none, tho' most of those who have in this Place acquir'd so much Learning as to distinguish them from *English*, pretended to an intimate Acquaintance with them. I then enquir'd of him, what could be the Reason why they continued vail'd, in this Place especially: He pointed to the Foot of the Throne, where I saw *Idleness,* attended with *Ignorance,* and these (he informed me) were they, who first vail'd them, and still kept them so.

Now I observed, that the whole Tribe who entred into the Temple with me, began to climb the Throne; but the Work proving troublesome and difficult to most of them, they withdrew their Hands from the Plow, and contented themselves to sit at the Foot, with Madam *Idleness* and her Maid *Ignorance,* until those who were assisted by Diligence and a docible Temper, had well nigh got up the first Step: But the Time drawing nigh in which they could no way avoid ascending, they were fain to crave the Assistance of those who had got up before them, and who, for the Reward perhaps of a *Pint of Milk,* or a *Piece of Plumb-Cake,* lent the Lubbers a helping Hand, and sat them in the Eye of the World, upon a Level with themselves.

The other Step being in the same Manner ascended, and the usual Ceremonies at an End, every Beetle-Scull seem'd well satisfy'd with his own Portion of Learning, tho' perhaps he was *e'en just* as ignorant as ever. And now the Time of their Departure being come, they march'd out of Doors to make Room for another Company, who waited for Entrance: And I, having seen all that was to be seen, quitted the Hall likewise, and went to make my Observations on those who were just gone out before me.

Some I perceiv'd took to Merchandizing, others to Travelling, some to one Thing, some to another, and some to Nothing; and many of them from henceforth, for want of Patrimony, liv'd as poor as church Mice, being unable to dig, and asham'd to beg, and to live by their Wits it was impossible. But the most Part of the Crowd went along a large beaten Path, which led to a Temple at the further End of the Plain, call'd, *The Temple of Theology.* The Business of those who were employ'd in this Temple being laborious and painful, I wonder'd exceedingly to see so many go towards it; but while I was pondering this Matter in my Mind, I spy'd *Pecunia* behind a Curtain, beckoning to them with her Hand, which Sight immediately satisfy'd me for whose Sake it was, that a great Part of them (I will not say all) travel'd that Road. In this Temple I saw nothing worth mentioning, except the ambitious and fraudulent Contrivances of *Plagius,* who (notwithstanding he had been severely reprehended for such Practices before) was diligently transcribing some eloquent Paragraphs out of *Tillotson's* Works, &c., to embellish his own.

Now I bethought my self in my Sleep, that it was Time to be at Home, and as I fancy'd I was travelling back thither, I reflected in my Mind on the extream Folly of those Parents, who, blind to their Children's Dulness, and insensible of the Solidity of their Skulls, because they think their Purses can afford it, will needs send them to the Temple of Learning, where, for want of a suitable Genius, they learn little more than how to carry themselves handsomely, and enter a Room genteely, (which might as well be acquir'd at a Dancing-School,) and from whence they return, after Abundance of Trouble and Charge, as great Blockheads as ever, only more proud and self-conceited.

While I was in the midst of these unpleasant Reflections, *Clericus* (who with a Book in his Hand was walking under the Trees) accidentally awak'd me; to him I related my Dream with all its Particulars, and he, without much Study, presently interpreted it, assuring me, *That it was a lively Representation of* HARVARD COL-LEGE, *Etcetera.* I remain, Sir,

Your Humble Servant,
SILENCE DOGOOD

THE BUSY-BODY NO. 4

On the Proper Length of a Visit

Ne quid nimis*

In my first Paper I invited the Learned and the Ingenious to join with me in this Undertaking; and I now repeat that Invitation. I would have such Gentlemen take this Opportunity, (by trying their Talent in Writing) of diverting themselves and their Friends, and improving the Taste of the Town. And because I would encourage all Wit of our own Growth and Produce, I hereby promise, that whoever shall send me a little Essay on some moral or other Subject, that is fit for publick View in this Manner (and not basely borrow'd from any other Author) I shall receive it with Candour, and take Care to place it to the best Advantage. It will be hard if we cannot muster up in the whole Country a sufficient Stock of Sense to supply the *Busy-Body* at least for a Twelvemonth.

*Not anything in excess

For my own Part, I have already profess'd, that I have the Good of my Country wholly at Heart in this Design, without the least sinister View; my chief Purpose being to inculcate the noble Principles of Virtue, and depreciate Vice of every kind. But as I know the Mob hate Instruction, and the Generality would never read beyond the first Line of my Lectures, if they were usually fill'd with nothing but wholesome Precepts and Advice, I must therefore sometimes humour them in their own Way. There are a Set of Great Names in the Province, who are the common Objects of Popular Dislike. If I can now and then overcome my Reluctance, and prevail with my self to Satyrize a little one of these Gentlemen, the Expectation of meeting with such a Gratification will induce many to read me through, who would otherwise proceed immediately to the Foreign News. As I am very well assured that the greatest Men among us have a sincere Love for their Country, notwithstanding its Ingratitude, and the Insinuations of the Envious and Malicious to the contrary, so I doubt not but they will chearfully tolerate me in the Liberty I design to take for the End above mentioned.

As yet I have but few Correspondents, tho' they begin now to increase. The following Letter, left for me at the Printer's, is one of the first I have receiv'd, which I regard the more for that it comes from one of the Fair Sex, and because I have my self oftentimes suffer'd under the Grievance therein complain'd of.

To the Busy-Body.

Sir,

You having set your self up for a *Censurer Morum* (as I think you call it), which is said to mean a *Reformer of Manners*, I know no Person more proper to be apply'd to for Redress in all the Grievances we suffer from Want of *Manners*, in some People. You must know I am a single Woman, and keep a Shop in this Town for a Livelyhood. There is a certain Neighbour of mine, who is really agreeable Company enough, and with whom I have had an Intimacy of some Time standing; but of late she makes her Visits so excessively often, and stays so very long every Visit, that I am tir'd out of all Patience. I have no Manner of Time at all to my self; and you, who seem to be a wise Man, must needs be sensible that every Person has little Secrets and Privacies, that are not proper to be expos'd even to the nearest Friend. Now I cannot do the least Thing in the World, but she must know all about it; and it is a Wonder I have found an Opportunity to write you this Letter. My Misfortune is, that I respect her very well, and know not how to disoblige her so much as to tell her I should be glad to have less of her Company; for if I should once hint such a Thing, I am afraid she would resent it so as never to darken my Door again.

But, alas, Sir, I have not yet told you half my Afflictions. She has two Children that are just big enough to run about and do pretty Mischief; these are continually along with Mamma, either in my Room or Shop, if I have never so many Customers or People with me about Business. Sometimes they pull the Goods off my low Shelves down to the Ground, and perhaps where one of them has just been making Water. My Friend takes up the Stuff, and cries, "Eh! thou little wicked mischievous Rogue! But however, it has done no great Damage; 'tis only wet a little"; and so puts it up upon the Shelf again. Sometimes they get to my Cask of Nails behind the Counter, and divert themselves, to my great Vexation, with mixing my Ten-penny, and Eight-penny, and Four-penny, together. I endeavour to conceal my Uneasiness as much as possible, and with a grave Look go to Sorting them out. She cries, "Don't thee trouble thyself, Neighbour: Let them play a little; I'll put all to rights my self before I go." But Things are never so put to rights but that I find a great deal of Work to do after they are gone. Thus, Sir, I have all the Trouble and Pesterment of Children, without the Pleasure of—calling them my own; and they are now so us'd to being here that they will be content no where else. If she would have been so kind as to have moderated her Visits to ten times a Day, and stay'd but half an hour at a Time, I should have been contented, and I believe never have given you this Trouble. But this very Morning they have so tormented me that I could bear no longer; for, while the Mother was asking me twenty impertinent Questions, the youngest got to my Nails, and with great Delight rattled them by handfuls all over the Floor; and the other, at the same Time, made such a terrible Din upon my Counter with a Hammer, that I grew half distracted. I was just then about to make my self a new Suit of Pinners, but in the Fret and Confusion I cut it quite out of all Manner of Shape, and utterly spoil'd a Piece of the first Muslin.

Pray, Sir, tell me what I shall do. And talk a little against such unreasonable Visiting in your next Paper; tho' I would not have her affronted with me for a great Deal, for sincerely I love her and her Children, as well, I think, as a Neighbour can, and she buys a great many Things in a Year at my Shop. But I would beg her to consider that she uses me unmercifully, Tho' I believe it is only for want to Thought. But I have twenty Things more to tell you besides all this; There is a handsome Gentleman, that has a Mind (I don't question) to make love to me, but he can't get the least Opportunity to—: O dear, here she comes again; I must conclude Yours, &c.

PATIENCE

Indeed, 'tis well enough, as it happens, that she is come to shorten this Complaint, which I think is full long enough already, and probably would otherwise have been as long again. However, I must confess I cannot help pitying my Correspondent's Case; and, in her Behalf, exhort the Visitor to remember and consider the Words of the Wise Man, "Withdraw thy Foot from the House of thy

Neighbour least he grow weary of thee, and so hate thee." It is, I
believe, a nice thing, and very difficult, to regulate our Visits in such
a Manner, as never to give Offence by coming too seldom, or too
often, or departing too abruptly, or staying too long. However, in my
Opinion, it is safest for most People in a general way, who are un-
willing to disoblige, to visit seldom, and tarry but a little while in a
Place, notwithstanding pressing invitations, which are many times
insincere. And tho' more of your Company should be really desir'd,
yet in this Case, too much Reservedness is a Fault more easily ex-
cus'd than the Contrary.

Men are subjected to various Inconveniences merely through
lack of a small Share of Courage, which is a Quality very necessary
in the common Occurences of Life, as well as in a Battle. How many
Impertinences do we daily suffer with great Uneasiness, because we
have not Courage enough to discover our Dislike? And why may not
a Man use the Boldness and Freedom of telling his Friends, that
their long Visits sometimes incommode him? On this Occasion, it
may be entertaining to some of my Readers, if I acquaint them with
the *Turkish* Manner of entertaining Visitors, which I have from an
author of unquestionable Veracity; who assures us, that even the
Turks are not so ignorant of Civility, and the Arts of Endearment,
but that they can practise them with as much Exactness as any
other Nation, whenever they have a Mind to shew themselves oblig-
ing.

"When you visit a Person of Quality," (says he) "and have talk'd
over your Business, or the Complements, or whatever Concern
brought you thither, he makes a Sign to have Things serv'd in for
the Entertainment, which is generally, a little Sweetmeat, a Dish of
Sherbet, and another of Coffee; all which are immediately brought
in by the Servants, and tender'd to all the Guests in Order, with the
greatest Care and Awfulness imaginable. At last comes the finishing
Part of your Entertainment, which is, Perfuming the Beards of the
Company; a Ceremony which is perform'd in this Manner. They
have for the Purpose a small Silver Chaffing-Dish, cover'd with a Lid
full of Holes, and fixed upon a handsome Plate. In this they put
some fresh Coals, and upon them a piece of *Lignum Aloes,* and
shutting it up, the Smoak immediately ascends with a grateful
Odour thro' the Holes of the Cover. This Smoak is held under every
one's Chin, and offer'd as it were a Sacrifice to his Beard. The bristly
Idol soon receives the Reverence done to it, and so greedily takes in
and incorporates the gummy Steam, that it retains the Savour of it,
and may serve for a Nosegay a good while after.

"This Ceremony may perhaps seem ridiculous at first hearing,
but it passes among the *Turks* for an high Gratification. And I will

say this in its Vindication, that its Design is very wise and useful. For it is understood to give a civil Dismission to the Visitants, intimating to them, that the Master of the House has Business to do, or some other Avocation, that permits them to go away as soon as they please, and the sooner after this Ceremony the better. By this Means you may, at any Time, without Offence, deliver your self from being detain'd from your Affairs by tedious and unseasonable Visits; and from being constrain'd to use that Piece of Hypocrisy, so common in the World, of pressing those to stay longer with you, whom perhaps in your Heart you wish a great Way off for having troubled you so long already."

Thus far my Author. For my own Part, I have taken such a Fancy to this Turkish Custom, that for the future I shall put something like it in Practice. I have provided a Bottle of right French Brandy for the Men, and Citron-Water for the Ladies. After I have treated with a Dram, and presented a Pinch of my best Snuff, I expect all Company will retire, and leave me to pursue my Studies for the Good of the Publick.

William Parks (c. 1698–1750)

Monitor

*T*HE **PRINTING CAREER** of William Parks was well established in his native England before he came to the Maryland colony in the mid-1720s. But the fact that he printed official laws and public documents is but a small part of his significance in the history of printing in early America. In 1727 he founded the *Maryland Gazette*, the first newspaper published south of Pennsylvania. It was followed in 1736 by the *Virginia Gazette*, the first newspaper published in that colony (Parks had established a press in Williamsburg in 1730 and had become public printer of Virginia in 1732).

Parks was, however, much more than an enterprising printer and journalist. He possessed an extraordinary mastery of book production, which distinguished his imprints as benchmarks of the art in colonial America. He also proved himself a major cultural influence in the Maryland and Virginia colonies, having published the poems of Richard Lewis and Ebenezer Cooke in Annapolis and those of Richard Markland and other talented Virginians in Williamsburg. His nonliterary imprints include the first sporting book and the first cookbook published in America, as well as William Stith's *The History of the First Discovery and Settlement of Virginia.*

His contributions to the cultural life of the colonies are most widely recognized in his newspapers, however, especially the *Virginia Gazette.* The literary fare that Parks printed reveals a familiarity with what was being carried in

---

The Parks selections are from *The Virginia Gazette,* 10 September 1736; 12 November 1736 (microfilm).

the London journals (he occasionally reprinted selections), as well as a broad knowledge of both classical and contemporary literature. Although not generally known outside the files of the *Virginia Gazette,* the Monitor essays were long thought to be of such high quality that they must have come from an English periodical. Elizabeth C. Cook, a leading authority on colonial American newspapers, has concluded that they are colonial originals, though she questions whether they were written by Parks himself (Cook 1912, 202).

Whatever the true facts of their provenance, the Monitor essays exhibit a high degree of imaginativeness and a graceful style and form. The club, or coterie of female "reporters" who interact with the Monitor, resembles similar groups of characters who made regular appearances in English literary journals. The Monitor himself functions as a rational, even-tempered adjudicator among his animated flock. Often the device of letters from anonymous readers is employed, thus giving the kindly sage an opportunity to deliver a response that puts all in perspective. Collectively, the Monitor essays suggest a readership concerned with manners, fashions, literature, and moral values—in short, a colonial audience with active intellectual interests and sophisticated tastes shaped largely by English trends of the day.

THE MONITOR NO. 6

The Monitor and His Club

Simia quam similis, turpissima bestia, nobis?*
—Cic. de Nat. Deorum

The other night, as I was lolling in my Elbow-Chair, in my Study, I was contriving some Method to give our Fair *Letitia Tattle* a View of my long Note; when, of a sudden, I was surpriz'd with Three Taps at the Door of my outward Chamber. My Man *Dominic* going to the Door, which was only half shut, flew back again in a great Fright, and told me he was sure it was the Devil, for he never saw

*How similar is an ape, the basest beast, to us?

such a Figure before. Pray, Sir, said I, desire the civil Gentleman to walk in; and do you set Chairs.

At the first Interview, I was inclin'd to my Man's Opinion, that 'twas a Devil; but whether Male, or Female, was in Doubt.

The Figure was upwards of Six Feet, a swarthy Complexion, a large Bottle-Nose, that spread so far on each Cheek, that took a great deal off from the Length of the Face; the Eyes no bigger than Ferrets, and full as Red, the Mouth very large, and the Under-Lip hung over the Chin. The Dress was a Man's Hat; a Woman's short Cloak, that hung loose down to the Waste, which play'd to and fro', and gave Air to the Body; (which was without Stays;) from the Waste downwards, was a large Pair of Trowsers fit for a Burgher-Master.

As soon as we were seated, Dominic trembling, got behind my Chair; and whisper'd me, the Candle burnt blue. I order'd him to withdraw, and shut the Door after him, which he was willing to comply with. After taking a thorough View, I desired to know in what Manner I was to address my self, Sir, or Madam? The answer was, I am a Woman, Sir, and Mistress of a large family; I find you are much surpriz'd at my Dress, therefore I shall explain it, and proceed to my Business.

You are to know, Sir, I am a Woman of Fashion; I was born and bred in *France*, and the Dress you see me in, was *French* originally, but now modeliz'd.

In the years 19 and 20, which were the Two Years, *France, Holland,* and *England,* were searching for the *Philosopher's Stone,* I was then at what we Women call, Years of Discretion; that is, to be capable of Distinguishing, to know what's Becoming, and what not. In the first Place we, One and All, agreed to shave our Heads; and to supply this Defect (if any were so stupid as to think it one), a Peruke was Propos'd, curl'd quite round, and very short, like unto that of a Shock Dog, which we call the *Tete de Mutton:* Upon this a Coif was sew'd; so that without any Trouble, we could dress, and undress the Head. This I left off upon my Arrival; and to supply the Place, betook me to the Man's Hat.

The next thing to complete our *French* Dress, was the Robe *Volante,* what the Vulgar call'd a *Sac.* This was a loose Gown full of Pleats, and without any Girdle: in which Habit we frequently took the Air on Horseback. I must inform you, our Manner there was to ride on Stride; therefore to answer that Part of the Dress, you see me loose to the Waste; As to my Breeches, they are an Improvement upon the Fashion, and what our Sex, when accustom'd to, will not dislike to wear.

I told her, I thank'd her for her Relation, but that I was going to be busy, therefore desired her to be Brief: to which she reply'd, Sir,

I'll take up as little of your time as possible, and therefore shall come to the Point.

I am informed you are acquainted with the MONITOR; and therefore what I have to propose, is to serve him: I love to do all the Good in my Power. I have Six Daughters (God bless them all!) and each of them capable of any Post he shall think proper to confer upon them.

Here I was more confounded than ever, and took the woman to be mad; to which I reply'd, Madam, What Post are they desirous of? O Sir, reply'd the Lady, they have different Talents. There's my Eldest Daughter Miss *Leer,* is as good a Girl at Attraction, as any in the Country; and will draw a Circle about her immediately where ever she goes.

Then my Second, Miss *Sly;* She has not one Bit of *French* in her, she's Secret as Death. Believe me, Sir, she was once in the company of 12 Women for 6 Hours, and never opened her Lips. You may set her down for some important Occasion.

My Third Daughter, Miss *Fidget;* She's here and there and every where; she never misses a Tea-Table, if there be Ten within the Compass of her Visits in a Day. There she hears Slander, Back-biting, and Scandal, which may turn out to some Use.

As to my Fourth Daughter, *Amoret;* She's a fine Girl, that's the Truth on't. She's forever moist'ning her Lips with her Tongue, that gives them a pouting Ripeness that tempts all the young Fellows in the Town; then she's a Girl of a very inquisitive Temper; so she may be excellent in her Way.

My fifth Daughter, *Phyllis,* She's an unaccountable Girl. The first Week of every Moon, she's dying for Love of some *Adonis,* or other.—She's for ever receiving or answering of *Billet-deux,* and Scraps of Poetry which may or may not be amiss.

As to my youngest Daughter, *Euphemia;* she's courted by Sir *Politick Wou'd-be;* he can inform her how Affairs stand in—(but no Matter). She's a good Girl of a bright Genius, and very willing; therefore I take her to be undeniable.

And now, Sir, I have given you an Account of my Family. I live a great Way off; and as this was my chief Errant, I hope you'll dispatch me to my Satisfaction. If you please to enjoin them or me to Secrecy, they're within Call.

To which I reply'd, since they were so desirous of Employment, I would engage them for the MONITOR; but could not put them into immediate Service 'til the MONITOR had weigh'd the Matter and considered their respective Qualifications: That if she pleas'd to send for them, I would talk to them: Upon which the good Lady, with the utmost Transport, seiz'd hold of a Pen, call'd for Half a

Sheet of Paper, and dispatch'd her Messenger directly. I importun'd her, in the mean-Time, to refresh her self, and recruit her Spirits with a Glass of Wine after her Fatigue; and in a short Space of Time the Ladies appear'd. After a little Discourse, they told me, if I distrusted their Honours, they were willing to be enjoin'd by Oath. Upon which I thought I could not administer any Oath upon the Occasion more binding than that of the Free Masons; and, after fast'ning the Door, and going thro' some of the usual Forms, I tender'd it to them, which they took with great Solemnity.

N.B. *Their different Emploiments will be settled as soon as possible.*

THE MONITOR NO. 13

Of Love and Reason

Nil admirari prope res est una Numici,
Solaque qua pusseracere & servare beatum.*
—HOR. EPIST. VI LIB. i

To the MONITOR

Worshipful Sir,

I Attack'd Miss *Fainwould* upon the Subject I mentioned to you some Time since; but she denied it in a particular Manner: I know my Sex pretty well, and therefore I let it breath a while. Last *Saturday* going into Church, she unluckily took out her Handkerchief, and drop'd the following Lines.

To Miss FAINWOULD.

Since first I beheld thy bright Eyes,
Which to Love my fond Heart did betray;
How swiftly the Happy Time flies!
'Tis no more than one Week and one Day.

Please to observe, Sir, that the King's Birth Day was Saturday was Sen'night.

*To wonder at nothing, Numicius, is perhaps the only thing which can make a man happy and keep him that way.

O! why was my Fate so severe,
To be parted when first we were met?
But adieu!—to complain I forbear,
Since you promis'd me, ne'er to forget.
W. Z.

I embrac'd the first Opportunity when Church was over, and delivered the Paper to her; she seem'd to be under some Confusion at the receiving of it, but after she had recovered herself, was extremely complaisant, and insisted upon my going home with her, where I have remained ever since, and am now let into the Secret. You are to know, Sir, that she has no less than Three Suitors, *viz. a Parson, a Doctor, and a Lawyer.* The young Lady is of a sprightly Genius, and lively Imagination; and has no Aversion to that *same Thing* call'd *Matrimony.* Tho' in my Opinion, I think she's a little too nice. She refutes the Parson absolutely, and says he's for ever lolling upon a Couch, with a Book in his Hand; and is inform'd by her Nurse that 'tis your active Men that make the best Husbands.

As to my Part, I think the Parson promises well; and were it not for this ill Habit (uncommon to the Profession) of studying too much, I believe he wou'd certainly be the Man. At present, indeed, she speaks in the Doctor's Favour: He's a strange Man that's the Truth on't; he's forever feeling of her Pulse; and were he let alone, I believe o' my Conscience he would trace it from Head to Foot.

As for the Mother of the younger Lady, she's for the Lawyer: Indeed he has a good deal to say for himself: He has promis'd to recover an Estate that was never in the Family. How this Matter will end, I know not; but this Morning the Parson was dismiss'd: He made his Exit with a tolerable good Grace, and behav'd with a proper Decorum; look'd wishfully; sigh'd reasonably; made his Honours, and so forth. Some Time after he was gone, we found a Letter upon the Table in the Room where he lay, with the following Poem, which I take to be his last Night's Soliloquy.

I am, with due Respect,
Sir, your Most Humble Servant,
PENELOPE LEER

I.
All hail, *ye fields, where constant Peace attends,*
    All hail, *ye sacred solitary Groves,*
All hail, *ye Books, my true my lasting Friends,*
    Whose Conversation pleases and improves.

II.

Cou'd one who studies your sublimer Rules,
　　Become so mad to seek for Joys abroad?
To run to Towns, to herd with Knaves and Fools,
　　And undistinguish'd pass among the Crowd.

III.

To wild Ambition many there a prey,
　　Think Happiness in great Preferment lies;
Nor fear for that, their Country to betray,
　　Gaz'd at by Fools, and laugh'd at by the Wise.

IV.

More still, when eager Hopes of Wealth bewitch,
　　Their precious Time consume, t'increase their Gains
And fancying wretched, all that are not rich,
　　Neglect the End of Life to get the Name.

V.

But most of all, soft Pleasure's Charms invite
　　In one gay Scene of sensual Joys to live,
Who vainly hope to find that long Delight
　　In Vice, which Virtue's Charms alone can give.

VI.

But how perplex'd, alas, is Humane Fate!
　　I, whom nor sordid Pelf, nor Pleasures move,
Who view with Scorn the Trophies of the Great,
　　Am made, my Self, a wretched Slave to Love.

VII.

If this dire Passion never will be gone,
　　If Beauty always must my Heart inthrall,
O! rather let me be confin'd to one,
　　Than madly thus become a Prey to all.

VIII.

One who has early known the Pomp of State,
　　(For Things unknown, 'tis Ignorance to condemn,)
And after having view'd the gaudy Bait,
　　Can boldly say, the Trifle I contemn.

IX.

In her blest Arms contented could I live,
  Contented could I dye.—But, O my Mind!
Imaginary Scenes of Bliss deceive,
  With Hopes of Things impossible to find.

X.

In Woman, how can Sense and Beauty meet?
  The wisest Men their Truth in Folly spend:
The best is he, who early knows the Cheat
  And finds his Error, while there's Time to mend.

There is no Time of Life we expose our Folly more, than at that Juncture we take it in our Heads to be in *Love*. This same Passion, which is called the Noblest of the Mind, I take to be an infectious Distemper, and bears a near Affinity to that obnoxious Disease, *the Small-Pox, The Physiologia, Pathologia,* and *Semeiotica* in Persons in Love, are the same with Those in the *Small-Pox.* The proper Time of Catching either of these Distempers, is when the Spirits are at the High Tide of the Flood; and, in my Opinion, tho' Mankind are less careful of the Former, they ought to ward against it as much as the Latter.

The one is a Drain to the Mind, the other to the Body; and the greatest Happiness that can attend us, is, that we can have them but once; the Cure of both depend upon Prudence and a proper Regimen.

2

FEDERALS

Philip Freneau (1752–1832)

Tomo Cheeki

*F*EW AMERICAN AUTHORS have written under more pseudonyms than Philip Freneau. However, like many of his contemporaries, Freneau made only occasional attempts at characterizing these pen names as recognizable personalities. One of the few was Tomo Cheeki, a Creek Indian who visited Philadelphia in the mid-1790s. Philadelphia was then the capital of the newly constituted Republic, and by having his simple yet eloquent spokesman comment upon events and customs of the city, Freneau could dissect the new body politic starting with the heart. He introduced his aboriginal ingenu on 23 May 1795 in the pages of the *Jersey Chronicle*, which he edited at the time. Like Steele and Franklin before him, Freneau immediately fixed his character in his designated setting. He then established a credible reason for a protracted series of writings (the Indian had left behind a cache of musings that his Philadelphia landlord had discovered).

The major segment of Freneau's literary career spans the final quarter of the eighteenth century, an epoch marked by residual characteristics of neoclassicism and by the burgeoning romantic movement. Both elements are evident in his work, and the Tomo Cheeki pieces are no exception. The character itself exemplifies obvious features of the Noble Savage, an idealized prototype suggesting the principle that the being who lives in a natural state is superior because of proximity to the Divine Presence that pervades the natural world it had originally created. Yet the observations of this

---

The Freneau selections are from *The Prose of Philip Freneau*, edited by Philip M. Marsh (New Brunswick, N.J.: Scarecrow Press, 1955).

American exponent constitute a simple criticism of the emerging society as being strange and unnatural. This suggests a basic belief in a naturally structured, well-ordered universe as perceived by the neoclassicists.

But above all, Freneau was a satirist and something of a radical. While an undergraduate at Princeton, he and H. H. Brackenridge had coauthored a class poem, "The Rising Glory of America." This was completed in 1771, and represented an affront to established English authority four years before revolutionary sentiments erupted into open war. By the mid-1790s, however, an independent America had become the establishment, and it was thus against its laws, its public officials, and its "civilized" patterns of emerging urban life that Tomo Cheeki's remarks were primarily aimed.

Introducing Tomo Cheeki

Some years ago, about thirty Indian chiefs of the Creek nation, attended by several squaws, came by land to Philadelphia, to settle a treaty of amity with the republican government of this country, and to solicit presents of looking-glasses, beads, brandy, blankets, hatchets, and a few other articles in general use and esteem among the various savage nations of this continent. During their residence in the above-named city, which was for several months, one of these chiefs was particularly noticed for the gravity of his deportment, his melancholy aspect, his pithy sayings, and a certain exotic peculiarity of character, which distinguished him in no small degree from his companions.—While they were amusing themselves in the streets with shooting arrows at half-pence, set perpendicularly on a post by the boys of the city, he employed himself in noting down observations on the buildings of the place, the character of the inhabitants, the policies of white men, and such other particulars as occurred from a situation, to him, so new and strange:—While his fellow deputies were carousing in taverns and dramshops, he would walk into the fields and woods, smoke his pipe—divert himself with fishing and such other rural employments as he found most inviting and agreeable to his savage fancy.

So singular a character could not escape observation, nor do otherwise than excite some degree of curiosity. After his departure, enquiry was made of the landlord of the house where he had lodged, for some particulars relative to this son of the woods. Little, however, could be got out of the publican concerning his guest except that he was fond of cyder and small beer, slept but five hours out of the twenty four; rose constantly at the first dawn of the day, walked several miles before sun rising, eat sparingly, seemed generally absorbed in thought, now & then noted down his remarks in his own language, expressed great disgust at the manners of civilized society,—and danced a whole hour, the evening before his departure, with a favourite squaw. The landlord added, that since the departure of Tomo Cheeki and his companions, a large bundle of papers had been discovered in an old hamper in a corner of the room where he had lodged, which he judged to be the notes and remarks this Indian had penned down while he resided in the city;—and that it had probably been forgotten at the time the savages departed for their own country. The landlord having intimated that the papers were now his sole property, his price for them was demanded; and on being answered that he would quit all claim to them for the value of ten French crowns, the sum was willingly paid, as it seemed more than probable that the notes and observations of a savage of his character, could not but afford some amusement, if a translator for such an abstruse body of writing could possibly be discovered. This, however, was for a long time found impracticable. No person offered, that had a sufficient knowledge of the Talassee, or Creek language, to give only a tolerable translation. The bundle of papers was consequently thrown aside, and for a long time lay forgotten. A prisoner, however, having since made his escape from among the Creek nation, who had resided nearly twenty years, has been engaged to undertake a translation. He promises to be close and literal, not to amplify in the least, but to be true and faithful to his original, as far as the idioms of the two languages will allow. As these translated papers come to hand they will be inserted in the JERSEY CHRONICLE, for the amusement and information of the curious.

The "Savage" Way of Life

As I travel through the streets and bye-ways of this village, I never fail hearing the condition of my brethren and myself commiserated by the men and women of the place, on account of what they call our savage way of life, when at home.

We, in turn, no less pity them for living cooped up in dark cages and narrow boxes, where they have scarcely room to turn or breathe, where the cheerful rays of the sun never yet penetrated but are concealed from the wretched inhabitant by walls of stupendous height and thickness.

The most unrelenting storm, the darkest mourning cloth of clouds that ever over shadowed the face of the Heavens, is sooner or later scattered & dissipated before the light of the great luminary: but in these deep alleys and narrow path-ways reigns a perpetual gloom, the source of pining discontent and peevish melancholy.

There sits the artist on his bench, pale as the grass beneath the thick spreading oak; actuated, like a machine, by the will of another, he moves not from place to place, but is restrained by an artificial necessity to his gloomy habitation.

But in our country, and with us, a tree, on occasion, will serve us for a house. Our largest wigwams are erected and finished in a day, and admit the light and air in abundance. In summer, we allow the winds to blow freely through the sides, made of cane and wattles: in the winter, the fire is placed in the middle, and all enjoy an equal share. Our woods supply us with plenty of fuel, and for nothing; while here it is brought to the inhabitant in little niggardly parcels, and at the cost of much money. In many of their habitations here we are not allowed to see the cheerful blaze—it is confined to a thick dark case of iron, and throws out a deadly smothering heat that never fails to deject & afflict my spirit.—In others, the fire place is in the side of the wall—the master of the wigwam only enjoyeth the heat, and looketh with a stern eye on those who approach to partake of his little sneaking fire of two sticks.

But before the night is advanced too far, and the taper that yet burns brightly before me shall grow dim in the socket, I will put down some few particulars of the manner of what is called the savage life, by the white men.

I feel a flow of re-animation at the recollection of the charming vision, and would instantly return to enjoy it, were I not restrained by the frowns of the big men of the council, who have strictly enjoined my brethren and myself not to return without at least the looking-glasses, blankets, and brandy.

In the morning early we rise from the bed of skins to hail the first dawn of the sun: We seize our bows and arrows—we fly hastily through the dews of the forests—we attack the deer, the stag, or the buffaloe, and return with abundance of food for the whole family. Wherever we run it is amidst the luxuriant vegetation of Nature, the delectable regale of flowers and blossoms, and beneath trees bending with plump and Joyous fruits.

By this time the stomach receives its food with a pleasure unknown to the puny sons of this huge village. Our drink is the milk of the goat, mingled with the clear water of the stream flowing over the white sand or yellow pebbles—It is that which every wise Indian prefers, because it is the drink prepared by the hand of NATURE.

Every desire of the heart is considered as a blessing of this our common mother. These desires are few and simple, and are almost always within our power to gratify. We can vary them at pleasure, and thus they are always new.

We are strangers to the cruel passion of jealousy, and consider that man as under the dominion of the foolish spirit who is distrustful of his wife. Our young women live constantly under the golden star of Love; nor do we think the less of them if, before they are married, they indulge in that amiable passion.

In the forests, we acknowledge no distinction of property. The woods are as free as the waters; and the odious land-mark was never seen to arrest the foot of the hunter.

We are carried along upon the great wheel of things. We trouble ourselves not about the uncertainties, or the seeming irregulations of its motions. When the comet extends its long glittering tail over our thick forests, or when the moon puts on her black mantle of mourning, we apprehend no cause of alarm. It is the work of the great spirit of the universe, who sleepeth not, but day and night guides his wonderful machine in the way that is best.

However numerous may be our wives, or our children around us, we afflict not our souls with trouble to know what will become of them when we are no more. Whether they shall be doomed to carry wood, as slaves, on the borders of the white men; or to bring the heavy load of waters from the springs of Owya menah, it is the same thing. We leave them to the care of that good Being who is the protector of the destitute.

We hear not the voice of the tax-gatherer at our doors, to take away our bed of skins to support the luxuries of the proud, and governments that riot on the spoils of the poor. We despise all tributes, and abhor those burthens which are imposed on the white men to tame and degrade the spirit.

Surrounded by forests that have no lines of boundary, we fear no storms—they blow far above us, and are spent in the regions over the tops of the trees. We are in dread of no droughts, for nature has so overshadowed the soil that the sunbeams cannot scorch it. It is therefore always moist, and favourable to the little gardens that give us the vegetables we want. The most impetuous torrents are arrested by the woods and thickets, and cannot sweep away our harvests before them.

Our manner of life renders us alert, cheerful, and courageous.

We live in the midst of content, and when the time comes that we must depart to the silent mansions of our fathers, we depart without regret, because we are sure that our sleep, though in reality it may be long, can be, to us, but a moment. When that interrupting pause of life is once made, a total oblivion of the past ensues; but we suppose we shall soon revive, young, vigorous, and beautiful, to enjoy once more the chace of the forest and the pleasures of the wigwam. This seems to be the oeconomy of Nature, at least with regard to the men of the woods.

Joseph Dennie (1768–1812)

The Lay Preacher

*H*AD IT NOT BEEN for the unprecedented literary success of Washington Irving in early nineteenth-century America, Joseph Dennie might be recognized as the stellar figure among journalists of the Federal period. He was a friend and close associate of such notable authors as Royall Tyler and T. G. Fessenden, and during the years that he edited the *Farmer's Weekly Museum* of Walpole, New Hampshire (1796–1798), he enjoyed a national reputation. This popularity derived in large measure from his authorship of a series of secular sermons delivered in the guise of the "Lay Preacher." According to Joseph T. Buckingham, a printer's devil during Dennie's tenure, large packages of the *Museum* were carried south each week to other states. The sermons, moreover, were published in "nearly all the newspapers in the nation," thus becoming among the first such journalism to be syndicated.

Despite his success as the Lay Preacher, Dennie had his share of disappointments as a literary man. Among these was an elaborate edition of the Lay Preacher pieces, which might have assured popularity beyond their appearance in the *Museum,* but which never materialized. (Not until the twentieth century was a collected edition published.) Frank Luther Mott, a leading historian of American newspapers, has proclaimed the pieces "probably the best periodical essays ever produced in America."

The Lay Preacher himself is a genial, engaging narrator whose parish is the world at large and whose texts are taken

---

The selection is from Joseph Dennie, *The Lay Preacher* (New York: Scholars' Facsimiles and Reprints, 1943).

from religious as well as secular sources. The topics upon which he discourses are often matters that concern the everyday lives of his readers. Thus, when delivering his New Year's sermon, the subject of contemporary politics is specifically treated (Dennie was an ardent Federalist, and thus an admirer of Washington). The overall tone is nevertheless moral, but never in a strictly didactic sense. Speaking from a broad base of morality, the Preacher was able to appeal to Puritan and secularist alike.

Design of the Preacher

> I will rise now and go about the city, in the streets, and in the broad ways.
>
> —*SONG OF SOLOMON* iii.2

In a walk so wide and various, the pondering preacher, perhaps, can moralize upon the shifting scenes more profitably, aye, and more pleasantly too, than a more heedless pedestrian. He who sallies out for the express purpose of speculation and remark, with his scrutinizing spectacles on and "with a patient ear," can note and describe, with greater accuracy than the individual who is cramped with the crowd or who, engrossed by some worldly care, is hurrying onward to his object.

I have long been of opinion that if I could traverse the market place, visit the mart, lounge at the coffee-houses, and explore, in the homely phrase of Sancho, "every creek and corner" of a great city, that I could profitably compose a little essay, and tell occasionally what I had seen and heard. With this opportunity, eagerly sought and long denied, I am now indulged. In the metropolis of my country I have found a sort of parsonage, which has been my shelter for more than a year. Having had time to visit many of my new parishioners, to compose my cares, and put my study in order, I have thought it expedient to shake off sluggishness, to rouse from the dreams of abstraction, and to resolve, as it seems Solomon, in my text, has done before me, to rise now and go about the city, in the streets, and in the broad ways.

Many years ago I stood in a rustic pulpit and was wont to address myself to the few villagers who thought my sermons worth listening to. It was literally "the voice of one crying in the wilderness," for the forest was frequently my study and my principal hearers a gurgling brook, a silent valley, or an aged tree. I had but few of the fathers to consult, and perused the best of books, not with Poole's, but my own commentary. My discourses, like the tedious narratives of farmer Flamborough in the "Vicar of Wakefield," began to be "very long, very dull, and all about myself." My hearers grew desperate, and I disheartened. I took an affectionate leave of them, migrated to the city, and sought preferment. Of the difficulty in obtaining it I quickly had occasion to meditate in the text of "Ye shall seek me, but ye shall not find me." Disappointed in my golden and romantic expectations of a benefice, I have become quietly submissive to the mandate of necessity; acquire, as fast as I can, "the knack of hoping;" and, like some cheery practical philosopher that I have read of, "draw upon content for the deficiencies of fortune."

But, though not translated to a see, nor even made chaplain to a bishop; though I neither snore with fat prebends in a stall, nor gloriously wake with a Watson or a Horsley, yet, as happy brides are wont to say, I have some reason to be pleased with the alteration of my condition. My study is enlarged, and I have received salary enough to purchase the works of St. Austin and a bible of better print than the little Scotch edition I used to twirl over in the country. Though the tithes of a Lay Preacher are very tardily collected, yet the more liberal parishioner does not always forget that "the labourer is worthy of his hire." Cheerfulness keeps pace with Patronage, and though there is not much danger that she will be outstripped by her companion, I have such good spirits and such agreeable reveries in my "Journeyings," whether from country to town, or "from Dan to Beersheba," that I often flatter myself I shall "From diocese to diocese, to Canterbury pass, sir."

But enough of this levity. It remains to speak of the profit, or the pleasure, which I propose to my readers from my habit of going about the city. If, either as a watchman or a lounger, I traverse its streets, or its broad ways, the utility of such a ramble need not long be doubted. It will enable me to variegate my speculations, to discern all the hues of "many coloured life," to turn gay subjects to moral purposes, and furnish copious materials for rebuke or exhortation.

On the decisive authority of the sagacious author of the text, we are told that wisdom crieth without and uttereth her voice in the streets, in the chief place of concourse, in the openings of the gates, in the city. We are repeatedly assured, by one who perfectly knew all her haunts, that she standeth in the top of high places, by the way, in the places of the paths, at the entry of the city and at the coming in at the doors. Now, if such places be her chief resort, it is surely laudable to look for her there, to go about, and strive to meet her, and persuade others to be companions in such a stroll. This is an invincible argument in support of the proposition; and if my readers, in their pride of logic, talk of sophisms and fallacy, they virtually vote the words of the wise, foolish; and Solomon himself, a simpleton!

3

YANKEES

Seba Smith's "Major Jack Downing" smiling wryly and surrounded by his military trappings and letters to his relatives. (from The Life and Writings of Major Jack Downing, *1834)*

Seba Smith (1792–1868)

Major Jack Downing

WHEN SEBA SMITH conceived the idea of Jack Downing, he was concerned about making a success of the *Portland Courier,* which he had founded in 1829. Portland was then the capital of Maine and when the legislators took their seats in January 1830, each party had an equal number of representatives. The natural result was a stalemate on every question, from choosing a speaker to actual legislating. It was a situation tailor-made for a satirist. Not wishing to take a partisan position (Smith maintained an apolitical stance), he fashioned a rustic ingenu who could convey in commonsense terms the views of the common man. And, true to the conventions of the genre, Smith provided him with a recognizable provenance. Jack Downing was a native of the mythical Downingville, a rural Maine village, who had come to Portland bearing a supply of goods produced by the cottage industries of his community. In typical Yankee fashion, he shrewdly dealt with the businessmen of Portland in bartering his axe helves and cheeses. In the process of familiarizing himself with the city, he wandered into the State "Legislater." Thus began the series of letters he wrote home to his family—his cousin Ephraim, his uncle Joshua, his father—and, somewhat later, to the editor of the *Courier.*

If imitation is the highest form of flattery, Smith must have been gratified. Almost immediately the letters were pirated by other newspapers, and spurious continuations began to appear (they persisted throughout much of Smith's

---

The selections are from Seba Smith, *The Life and Writings of Major Jack Downing* (Boston: Lily, Wait, Colman, & Holden, 1834).

career). Smith soon realized that his surrogate had attracted interest far beyond his local environs; therefore, he wisely sent him off to Washington, where he became an intimate of President Andrew Jackson and one of the cronies in his "kitchen cabinet." Thus, despite his provincial upbringing, Jack Downing became a sort of folk hero of national scope. One of the most interesting sidelights in his career is the fact that hosts of readers took him to be a real person. This is a tribute to Smith's ability to select genuine raw materials and fashion them into a credible figure so true to actual type as to be indistinguishable from it. It is thus the realness of Jack Downing that makes him a kind of paradigm that succeeding writers tried to emulate, often with uneven results.

The creation of the Yankee Jack Downing for the *Portland Courier* in 1830 represented a rite of passage for the fictional personality in American newspapers. Downing was fashioned from distinctly American materials: his dialect that of the Down-Easter, his native Downingville a typical New England pioneering community, his instincts those of the Yankee trader. Moreover, Downing was the first such character to become a national craze, and the first to have his newspaper letters collected into a separate volume. By 1830, then, authors who devised masks might still owe a vague debt to English prototypes, but for raw material and for popularization they could rely completely upon native resources.

Choosing a Speaker*

Portland, Monday, Jan. 18, 1830.

To Cousin Ephraim Downin up in Downingville.

DEAR COUSIN EPHRAIM.—I now take my pen in hand to let you know that I am well, hoping these few lines will find you enjoying the same blessing. When I come down to Portland I did n't think o' staying more than three or four days, if I could sell my load of ax handles, and mother's cheese, and cousin Nabby's bundle of footings; but when I got here I found Uncle Nat was gone a freighting down to Quoddy, and ant Sally said as how I should n't stir a step home till he come back agin, which wont be this month. So here I am, loitering about this great town, as lazy as an ox. Ax handles dont fetch nothing, I could n't hardly give 'em away. Tell cousin Nabby I sold her footings for nine-pence a pair, and took it all in cotton cloth. Mother's cheese come to five-and-sixpence; I got her half a pound of shushon, and two ounces of snuff, and the rest in sugar. When uncle Nat comes home I shall put my ax handles aboard of him, and let him take 'em to Boston next time he goes; I saw a feller tother day, that told me they'd fetch a good price there.—I've been here now a whole fortnight, and if I could tell ye one half I've seen, I guess you'd stare worse than if you'd seen a catamount. I've been to meeting, and to the museum, and to both Legislaters, the one they call the House, and the one they call the

*[The political struggle in the Legislature of Maine in the winter of 1830 will long be remembered. The preceding electioneering campaign had been carried on with a bitterness and personality unprecedented in the State, and so nearly were the parties divided, that before the meeting of the Legislature to count the votes for Governor both sides confidently claimed the victory. Hence the members came together with feelings highly excited, prepared to dispute every inch of ground, and ready to take fire at the first spark which collision might produce. A fierce war commenced at the first moment of the meeting, and continued for about six weeks without intermission, before they succeeded in organizing the government. It was during this state of things that Mr. Downing fortunately happened to drop into the Legislature, when his prolific genius was at once fired to record the scenes that were passing before him, for the edification not only of the present generation but of remote posterity. In explanation of the first letter, it may be remarked, that as soon as the Representatives had assembled, Albert Smith, Esq. of Nobleborough, the present Marshal of Maine, called them to order, and nominated Mr. White of Monmouth, Chairman, who was declared elected without ceremony, and took the chair. After he had occupied it two days Mr. Goodenow was elected Speaker.]—Smith's note.

Sinnet. I spose uncle Joshua is in a great hurry to hear something about these Legislaters; for you know he's always reading newspapers, and talking politics, when he can get any body to talk with him. I've seen him, when he had five tons of hay in the field well made, and a heavy shower coming up, stand two hours disputing with squire W. about Adams and Jackson, one calling Adams a tory and a fed, and the other saying Jackson was a murderer and a fool; so they kept it up, till the rain began to pour down, and about spoilt all his hay.

Uncle Joshua may set his heart at rest about the bushel of corn that he bet long with the post-master, that Mr. Ruggles would be Speaker of that Legislater, they call the House; for he's lost it, slick as a whistle. As I had n't much to do, I've been there every day since they've been a setting. A Mr. White of Monmouth was the Speaker the two first days; and I cant see why they did n't keep him in all the time; for he seemed to be a very clever good-natured sort of man, and he had such a smooth pleasant way with him, that I could n't help feeling sorry when they turned him out and put in another. But some said he was n't put in hardly fair; and I dont know as he was, for the first day when they were all coming in and crowding round, there was a large fat man, with a round, full, jolly sort of a face, I suppose he was the captain, for he got up and commanded them to come to order, and then he told this Mr. White to whip into the chair quicker than you could say Jack Robinson. Some of 'em scolded about it, and I heard some, in a little room they called the lobby, say 'twas a mean trick; but I could n't see why, for I thought Mr. White made a capital Speaker, and when our company turns out you know the captain always has a right to do as he 's a mind to.

They kept disputing most all the time the two first days about a poor Mr. Roberts from Waterborough. Some said he should n't have a seat, because he adjourned the town meeting, and was n't fairly elected. Others said it was no such thing, and that he was elected as fairly as any of 'em.—And Mr. Roberts himself said he was, and said he could bring men that would swear to it, and good men too. But notwithstanding all this, when they came to vote, they got three or four majority that he should n't have a seat. And I thought it a needless piece of cruelty, for they want crowded, and there was a number of seats empty. But they would have it so, and the poor man had to go and stand up in the lobby.

Then they disputed awhile about a Mr. Fowler's having a seat. Some said he should n't have a seat, because when he was elected some of his votes were given for his father. But they were more kind to him than they were to Mr. Roberts; for they voted that he should have a seat; and I suppose it was because they thought he had a lawful right to inherit whatever was his father's. They all declared there was no party politics about it, and I dont think there was; for I noticed that all who voted that Mr. Roberts should have a seat, voted that Mr. Fowler should not; and all who voted that Mr. Roberts should not have a seat, voted that Mr. Fowler should. So, as they all voted both ways, they must have acted as their consciences told them, and I dont see how there could be any party about it.

It's a pity they could n't be allowed to have two speakers, for they seemed to be very anxious to choose Mr. Ruggles and Mr. Goodenow. They two had every vote, except one, and if they had had that, I believe they would both have been chosen; as it was, however, they both came within a humbird's eye of it. Whether it was Mr. Ruggles that voted for Mr. Goodenow, or Mr. Goodenow for Mr. Ruggles, I can't exactly tell; but I rather guess it was Mr. Ruggles voted for Mr. Goodenow, for he appeared to be very glad that Mr. Goodenow was elected, and went up to him soon after Mr. Goodenow took the chair, and shook hands with him as goodnatured as could be. I would have given half my load of ax handles, if they could both have been elected and set up there together, they would have been so happy. But as they can't have but one speaker at a time, and as Mr. Goodenow appears to understand the business very well, it is not likely Mr. Ruggles will be speaker any this winter. So Uncle Joshua will have to shell out his bushel of corn, and I hope it will learn him better than to bet about politics again. If he had not been a goose, he might have known he would loose it, even if he had been ever so sure of getting it; for in these politics there's never any telling which way the cat will jump. You know, before the last September election, some of the papers that came to our town had found out that Mr. Hunton would have five thousand majority of the votes. And some of the other papers had found out that Mr. Smith would have five thousand majority. But the cat jumped 'tother way to *both* of 'em; for I cant find yet as either of 'em has got any majority. Some say Mr. Hunton has got a little majority, but as far from five thousand as I am from home. And as for Mr. Smith, they dont think he has any majority at all. You remember, too, before I came from home, some of the papers said how there was a majority of ten or fifteen national republicans in the Legislater, and the other papers said there was a pretty clever little majority of democratic republicans. Well, now every body says it has turned out jest as that queer little paper, called the *Daily Courier*, said 't would. That paper said it was such a close rub, it could n't hardly tell which side would beat. And it 's jest so, for they 've been here now most a fortnight acting jest like two boys playin see-saw on a rail. First one goes up, then 'tother; but I reckon one of the boys is rather heaviest, for once in awhile he comes down chuck, and throws the other up into the air as though he would pitch him head over heels.

In that 'tother Legislater they call the Sinnet, there has been some of the drollest carryins on that you ever heard of. If I can get time I 'll write you something about it, pretty soon. So I subscribe myself, in haste, your loving cousin till death.

JACK DOWNING

Major Downing and Mr. Van Buren Quarrel

Washington City, July 20, 1833.

To my old friend, the editor of the *Portland Courier*, away down east in the State of Maine.

MY DEAR OLD FRIEND, YOU.—I dont know but you might think strange on 't, that I should be back here to Washington more than a fortnight, and not write to you. But I hant forgot you. You need n't never be afraid of that. We aint very apt to forget our best friends; and you may depend upon it Jack Downing will never forget the editor of the *Portland Courier* any more than Andrew Jackson will forget Jack Downing. You was the first person that ever give me a lift into public life, and you 've been a boosting me along ever since. And jest between you and me I think I'm getting into a way now where I shall be able by and by to do something to pay you for it. The reason that I have n't writ to you before, is, that we have had pretty serious business to attend to since we got back. But we 've jest got through with it, and Mr. Van Buren has cleared out and gone back about the quickest to New York, and I guess with a bed-bug in his ear. Now jest between you and me in confidence, I'll tell you how 't is; but pray dont let on about it to any body else for the world. Did n't you think plaguy strange what made us cut back so quick from Concord without going to Portland or Portsmouth or Downingville? You know the papers have said it was because the President want very well, and the President had to make that excuse himself in some of his letters; but it was no such thing. The President could a marched on foot twenty miles a day then, and only let him been at the head of my Downingville company and he 'd a made a whole British regiment scamper like a flock of sheep.

But you see the trouble ont was, there was some difficulty between I and Mr. Van Buren. Some how or other Mr. Van Buren always looked kind of jealous at me all the time after he met us at New York; and I could n't help minding every time the folks hollered 'hoorah for Major Downing' he would turn as red as a blaze of fire.

And wherever we stopped to take a bite or to have a chat, he would always work it, if he could, somehow or other so as to crowd in between me and the President. Well, ye see, I wouldn't mind much about it, but would jest step round 'tother side. And though I say it myself, the folks would look at me, let me be on which side I would; and after they'd cried hoorah for the President, they'd most always sing out 'hoorah for Major Downing.' Mr. Van Buren kept growing more and more fidgety till we got to Concord. And there we had a room full of sturdy old democrats of New Hampshire, and after they had all flocked round the old President and shook hands with him, he happened to introduce me to some of 'em before he did Mr. Van Buren. At that the fat was all in the fire. Mr. Van Buren wheeled about and marched out of the room looking as though he could bite a board nail off. The President had to send for him three times before he could get him back into the room again. And when he did come, he didn't speak to me for the whole evening. However we kept it from the company pretty much; but when we come to go up to bed that night, we had a real quarrel. It was nothing but jaw, jaw, the whole night. Mr. Woodbury and Mr. Cass tried to pacify us all they could, but it was all in vain, we didn't one of us get a wink of sleep, and shouldn't if the night had lasted a fortnight. Mr. Van Buren said the President had dishonored the country by placing a military Major on half pay before the second officer of the government. The President begged him to consider that I was a very particular friend of his; that I had been a great help to him at both ends of the country; that I had kept the British out of Madawaska away down in Maine, and had marched my company clear from Downingville to Washington, on my way to South Carolina, to put down the nullifiers; and he thought I was entitled to as much respect as any man in the country.

This nettled Mr. Van Buren peskily.—He said he thought it was a fine time of day if a raw jockey from an obscure village away down east, jest because he had a Major's commission, was going to throw the Vice President of the United States and the heads of Departments into the back ground. At this my dander began to rise, and I stepped right up to him; and says I, Mr. Van Buren, you are the last man that ought to call me a jockey. And if you'll go to Downingville and stand up before my company with Sarjeant Joel at their head, and call Downingville an obscure village, I'll let you use my head for a foot-ball as long as you live afterwards. For if they wouldn't blow you into ten thousand atoms, I'll never guess again. We got so high at last that the old President hopt off the bed like a boy; for he had laid down to rest him, bein it was near daylight, though he couldn't get to sleep. And says he, Mr. Donaldson, set down and write Mr. Anderson at Portland, and my friend Joshua Downing at Downingville, that I can't come. I'm going to start for Washington this morning. What, says Mr. Cass, and not go to Portsmouth and Exeter and round there! I tell you, says the President, I'm going to start for Washington this morning, and in three days I'll be there. What, says Mr. Woodbury, and not got to Portland, where they have spent so much money to get ready for us! I tell you, says the President, my foot is down: I go not a step further, but turn about this morning for Washington. What, says I, and not go to Downingville, what will Uncle Joshua say? At this the President looked a little hurt; and says he, Major Downing, I can't help it. As for going any further with such a din as this about my ears, I cannot, and will not, and I am resolved not to budge another inch. And sure enough the President was as good as his word, and we were all packed up by sunrise, and in three days we were in Washington.

And here we've been ever since, battling the watch about the next Presidency. Mr. Van Buren says the President promised it to him, and now he charges me and the President with a plot to work myself into it and leave him out. It's true I've been nominated in a good many papers, in the *National Intelligencer,* and in the *Munch Chunk Courier* printed away off among the coal diggers in Pennsylvany, and a good many more. And them are Pennsylvany chaps are real pealers for electing folks when they take hold; and that's what makes Mr. Van Buren so uneasy. The President tells him as he has promised to help him, he shall do what he can for him; but if the folks will vote for me he can't help it. Mr. Van Buren wanted I should come out in the *National Intelligencer* and resign, and so be put up for Vice President under him. But I told him no; bein it had gone so fur I wouldn't do nothing about it. I hadn't asked for the office, and if the folks had a mind to give it to me I wouldn't refuse it. So after we had battled it about a fortnight, Mr. Van Buren found it was no use to try to dicker with me, and he's cleared out and gone to New York to see what he can do there.

I never thought of getting in to be President so soon, though I've had a kind of hankering for it this two years. But now, seeing it's turned out as it has, I'm determined to make a bold push, and if I can get in by the free votes of the people, I mean to. The President says he rather I should have it than any body else, and if he hadn't promised Mr. Van Buren beforehand, he would use his influence for me.

I remember when I was a boy about a dozen years old, there was an old woman come to our house to tell fortunes. And after she'd told the rest of 'em, father says he, here's Jack, you haven't told his fortune yet, and I dont spose it's worth a telling, for he's a real mutton-headed boy. At that the old woman catched hold of my hair, and pulled my head back and looked into my face, and I never shall forget how she looked right through me, as long as I live. At last, says she, and she gin me a shove that sent me almost through the side of the house, Jack will beat the whole of you. He'll be a famous climber in his day, and wherever he sets out to climb, you may depend upon it, he will go to the top of the ladder. Now, putting all these things together, and the nominations in the papers, and the 'for Major Downing,' I dont know what it means, unless it means that I must be President. So, as I said afore, I'm determined to make a bold push. I've writ to Col. Crockett to see if I can get the support of the western States, and his reply is, 'go ahead.' I shall depend upon you and uncle Joshua to carry the State of Maine for me; and, in order to secure the other States, I spose it will be necessary to publish my life and writings. President Jackson had his life published before he was elected, and when Mr. Clay was a candidate he had hisn published. I've talked with the President about it, and he says, publish it by all means, and set the printer of the *Portland Courier* right about it.

So I want you to go to work as soon as you get this, and pick up my letters, and begin to print 'em in a book; and I'll set down and write a history of my life to put into it, and send it along as fast as I can get it done. But I want you to be very careful not to get any of them are confounded counterfeit letters, that the rascally fellers have been sending to the printers, mixed in long with mine. It would be as bad as breaking a rotten egg in long with the good ones; it would spile the whole pudding. You can tell all my letters, for they were all sent to you first.

The President says I must have a picter of me made and put into the book.—He says he had one put into his, and Mr. Clay had one put into his. So I believe I shall write to Mr. Thatcher that prints the little *Journal* paper in Boston, and get him to go to some of the best picter-makers there, and get them to do me up some as slick as they can. These things, you know, will all help get the free votes of the people; and that's all I want. For I tell you now, right up and down, I never will take any office that doesn't come by the free votes of the people. I'm a genuine democratic republican, and always was, and so was my father before me, and uncle Joshua besides.

There's a few more things that I want to speak to you about in this letter, but I'm afraid it will get to be too lengthy. That are story that they got in the newspapers about my being married in Philadelphy is all a hoax. I aint married yet, nor I shant be till a little blue-eyed gal, that used to run about with me, and go to school and slide down hill in Downingville is the wife of President Downing. And that are other story, that the President give me a Curnel's commission jest before we started down east, isn't exactly true. The President did offer me one, but I thanked him, and told him if he would excuse me, I should rather not take it, for I had always noticed that Majors were more apt to rise in the world than Curnels.

I wish you would take a little pains to send up to Downingville and get uncle Joshua to call a public meeting, and have me nominated there. I'm so well known there, it would have a great effect in other places. And I want to have it particularly understood, and so stated in their resolutions, that I am the genuine democratic republican candidate. I know you will put your shoulder to the wheel in this business and do all you can for me, for you was always a good friend to me, and, just between you and me, when I get in to be President you may depend upon it you shall have as good an office as you want.

But I see it's time for me to end this letter. The President is quite comfortable, and sends his respects to you and uncle Joshua.

I remain your sincere friend.

JACK DOWNING

James Russell Lowell (1819–1891)

Hosy Biglow

THE FIRST POETIC INSTALLMENT of what was to become known as "The Biglow Papers" appeared in the *Boston Courier* on 17 June 1846, more than sixteen years after the first Jack Downing letter had appeared in the *Portland Courier*. During this period the Downing pieces had achieved celebrity status, a fact that may have spurred the popularity of the Biglow material. Both Jack Downing and Hosea ("Hosy") Biglow were unlettered Yankee bumpkins whose dialect, no less than their unvarnished sentiments, appealed to a broad spectrum of newspaper readers. But whereas Downing had taken many aspects of national politics as his province, Hosy Biglow was concerned mainly with the Mexican War. He served, essentially, as a voice of protest for Lowell, whose humanitarian principles were offended by war in general and especially by fighting for land that would expand America's slave-holding territory.

Though a recognizable scion of the Yankee species Biglow, unlike Jack Downing, is primarily a caricature, exaggerated in order to emphasize the issues he expounds upon. While the dimensions of his character are thus limited, he is nonetheless a vivid creation, whose sentiments concerning the unpopular Mexican War (the same conflict that Henry David Thoreau repudiated by refusing to pay his poll tax), seemed to jibe with those of his public. The Biglow pieces achieved almost instantaneous success. Lowell, who heard them discussed and saw them posted on the walls of public buildings, published the Biglow papers in book form in 1848.

The selection is from James Russell Lowell, *Writings*, vol. 8 (Boston: Houghton, Mifflin, 1893).

At the outbreak of the Civil War he began a new series, which excoriated the Southern cause.

Several characters appear in the Biglow papers. Hosy's father, Ezekiel, introduces the first of the poems; Parson Homer Wilbur, the putative editor, windily explains the texts; Birdofredom Sawin, a friend of Hosy, heeds the call to arms and returns from the war a physical wreck. But none overshadows Hosy who, in true democratic fashion, boldly and unabashedly expresses the common person's point of view for all the mighty to hear.

Taps for the Mexican War

Thrash away, you'll hev to rattle
    On them kittle-drums o' yourn,—
'Taint a knowin' kind o' cattle
    Ther is ketched with mouldy corn;
Put in stiff, you fifer feller,
    Let folks see how spry you be,—
Guess you'll toot till you are yeller
    'Fore you git ahold o' me!
Thet air flag s a leetle rotten,
    Hope it aint your Sunday's best;—
Fact! it takes a sight o' cotton
    To stuff out a soger's chest:
Sence we farmers hev to pay fer 't,
    Ef you must wear humps like these,
S'posin' you should try salt hay fer 't,
    It would du ez slick ez grease.

'T would n't suit them Southun fellers,
    They're a dreffle graspin' set,
We must ollers blow the bellers
    Wen they want their irons het;
May be it's all right ez preachin',
    But my narves it kind o' grates,
Wen I see the overreachin'
    O' them nigger-drivin' States.

Them thet rule us, them slave-traders,
    Haint they cut a thunderin' swarth
(Helped by Yankee renegaders),
    Thru the vartu o' the North!
We begin to think it's nater
    To take sarse an' not be riled;—
Who'd expect to see a tater
    All on eend at bein' biled?

Ez fer war, I call it murder,—
    There you hev it plain an' flat;
I don't want to go no furder
    Than my Testyment fer that;
God hez sed so plump an' fairly,
    It's ez long ez it is broad,
An' you've gut to git up airly
    Ef you want to take in God.

'Taint your eppyletts an' feathers
    Make the thing a grain more right;
'Taint afollerin' your bell-wethers
    Will excuse ye in His sight;
Ef you take a sword an' dror it,
    An' go stick a feller thru,
Guv'ment aint to answer for it,
    God'll send the bill to you.

Wut's the use o' meetin'-goin'
    Every Sabbath, wet or dry,
Ef it's right to go amowin'
    Feller-men like oats an' rye?
I dunno but wut it's pooty
    Trainin' round in bobtail coats,—
But it's curus Christian dooty
    This 'ere cuttin' folks's throats.

They may talk o' Freedom's airy
    Tell they're pupple in the face,—
It's a grand gret cemetary
    Fer the barthrights of our race;
They jest want this Californy
    So's to lug new slave-states in
To abuse ye, an' to scorn ye,
    An' to plunder ye like sin.

Aint it cute to see a Yankee
 Take sech everlastin' pains,
All to git the Devil's thankee
 Helpin' on 'em weld their chains?
Wy, it's jest ez clear ez figgers,
 Clear ez one an' one make two,
Chaps thet make black slaves o' niggers
 Want to make wite slaves o' you.

Tell ye Jest the eend I've come to
 Arter cipherin' plaguy smart,
An' it makes a handy sum, tu,
 Any gump could larn by heart;
Laborin' man an' laborin' woman
 Hev one glory an' one shame.
Ev'y thin' thet's done inhuman
 Injers all on 'em the same.

'Taint by turnin' out to hack folks
 You're agoin' to git your right,
Nor by lookin' down on black folks
 Coz you're put upon by wite;
Slavery aint o' nary color,
 'Taint the hide thet makes it wus,
All it keers fer in a feller
 'S jest to make him fill its pus.

Want to tackle *me* in, du ye?
 I expect you'll hev to wait;
Wen cold lead puts daylight thru ye
 You'll begin to kal'late;
S'pose the crows wun't fall to pickin'
 All the carkiss from your bones,
Coz you helped to give a lickin'
 To them poor half-Spanish drones?

Jest go home an' ask our Nancy
 Wether I'd be sech a goose
Ez to jine ye,—guess you'd fancy
 The etarnal bung wuz loose!
She wants me fer home consumption,
 Let alone the hay's to mow,—
Ef you're arter folks o' gumption,
 You've a darned long row to hoe.

Take them editors thet's crowin'
    Like a cockerel three months old,—
Don't ketch any on 'em goin',
    Though they be so blasted bold;
Aint they a prime lot o' fellers?
    'Fore they think on 't guess they'll sprout
(Like a peach thet's got the yellers),
    With the meanness bustin' out.

Wal, go 'long to help 'em stealin'
    Bigger pens to cram with slaves,
Help the men thet's ollers dealin'
    Insults on your fathers' graves;
Help the strong to grind the feeble,
    Help the many agin the few,
Help the men thet call your people
    Witewashed slaves an' peddlin' crew!

Massachusetts, God forgive her,
    She's akneelin' with the rest,
She, thet ough' to ha' clung ferever
    In her grand old eagle-nest;
She thet ough' to stand so fearless
    W'ile the wracks are round her hurled,
Holdin' up a beacon peerless
    To the oppressed of all the world!

Ha'n't they sold your colored seamen?
    Ha'n't they made your env'ys w'iz?
Wut'll make ye act like freemen?
    Wut'll git your dander riz?
Come, I'll tell ye wut I'm thinkin'
    Is our dooty in this fix,
They'd ha' done 't ez quick ez winkin'
    In the days o' seventy-six.

Clang the bells in every steeple,
    Call all true men to disown
The tradoocers of our people,
    The enslavers o' their own;
Let our dear old Bay State proudly
    Put the trumpet to her mouth,
Let her ring this messidge loudly
    In the ears of all the South:—

"I'll return ye good fer evil
    Much ez we frail mortils can,
But I wun't go help the Devil
    Makin' man the cus o' man;
Call me coward, call me traiter,
    Jest ez suits your mean idees,—
Here I stand a tyrant-hater,
    An' the friend o' God an' Peace!"

Ef I'd my way I hed ruther
    We should go to work an' part,
They take one way, we take t' other,
    Guess it would n't break my heart;
Man hed ough' to put asunder
    Them thet God has noways jined;
An' I should n't gretly wonder
    Ef there's thousands o' my mind.

Frances M. Whitcher (1814–1852)

Widow Bedott

*T*HE CREATION of fictional journalistic personalities, like many other literary endeavors in pre-twentieth-century America, was largely a masculine enterprise. A happy and welcome exception was the field of Yankee humor, which was enhanced both by female characters and contributors. Some of these characters enjoyed extensive and enduring fame, a good example being Benjamin P. Shillaber's Mrs. Partington, whose exploits were widely read, beginning with their initial appearance in 1847. Mrs. Partington bore a fairly close resemblance to another Yankee lady who had emerged the year before in Joseph C. Neal's *Saturday Gazette* of Philadelphia. This was Priscilla Bedott, a garrulous widow whose cap is constantly set and whose loquacity apparently knows no bounds.

The Widow Bedott is of course farcical, but her resemblance to actual prototypes is nevertheless recognizable. Like other Yankee characters, she speaks in authentic dialect, yet her monologues are peppered with malapropisms. Her literary ancestry is traceable to two possible forebears: Silence Dogood, the widowed surrogate employed by Benjamin Franklin in the *New England Courant* more than a century before, and Mrs. Malaprop, whose inept expressions flavor Richard Brinsley Sheridan's play *The Rivals*.

Frances Whitcher had first tried her hand at humorous writing with a series of sketches spoken by a Widow Spriggins, which were first read to members of a literary society in her hometown. In the character of the earlier narrator, one

---

The selections are from Frances M. Whitcher, *The Widow Bedott Papers* (New York: Hurst, 1883).

can see the outlines of the more popular Widow Bedott. Both narrators are essentially Yankee caricatures; both are voluble; yet both reveal a certain quaint charm behind the dense screen of verbiage.

The Bedott pieces were written in a loose sequence, so that the reader may follow the widow's attempts at catching a second husband all the way to the altar and beyond. Her second spouse was the Reverend Shadrack Sniffles, whose life changed markedly after the widow took hold of its reins. So enduring were the sketches with American audiences that in 1879, twenty-seven years after Mrs. Whitcher's untimely death, they were turned into a four-act play by David Ross Locke ("Petroleum V. Nasby"), and enjoyed a successful run on the stage.

My Dear Correspondent Bedott

Philadelphia, September 10th, 1846.

MY DEAR CORRESPONDENT BEDOTT:

Your last contributions have been received, and are truly welcome. The "Gazette" is again deeply your debtor; for your aid has been indeed truly valuable to "Neal." But I regret to find that Duberly Doubtington has cast a "glamour" over you about continuing in the comic vein, just at the moment too, when all the world is full of Bedott. Our readers talk of nothing else, and almost despise "Neal" if the Widow be not there. An excellent critic in these matters, said to me the other day, that he regarded them as the best Yankee papers yet written, and such is indeed the general sentiment. I know for instance, of a lady who for several days after reading one of them, was continually, and often, at moments the most inopportune, bursting forth into fits of violent laughter, and believe me that you, gifted with such powers, ought not to speak disparagingly of the gift which thus brings wholesome satire home to every reader. It is a theory of mine that those gifted with truly humorous genius, like ourself, are most useful as moralists, philosophers, and teachers, than whole legions of the gravest preachers. They speak more effectually to the general ear and heart even though they who hear are not aware of the fact that they are imbibing wisdom.

To be sure, if you have more imperative duties, I should be the last to wish that you should neglect them; but if your hesitations arise from other scruples, it appears to me that if you were to weigh them well they may be found mere intangibilities. But of all this you, of course, must be the judge, and any interference on my part would be intrusive and impertinent.

But I would add that Mr. Godey called on me to inquire as to the authorship of the "Bedott Papers" wishing evidently to obtain you for a correspondent to the "Lady's Book." I declined giving him the name, etc., until I had consulted you, checking the selfish impulse that would have denied him, that "Neal" might monopolize a correspondent so valued as "Frank."* Would you like to hear from him on the subject?

Think on it then before yielding up the pen of comedy, but in any event, whether you conclude to be either serious or comic,

Believe me ever yours,
Joseph C. Neal

[*Mrs. Whitcher had signed the pieces "Frank."—Ed.]

The Rev. Mrs. Sniffles Abroad

Left Scrabble Hill this mornin' in the stage for Libertyville. Felt like death about leavin' my beloved companion, but he insisted on 't; said 't would be onpleasant for me to stay to hum while the parsonage was undergwine repairs; and, besides the journey'd be for my health; so at last I yealded to conformity and went. 'T was determined I should visit the Crippinses, at Libertyville—Mrs. Crippin bein' my husband's cousin.

The mornin was derlicious, and Aurory shone with undiminished lusture. The feathered songsters wobbled in the groves; the breezes was ladened with the fragrance of ten thousand flowers, while natur seemed to vie with creation to render the scene one of unmitigated splendor. But I scercely noticed it a bit; for I wa'n't in a sittiwation to enjoy it a mite. Alas! my hull soul was with Shadrack.

Ther wa'n't but tew individiwals besides me in the stage, and they was men folks. I should a found the journey awful tejus if I hadent amused myself by courtin' the muses, as Shadrack calls it. I had a pencil and a piece o' paper in my ridicule, and I axed one o' the gentlemen to lend me his hat to write on. He handed it out very perlitely, and I composed the follerin' stanzys:

To My Own One

Farewell to Scrabble Hill!
　　Farewell to my dear Shad!
I leave you much against my will,
　　And so I feel quite bad.

O Shadrack think o' me
　　When I am far away;
I sartingly shall think o' thee
　　Wherever I do stray.

Adoo! a fond adoo!
　　Dear pardner o' my heart.
The idee o' comin' back to you
　　Sustains me while we part.

O if my Shad should be
　　Onwell while I'm from home,
I shall feel most onpleasantlee,
　　And wish I had n't a come.

But I will hope and pray
　　That we may both be able
To meet agin some futur day,
　　Alive and comfortable.

FRIDAY.—Last night attended the literary swearee at Cousin Briggs-
ses, and was highly intertained. Ther was ten or a dozen present,
and four on 'em had original producations. The most extinguished
article was the Widder Reade's. She signs her perductions "Nell
Nox." She's a very fleshy woman, with a wonderful small head. I
took particular notice of her 'cause she's so notorious in a literary
point o' view. She had a singlar lookin' head-dress stuck atop of her
head. Her nose is awful long, and turns up at the eend; very handy,
saves her the trouble o' turnin' on 't it up every time she reads a
poor piece o' poetry, and she don't seem to read no other exceptin'
Cousin Briggses. She was drest in a sky blue muslin dress with
flounces almost up to her waist, that made her look shorter and
fleshyer than she actilly was. She had a dretful severe critisism on
the American poits, espeshially a certing long-feller, as she called
him, some tall individiwal I s'pose. She cut him all to pieces, de-
claring that he had never writ a line that could be call poitry in all
his born days. She said that his Eve Angeline was a perfectly non-
sensical humbug. I presume that's some young woman he's in-
gaged to. I thought if she was a mind to whale away aginst the long-
feller she might, but she might a let his intended alone. Cousin

Susan Ann axed me afterwards if I dident think Nell Nox was awful cuttin'. She said *she* shouldent like to come under her lash. She wondered what long-feller 'd say when he come to see that critisism, as he ondoubtedly would, for 't would come out in "The Reflector" afore long; Nell contribbits to that paper. Thinksme I ain't afeared of her; I guess she'll change her sentiments when she hears my piece. She'll think ther is such a thing as poitry in Ameriky then. For I had in my pocket the stanzys I writ in the stage—I'd brought 'em along, thinkin' like enough I should be called on to read something.

The editor of "The Reflector" was there; he's president of the swearees. A wonderful small, jandery-lookin' young man, with blazin' red hair, and exceedinly pompous, but oncommon talented. He had an article on the prospects of the literary horizon throughout the world. His sentiments differed from Nell Noxes inasmuch as he held that Americky was the only country where poitry had reached the hight of its zenith. To prove it, he brought forrard Cousin Briggses writins, said that even Nell Nox, the severest critic of the age, spared her; ther wa'n't nothing in her poitry that no critic could git hold of. He wound up, at last, by glorifyin', in a most eloquent manner, that both o' these remarkable writers were contribbitors to his paper.

Next come Cousin Susan Ann Briggs with her article. 'T was a very affectin' poim on, the death o' Deacon Paine's daughter. I don't remember but one stanzy, and that come in at the eend of every alternative verse. It runs thus:

> Fond parents weep for me no more,
> That I no more am given;
> We'll surely shall meet when life is ore,
> High up above in heaven.

I must ax Cousin Briggs for a copy on 't, it's very good, though I actilly think I can beat it; 't ain't for me to say so, however. Her newspaper name is "Fenella Fitzallen."

The last individiwal that read was an olderly young woman, named Samanthy Hocum, a wonderful tall, slab-sided, coarse lookin' critter. Her hair looked singular, 't was all raked back off her forrard, and made her phizmahogany look amazin' broad and brazen. She certainly was oncommon odd and ornary lookin'. Had on a red calico dress, and a queer kind of a bobtailed little thing, made o' green silk, with brass buttons down it. Take her altogether, she was about as singular a critter in her appearance as I've seen in some time.

But she's oncommon smart. She had an article on the subject o'

"Woman's Rights." 'T was a powerful perduction. She hild that the men hadent no bizness to monopolize every thing, and trammil the female sect. I thought to myself they hadent showed no great disposition to *trammil* her so far. She writes for the "pidgin Pint Record of Genius," and signs Kate Kenype.

Them was all the articles that was read last night, though ther was several more literary individiwals ther. A fat, pudden-faced young man that writes poetry for the "Newville Star and Trumpet," and signs "Phil Philpotts." And then ther was a ruther good lookin' young woman that writes the amusin' articles for the same paper, and signs 'em "Betsy Buttertub," and some more, but I disremember their newspaper names.

After the readin' was over, the company diverted the time till the refreshments come in to walkin' round and round through the foldin' doors to the hall, and then from the hall through the foldin' doors agin, as if ther lives depended on 't. The editor, he walked with Nell Nox, and Phil Philpotts with Betsy Buttertub, and Kate Kenype, she stramanaded round alone, wonderful independent. I sot on the sofy and talked to the Briggses till I got as dizzy as a fool, seein' 'em go round and round. I wanted to read my poim, and I seed plainly that Cousin Susan Ann dident mean to ax me to (shouldent wonder if she was a little jealous). So I determined I would read it whether or no; so when the company sot down to take refreshment, I speaks up and says, that seein' I'd ben so eddified myself, I thought I'd ought to contribute my share to the evenin's intertainment; and then without furder ado, I takes out my piece and reads it. 'T was very much admired. Nell Nox declared 't was what she called poitry, and the editor requested a coppy on 't to put in "The Reflector." I gi'n it tew him. It dident strike me till after I got hum that I'd gi'n it the Reverend Mr. Beadle, to be printed in the "Punkin Hook Patriot and Journal." So I s'pose the tew papers'll be accusin' one another o' stealin' on 't, and there'll be a reglar newspaper quarril about it; and I shall be drawn into public notice in a manner very imbarrassin' to my retirin' disposition. But I can't he'p it. We literary characters must expect to be subjected to a great many more onpleasant things than falls to the lot o' privit individiwals —it's the fate o' genius.

Don't know but what I'd try git up a Literary Swearee Society in Scrabble Hill, if I dident s'pose Sally Hugle'd make herself so conspickiwous in it. But I know she would. She's so awful vain, and thinks herself such an amazin' poitess, though as to that, every body knows she can't write. I feel kinder sorry for her, she mistakes her calling so. I should lament to have her make such a laffin' stock of herself as she would if ther was any literary dewins there.

4

FRONTIERSMEN

George Washington Harris (1814–1869)

Sut Lovingood

𝒜MONG THE HUMOROUS CREATIONS of the south-western frontier, Sut Lovingood stands out as the ultimate extreme. This brand of humor, founded upon the oral tradition of the tall tale and characterized by such legendary figures as Davy Crockett and Daniel Boone, naturally tends toward hyperbole. The protagonists of such stories are often superhuman in scope and exceed the limits of mere mortals in their exploits. Though certainly never heroic, and often not even respectable, in a sense Sut does resemble the figures of his region by exceeding normal limitations in his knavery and outlandish pranks. His misadventures, narrated in the typical exaggerated style of the genre, often border on the ridiculous and cruel, with the result that modern readers, though part of a very tolerant literary epoch, are repulsed.

Such was not the intention of the author, George Washington Harris. But Harris had grown up in the Tennessee mountains during the first half of the nineteenth century when flesh-and-blood prototypes of Sut Lovingood were no rarity. Harris seems to have been true to the prototype. Sut was based, at least in part, upon the real-life Sut Miller, whom Harris had met by chance on a business excursion. The Lovingood sketches, which began in the autumn of 1854, attracted both a local and a national audience. They were enjoyed, understandably, by readers of the Nashville *Union and American*, but many were also carried by *The Spirit of the*

The selection is from George W. Harris, *Sut Lovingood. Yarns Spun by a Nat'ral Born Durn'd Fool. Warped and Wove for Public Wear* (New York: Dick & Fitzgerald, 1867).

Times, a New York journal concentrating on sport, drama, and humor, which carried the work of a number of other southwestern humorists.

George Washington Harris was himself a colorful character. Trained as a metal worker, he was for a time captain of a steamboat, and at the end of his life was working for a railroad. Though marked by short periods of success, his career was on the whole uneven and unstable. The frequent upheavals imposed upon him by the Civil War produced a bitterness that is evident in his later work. Whereas he had had Sut narrate tales of ridiculous rascality early in the series, the narratives depicting Sut in the presence of Lincoln show a crude vindictiveness. After the Civil War, the sketches were collected into a volume titled *Sut Lovingood. Yarns Spun by a Nat'ral Born Durn'd Fool* (1867). A second collection was completed, but the manuscript disappeared during a trip that Harris made to a prospective printer in Virginia. On the same journey, Harris was taken ill and died shortly after returning home.

The Widow McCloud's Mare

"Thar cum tu this country, onst, a cussed sneakin lookin reptile, name Stilyards. He wer hatched in a crack—in the frosty rocks, whar nutmaigs am made outen maple, an' whar wimmin paints clock-faces an' pints shoe-paigs, an' the men invents rat-traps, mantraps, an' new fangled doctrins fur the aid of the Devil. In fac' hit am his garden, whar he kin grow what won't sprout eny whar else.

"Well, this critter look't like a cross atween a black snake an' a fireman's ladder. He wer eighteen an' a 'alf hans high, an' modeled like ontu a shingle maker's shavin horse, an' wer as yaller as a warter dorg wif the janders. His eyes wer like ontu a coon's, an' his foot wer the biggest chunk ove meat an' knotty bones I ever seed tu hev no guts intu hit. Now ef he hed wun gif what wud make yu take tu him, I never seed hit, an' ef he ever did a good ur a straight ahead thing, I never hearn ove hit. He cud praps be skar'd intu actin rite fur a minit ur two at a time, but hit wudn't las'. He cum amung us a ole field school-marster—soon shed that shell, an' cum out es oily, slippery a lawyer as ever tuck a fee. Why, he'd a hilt his own in a pond full ove eels, an' a swallerd the las durn one ove em, an' then sot the pond tu turnin a shoe-paig mill. Well he practiced on all the misfortinat devils round that sarkit, till he got sassy, got niggers, got rich, got forty maulins for his nastiness, an' tu put a cap sheaf ontu his stack ove raskallity, got religion, and got tu Congress.

"The fust thing he did thar, wer to proffer tu tend the Capitol grounds in inyuns an' beans, on the shears, an' tu sell the statoot ove Columbus tu a tenpin alley, fur a sign, an' the she injun wif him, tu send back the balls. He stole the Romun swoard ofen the stone picter ove War thar, an' fotch hit tu his wife fur a meat-chopper. He practiced lor ontu yu fur eny thing yu hed, frum a handful ove chestnuts tu a plantashun, an' tu tell hit all in a minit, when he dies, he'll make the fastes' trip tu the senter ove soot, sorrer, an' smoke, on record, not even sceptin ole Iskariott's fas' time.

"Well, a misfortinit devil happen'd tu steal a hoss by accidint, got Stilyards tu 'fend him, got intu the penitensary, an' Stilyards got all he hed—a half houn' dorg, an' a ole eight day Yankee clock, fur sendin' him thar.

"He tuck a big young mar frum a widdar name McCloud, fur losin a land case. So he walked out intu that neighborhood tu gether up an' tote home his fees, an' I met up wif him. He hed the clock tied ontu his back pedler fashun, leadin' the mar in wun han' an' the dorg by a rope wif tuther. The dorg wer interprisin' an' led too fas'— the mar wer sulky an' led tu slow, an' the clock wer heavy, an' the day hot, an' he wer hevin' ove a good time gineraly wif his fees, his sweat, an' his mean thoughts. So he cumenced tryin' tu hire me tu help him tu town, fur a gill ove whisky.

"Now, who the devil ever hearn tell ove a gill ove whisky, in these parts afore? Why hit sounded sorter like a inch ove cord-wood, ur a ounce uv corn-shucks. Hit 'sulted me. So I sot in tu fix a way tu put a gill ur so ove pussonal discomfort onder his shut, an' I did hit. Sez I, 'Yu mout save that whisky ef yu dus' es I tells yu':

" 'Jis yu git atop, an' outside that she hoss thar, tie that ar dorg's rope roun her neck, set the time-mill up ontu her back, ahine yu, an' tie hit roun yersef; that makes her tote the furniture, tote yu, an' lead yer valerabil dorg, while yu governs the muvemint wif a good hickory, an' them bridil strings, don't yu see?'

"He pouched out his mouf, nodded his hed five ur six times, a-bendin' but one jint 'bout the midil ove that long yaller neck ove hisn, an' said, 'Yas, a good surgistshun, mister Lovingood,' an' I sot in tu help him fix things. I peeled lots ove good bark, sot the clock on aind, back tu back wif him ontu the mar's bar cupplin, an' I tied hit roun his cackus like I ment them to stick es long es hit run, ur he lived, an' hit cum durnd ni' doin hit. He sed he thot the thing wud work, *an' so did I*. By golly, I seed the redish brown fire a plain in the mar's eyes, an' a quick twitchin in her flank, what I knowd, an' onderstood tu mean, that she'd make orful things happen purty durn'd soon. The sharp pint ove Stilyard's tail bone, an' the clock laigs wer a makin lively surgistshins tu a devil intu her es big es a yearlin.

"All wer redy fur the show tu begin. 'Yu git up, yu pesky critter,' sed he, a-makin his heels meet, an' crack onder her belly. Well she did 'git up,' rite then an' thar, an' staid up long enuf to lite twenty foot further away, in a broad trimblin squat, her tail hid a-tween her thighs, an' her years a dancin a-pas' each uther, like scissors a-cuttin. The jolt ove the litin sot the clock tu strikin. Bang-see-bang-zee whang-zee. She listined pow-ful 'tentive to the three fus' licks, an' they seemed tu go thru an' thru her es quick es quicksilver wud git thru a sifter. She waited fur no more, but jus' gin her hole soul up to the wun job ove runnin from onder that infunnel Yankee, an' his hive ove bumble bees, ratil snakes, an' other orful hurtin things, es she tuk hit tu be. I knows how she felt; I'se been in the same 'bout five hundred times, an' durn my cackus ef she didn't kerry out my idears ove gittin outen trubil fus' rate.

"Every jump she made, she jerk't that misfurtinat dorg six foot upard, an' thurty foot onward. Sumtimes he lit on his starn, sumtimes on his snout, then ontu bof ainds at wunst. He changed sides every uther lunge, clar over Stilyards, an' his hour-mill tu. He sed 'O! Outch!' every time he lit, in houn talk loud enuff to skeer the Devil. An' the road wer sprinkled worm fence fashun, like ontu a drunken man a-totin a leaky jug.

"The durn'd ole clock, hit got exhited too, an' los' control ove hits sef, an' furgot tu stop, but jis scizzed an' whang'd away strait along, an' the mar a hearin hit all, an' a b'levin the soun' tu be comin nigher tu her inards every pop. She thort, too, that four hundred black an' tan houn' dorgs wer cumpassin her etarnal ruin.

"She seed em ebove her, below her—behine her—afore her—an' on bof sides ove her, eny whar, every whar, nuffin but houn' dorgs. An she jis' tried tu run outen her sorril hide. I seed her two hine shoes shinin way up in the a'r, like two new moons. I know'd she wer a-mixin in sum high pressure vishus kickin, wif a heap ove as yearnest, an' fas' runnin es hosses ever 'dulges in.

" 'Wo yeow now!' I hearn this, sprinkled in now an' then wif the yowls ove the dorg, an' the whangin' ove the clock, an' all hit outdun wif the mity nise ove clatterin huffs, an' crashin brush.

"Stilyards sot humpt up, his puddin foots lock'd onder that skeerd critter's belly, an' his paws wove intu her mane double twill'd. I speck she thot the Devil wer a-huggin her, an' she wer durnd near right.

"Thinks I, ole feller, *if* yu gain *this* suit, yu may ax Satun, when yu sees him, fur a par ove lisence tu practice at his cort. He'll sign em, sure.

"I cut acrost the ridge, what the road woun roun', an' got whar I cud see em a cummin, sorter to'ards me agin. She wer stretched out strait as a string, an' so wer he—he wer roostin pow'ful low ontu her withers, his long arms locked roun her neck, his big feet a flyin about in the air, each side ove her tail, sorter limber like, an' the dorg mus' hev been nigh ontu killed dead, fur bof his hine laigs wer gone plumpt up tu his cuplin. . . . His paunch wer a bobbin up an' down about a foot ahine whar the pint ove his tail used tu be. Ef he yowled any now, I didn't hear hit.

"That clock, the cussed mischeaf-makin mercheen, the cause ove all this onyeathly nise, trubbil, an' vexation ove sperit, wer still ontu ole Stilyards's back, an' a maulin away as ef hit wer in the strait line ove a houshole juty, an' the bark wer a holdin hits holt pow'ful well, considerin the strain. They met a ole bald-heded, thick-sot feller a-cummin frum mill, a-ridin ontu a grist ove meal, an' hit on a blaze-face hoss, wif burs in his tail. He wer totin a kaig ove strain'd honey in his lap, an' a 'oman behine him, wif a spinnin wheel ontu her hip. The mar run squar intu the millin experdishun. Jis' es she did hit, Stilyards holler'd, 'Yeow, cut the bar—' He never addid the 'K' tu that word, fur somethin' happen'd, jis' then an' tharabouts."

Sut scratched his head, and seemed to be in deep thought.

"Well, Sut, go on."

"I wer jis' a-studyin yu a sorter udear ove how things look'd arter them two hoss beastes mixed. Spose you take a comon size frame doggery, sortar old an' rotten, wif all the truck generly inside them necessary instertushuns; sit hit down squar ontu a railroad track, jis *so*—an' du hit jis' in time fur the kerrs a-cummin forty miles a hour, an thar whistil string broke. How du yu say things wud look bout a minit arterards?"

"Very much injured, I'd say, Sut."

"An' pow'fuly mix'd?"

"Yes."

"An' tremenjusly scattered?"

"Yes."

"An' orfully changed in shape?"

"Yes."

"An' in nater?"

"Yes."

"An' in valuer?"

"Yes."

"An' a heap more pieces?"

"Yes."

"An smaller wuns?"

"Yes."

"Splinters, an' scraps perdominant?"

"Yes."

"An' not wuf a durn by a dullar an' a 'alf?"

"Yes."

"Well, yu kin sorter take in the tremenjus idear ove that spot ove sandy road, whar Stilyards met the bald-heded man. That on-lucky ole cuss lit twenty foot out in the woods, never look'd back, but sot his trampers tu work, an' distributed hissef sumwhar to-ward the Black Oak Ridge. The 'oman hung by wun foot in the fork ove a black-jack, an' a-holdin tu a dogwood lim' wif her hans, an' she hollerin surter spiteful like—'Split the black-jack, ur fetch a quilt!' Nuffin ove the sort wer dun whilest I wer thar, es I knows on. Stilyards wer ni tuther side ove the road, flat ontu his back, fainted cumfortabil, an' quiet as a sick sow in a snow storm, his arms an' laigs stretched till he look'd like a big letter X. His hat wur sumwhar, an' a boot sumwhar else. His clothes wer in strings, like he'd been shot thru a thorn thicket, outen a canyun. His nose wer a bleedin' jis' bout rite tu bring 'im too sumtime to'ards the middil ove the arternoon. His eyes wer shot up, an' his face wer pucker'd like a wet sheep-skin afore a hot fire, an' he look'd sorter like he'd been stu-dyin a deep plan tu cheat sumbody, an' hed miss'd. The dorg—that is what wer lef' ove him—wer a-lyin bent over the top ove a saplin stump, an' the . . . [mar] wer streched out in runnin shape, not hurt a bit, only her naik wer broke, an' a spinnin-wheel spoke a-stickin atween her ribs a foot ur so deep. Ole Ball-face wer ontu his side, now an' then liftin his head an' takin a look at the surroundin de-serlashun an' sorrer. The ole time counter wer a-leanin up agin a tree, sum bark still roun hit, the door gone, the face smashed, but still true tu what hit thort hits juty, jis bangin away es reguler es ef hit wer at home; an' I reckon hits at hit yet. Ther wer honey-kaig hoops, heads, an' staves, an' spinnin-wheel spokes, permiskusly scattered all about, an' meal sprinkled over everybody, an' every-thing.

"Jis' then a feller what Look't like he mout be a tract sower, ur a map agent, rid up an' tuk a *big* look all roun. Sez he, 'Mister, did the litenin hurt *yu*?' Sez, I, 'Wus nur litenin; a powder mill busted.' The 'oman in the black-jack holler'd at him jis' then, savidge as a cat, 'Look tuther way, yu cussed imperdint houn!' He hed tu turn his hed tu see whar the vise cam frum; he jis' look't one squint, an' sed, 'Great hevings!' an' gin his hoss a orful dost ove whip an' spurs, an' lef' a-flyin, an' he tolt at town what he'd seed. The feller wer orful skeer'd, an' no wonder; he'd seed enuf tu skeer a saw-mill plum offen the krik.

"I now tuck the meal-bag, put the remnant of the dorg, an' sich ove the honey es I cud scoop up, an' draw'd hit over Stilyard's head, tied hit tite roun his naik, in hopes hit mout help fetch him tu sooner; split the black-jack, an' lef' in a lope. I hearn the 'oman squall arter me, 'Never mind, laigs, *I'll pay yu!*' She haint dun hit *yet.*

"I tuck the road Stilyards, an' the mar, an' his tuther geer, hed cum over so fur, an' pass'd a cabin what a ole 'oman dress'd in a pipe an' a stripid aprun wer a-standin on the ash-hopper lookin up the road like she wer 'spectin tu see sumthin soon. Sez she, talkin 'bout es fas' es a flutter-mill: 'Say yu, mister, did yu meet enything onkimon up thar?' I shook my head. 'Well,' sez she, jumpin ofen the hopper an' a-shakin the ashes outen her coteail, an' settin her specs back, 'Mister, I'se plum outdun. Thar's sumthin pow'ful wickid gwine on. A crazy organ-grinder cum a-pas' yere jis' a small scrimpshun slower nur chain litenin, on a hoss wif no tail. His organ wer tied ontu his back, an' wer a-playin that good tchune, 'Sugar in the Gourd,' ur 'Barbary Allin,' I dunno which, an' his monkey wer a-dancin Hail Columby all over the road. . . . He hed no hat on, an' one of his boots flew off as he passed yere, an' lit on the smoke-'ous. Thar hit is; he mus' been a pow'ful big man, fur hits like ontu a indigo ceroon.'

"All this wer said wifout takin one breff.

"I tole her hit wer the advance gard ove a big sarkis purclaimin hits cummin, ur the merlennium, an' durn'd ef I know'd which.

"She 'lowed hit cudent be the merlennium, fur hit warnt a playin hyme-tchunes; nur a sarkis either, fur the hoss warn't spotted. But hit mout be the Devil arter a tax collector, ur a missionary on his way tu China; hit look't ugly enuf tu be one, an' fool enuf tu be tuther. She wer pow'fully exercised; she sweat an' snorted onder hit.

"Now don't yu b'leve, es soon es Stilyards cum tu, an' got outen the bag, he sot in an' buried the mar so es tu hide her, an' then, at nex' cort, *indited me fur stealin her,* an' durn'd ni provin hit; now hain't that the Devil?"

"What ever become of Stilyards, Sut, anyhow?"

"I dono; ef he haint in Congriss he's gone to h—l."

William Tappan Thompson (1812–1882)

Major Jones

ILLIAM TAPPAN THOMPSON was one of the earliest southwestern humorists, and probably the first to channel his humor into a fictional newspaper personality endemic to the region. Though not formally educated, Thompson had the benefit of a literary apprenticeship of sorts by working for Augustus Baldwin Longstreet on the *States' Rights Sentinel* in Augusta, Georgia, beginning in 1835. In the same year, Longstreet published *Georgia Scenes*, a collection of humorous frontier sketches that soon became a classic of the region and of the genre. Obviously inspired by Longstreet's treatment of this ambiance, Thompson eventually left the *Sentinel* and founded a newspaper that became known as the *Family Companion and Ladies' Mirror*. It was here, in June, 1842, that the first letter from Joseph Jones appeared. The letters continued in the *Mirror* and after the demise of that paper, in the *Southern Miscellany*, which Thompson edited next. In 1843, sixteen letters appeared in a separate pamphlet edition, which sold out almost immediately. This was the first of numerous editions, some thirty of which had appeared by 1900.

By Thompson's own admission, Jones was intended to be a simple farmer, unpolished in manner but pure in heart—a class that Thompson admired. Jones is a spirited raconteur in the letters he writes to Thompson, but his words and deeds are never offensive. They rather reflect a gentle good humor and a broad-based humanity that have appealed to many kinds of readers through the years.

The selection is from [William T. Thompson], *Major Jones's Courtship and Travels* (Philadelphia: Peterson, 1848).

Much of the interest in the letters comes from his courtship of Mary Stallings, whose family owns the adjoining plantation. The best-known episode is that in which Mary promises to accept and keep for life anything that Jones gives her
for Christmas. On Christmas Eve, he hangs a large sack on
her back porch and crawls into it. After an initial shock the
following morning, she lives up to her promise. This jest
must have particularly pleased contemporary readers, as the
first three editions of the letters were entitled *Major Jones's
Courtship.* But the two lovers are depicted from the very first
letter, when Jones pays Mary a visit after her return from her
first year at "the Female College down to Macon," and exhibits his woeful ignorance while attempting to express his
tenderest feelings.

Major Jones to Mr. Thompson

Pineville, May 28th, 1842

To Mr. Thompson:—Dear Sir—Ever sense you was down to
Pineville, it's been on my mind to rite you a letter, but the boys
lowed I'd better not, cause you mought take me off bout my spellin
and dictionary. But something happened to me tother night, so
monstrous provokin, that I can't help tellin you about it, so you can
put other young chaps on ther gard. It all come of chawin so much
tobacker, and I reckon I've wished there was no sich plagy stuff,
more'n five hundred times sense it happened.
    You know the Stallinses lives on the plantation in the summer
and goes to town in the winter. Well, Miss Mary Stallins, who you
know is the darlinest gal in the county, come home tother day to see
her folks. You know she's been to the Female College, down to Macon, for most a year now. Before she went, she used to be jest as
plain as a old shoe, and used to go fishin and huckleberryin with us,
with nothin but a calico sun-bonnet on, and was the wildest thing
you ever saw. Well, I always used to have a sort of a sneakin notion
of Mary Stallins; and so when she come, I brushed up, and was
termined to have a rite serious talk with her bout old matters; not
knowin but she mought be captivated by some of them Macon fellers.
    So, sure enough, off I started, unbeknowin to anybody, and rode

rite over to the plantation—(you know ours is rite jinin the widder Stallinses). Well, when I got thar, I felt a little sort o' sheepish; but I soon got over that, when Miss Carline said, (but she didn't mean me to hear her), "There, Pinny, (that's Miss Mary's nick-name, you know), there's your bo come."

Miss Mary looked mighty sort o' redish when I shuck her hand and told her howdy; and she made a sort of a stoop over and a dodge back, like the little gals does to the school-marm, and said, "Good evenin, Mr. Jones," (she used to always call me jest Joe).

"Take a chair, Joseph," said Miss Carline; and we sot down in the parlor, and I begun talkin to Miss Mary bout Macon, and the long ride she had, and the bad roads, and the monstrous hot weather, and the like.

She didn't say much, but was in a mighty good humor and laughed a heap. I told her I never seed sich a change in anybody. Nor I never did. Why, she didn't look like the same gal—good gracious! she looked so nice and trim—jest like some of them pictures what they have in Mr. Graham's Magazine—with her hair all komed down longside of her face, as slick and shiny as a mahogany burow. When she laughed she didn't open her mouth like she used to; and she set up strait and still in her chair, and looked so different, but so monstrous pretty! I ax'd her a heap of questions, bout how she liked Macon, and the Female College, and so forth; and she told me a heap bout 'em. But old Miss Stallins and Miss Carline and Miss Kesiah, and all of 'em, kep all the time interruptin us, axin bout mother—if she was well, and if she was gwine to the Spring church next Sunday, and what luck she had with her soap, and all sich stuff—and I do believe I told the old woman more'n twenty times that mother's old turky-hen was settin on fourteen eggs.

Well, I wasn't to be backed out that-a-way—so I kep it a goin the best I could, til bimeby old Miss Stallins let her knitin fall three or four times, and then begun to nod and snap back like a fishin-pole that was all the time gitin bites. I seed the gals lookin at one another and pinchin one another's elbows, and Miss Mary said she wondered what time it was, and said the College disciplines, or somethin like that, didn't low late hours. I seed how the game was gwine—but howsumever, I kep talkin to her like a cotton gin in packin time, as hard as I could clip it, til bimeby the old lady went to bed, and arter a bit the gals all cleared, and left Miss Mary to herself. That was jest the thing I wanted.

Well, she sot on one side of the fire-place, and I sot on tother, so I could spit on the hath, whar ther was nothin but a lighterd chunk burnin to give light. Well, we talked and talked, and I know you would like to hear all we talked about, but that would be too long.

When I'm very interested in any thing, or git bother'd about any-thing, I can't help chawin a heap o' tobacker, and then I spits uncon-tionable, specially if I'm talkin. Well, we sot thar and talked, and the way I spit, was larmen to the crickets! I axed her if she had any bos down in Macon.

"Oh, yes," she said, and then she went on and named over Mat-thew Matix, Nat. Filosofy, Al. Geber, Retric Stronomy, and a whole heap of fellers, that she'd been keepin company with most all her time.

"Well," ses I, "I spose they're mazin poplar with you, aint they, Miss Mary?" for I felt mighty oneasy, and begin to spit a great deal worse.

"Yes," ses she, "they're the most interestin companions I ever had, and I am anxious to resume their pleasant sciety."

I tell you what, that sort o' stumped me, and I spit rite slap on the chunk and made it "flicker and flare" like the mischief; it was a good thing it did, for I blushed as blue as a Ginny squash.

I turned my tobacker round in my mouth, and spit two or three times, and the old chunk kep up a most bominable fryin.

"Then I spose your gwine to forget old acquaintances," ses I, "sense you's been to Macon, mong them lawyers and doctors; is you, Miss Mary? You thinks more of them than you does of anybody else, I spose."

"Oh," ses she, "I am devoted to them—I think of them day and night!"

That was too much—it shot me right up, and I sot as still as could be for more'n a minute. I never felt so warm behind the ears afore in all my life. Thunder! how my blood did bile up all over me, and I felt like I could knock Matthew Matix into a greas-spot, if he'd only been thar. Miss Mary sot with her handkercher up to her face, and I looked rite into the fire-place. The blue blazes was runnin round over the old chunk, ketchin hold here and lettin go thar, sometimes gwine most out, and then blazin up a little—I couldn't speak—I was makin up my mind for tellin her the siteation of my hart—I was jest gwine to tell her my feelins, but my mouth was full of tobacker, so I had to spit, and slap it went, rite on the lightwood chunk, and out *it* went, spang! I swar, I never did feel so in all my born days. I didn't know what to do.

"My Lord, Miss Mary," ses I, "I didn't go to do it—jest tell me the way to the kitchen, and I'll go and git a light."

But she never said nothin, so I sot down agin, thinkin she'd gone to get one herself, for it was pitch dark, and I couldn't see my hand afore my face.

Well, I sot thar and ruminated, and waited a long time, but she didn't come, so I begun to think maybe she wasn't gone. I couldn't hear nothin, nor I couldn't see nothin; so bimeby ses I, very low, for I didn't want to wake up the family—ses I,

"Miss Mary! Miss Mary!" but nobody answered.

Thinks I, what's to be done? I tryed agin. "Miss Mary! Miss Mary!" ses I; but it was no use.

Then I heard the gals snickerin and laughin in the next room, and I begun to see how it was; Miss Mary was gone and left me thar alone.

"Whar's my hat?" ses I, pretty loud, so somebody might tell me; but they only laughed worse.

I begun to feel about the room, and the fust thing I knew, spang! goes my head, rite agin the edge of a dore that was standin open. The fire flew, and I couldn't help but swar a little—"d—n the dore," ses I, "whar's my hat?" But nobody said nothin, so I begun to think it was best to git out the best way I could, and never mind my hat. Well, I got through the parlor dore after rakin my shins three or four times agin the chairs, and was feelin along through the entry for the frunt dore; but somehow I was so flustrated that I tuck the rong way, and bimeby kerslash I went, rite over old Miss Stallinses spinnin-wheel, onto the floor! I hurt myself a good deal; but that didn't make me half so mad as to hear them confounded gals a gigglin and laughin at me.

"Oh," said one of 'em, (it was Miss Kesiah, for I knowed her voice), "there goes mother's wheel! my Lord!"

I tried to set the cussed thing up, but it seemed to have more'n twenty legs, and wouldn't stand up no how—maybe it was broke. I went out of the dore; but I hadn't more'n got down the steps, when bow! wow! wow! comes four or five infurnal grate big coon-dogs, rite at me. "Git out! git out! hellow, Cato! call off your dogs!" ses I, as loud as I could. But Cato was sound asleep, and if I hadn't a run back into the hall, and got out of the frunt way as quick as I could, them devils would o' chawed my bones for true.

When I got to my horse, I felt like a feller jest out of a hornet's nest; and I reckon I went home a little of the quickest. Next mornin old Miss Stallins sent my hat by a little nigger; but I haint seed Mary Stallins sense. Now you see what comes of chawin tobacker! No more from,

Your frend, till deth,
Jos. Jones

p.s. I blieve Miss Mary's gone to the Female College agin. If you see her, I wish you would say a good word to her for me, and tell her

I forgives her all, and I hope she will do the same by me. Don't you think I better rite her a letter, and explain matters to her?

NOTABEMY.—This letter was rit to my pertickeler frend Mr. Thompson, when he was editen the *Family Companion* magazine, down in Macon. I had no notion of turnin author then; but when it come out with my name to it, and ther want no use in denyin it, and specially as he rit me a letter beggin I would go on and rite for the *Miscellany,* I felt a obligation restin on me to continue my correspondence to that paper. All my other letters was rit to Mr. Thompson, in Madison.

J. J.

Francis Bartow Lloyd (1861–1897)

Rufus Saunders

*F*RANCIS BARTOW LLOYD created the rural philosopher Rufus Saunders during the last quarter of the nineteenth century, at a time when the humor of the old Southwest was waning. But in a sense Rufus, the embodiment of the Southern yeoman farmer, brings to full circle the type of humor begun in the 1830s by Augustus Baldwin Longstreet and William Tappan Thompson. The simple, good-hearted guise of the small Southern farmer had proved a durable alter ego for authors and a popular character for audiences of the Southern rural press.

Rufus came into being almost by accident, but in a manner resembling the creation of Bill Arp and Sut Lovingood. Francis Bartow Lloyd was city editor for the *Montgomery* (Alabama) *Advertiser,* for which he wrote occasional homey features lacking any particular characterization. Then, one day "his eye was caught by the quaint, but thoroughly wholesome and manly face of a Montgomery County farmer, Mr. George S. Morrison. He adopted this gentleman's photograph as his ideal for the face and form of a sound and commonsense countryman, called him 'Rufus Saunders,' and made this simple name for the quaint-faced old tiller of the soil a synonym for household philosophy in many thousand American homes" (Lloyd 1898, 9).

Like many similar journalistic vehicles before him, Rufus made considerable money for his creator. Lloyd left journalism, bought a farm, and entered state politics. However, in

---

The selection is from Francis Bartow Lloyd, *Sketches of Country Life; Humor, Wisdom and Pathos from the 'Sage of Rocky Creek'* (Birmingham, Ala: Roberts & Son, 1898).

August 1897 he was assassinated by a man who presumably bore a political grudge.

Rufus Goes to College

To be certainly I believes in education. There is nothin like it and nothin better—exceptin a little more of it. The campaign of education is bound to win in the long run, if not in 1892.

But great is economy, too. There is the winnin card in the farmer's hand. Happy is the man with a head on him big enough to git on the outside of the absorbin question. Savin is a great art. It will beat hard work and close fist and big talk any day in the year and give them three in the game to start on. Economy don't mean for a man to be pizen stingy and selfish, as some folks that don't know no better seems to think. It never did pay a man to run very deep in stinginess.

Old man Zeke Strickle, that used to live down on Bear Creek, was about the stingiest man I ever had the hard luck to run up with. He used to run a little old water mill down on the creek, and in the summer time when the water was runnin low he would get his drinkin water below the dam and spit and pour the slops in the pond above the mill to keep up his head of water. And he used to go around and climb over the back fence to keep from openin the front gate and wearin out the hinges.

But old Zeke lived hard and died poor. He was stingy enough, but he didnt know nothin about economy. Real genuine economy is a mighty good thing for a man to have in his business. Every man ought to be savin—savin with his money, savin with his talk, savin with everything. I was always a great hand for cuttin across lots. It's about the easiest and quickest way to get there.

FOR INSTANCE

Me and Tom Dick Simkins was boys together in our growin up. We was born on the same day and on adjoinin farms, and came up neck and neck together. Tom Dick's ma used to say we was as thick as four in a bed, and I reckon she knowed what that meant. We played in the same sand bed, waded in the same branch, rode the same flyin jenny, went fishin and played marbles and raided neighboring orchards together. We came mighty nigh bein twins, and when I want at Tom Dick's house he was at our house.

But I was always lookin ahead and thinkin the time was comin when we would git to a fork in the road—a time for partin of the ways. And it was even so. After we got up in our teens past the quarter-pole, the turn come. The same blanket wouldnt cover both of us any longer.

Tom Dick was powerful quick and smart in books. His folks said he was a genius, whatever that is. He was apt-headed and bright and always breakin out in a fresh pace. Jerushy, how he could make poetry, say speeches and quote scripture! Well, old man Simpkins he was most tickled to death, and he says how he was goin to give Tom Dick full swing and the best education the country would afford. After a while he would be the greatest man in the settlement, and then he could be a governor, or a president, or maybe a general. We went to school together over at the Cross Roads, and there's where the partin of the ways comes in. I couldn't hold Tom Dick a light in the books. I didn't fly the track any, but he jest run away from me like a quarter horse.

Bye and bye Tom Dick played his hand plum out over at the Cross Roads. He got smarter than the professor, and then the old man fixes him up to go off to college.

Now my good old father was like a heap of folks you know— poor, but proud and high spirited. He had been keepin the run of things, and hearin that old man Simpkins was goin to send Tom Dick off to college, he took me down to the horse lot soon one mornin and had a plain family talk with me.

STILL IN THE RACE

"Your old daddy is proud of you, Ruf," says he, "and its mighty hurtin to me that Sol Simpkinses boy Tom Dick has got ahead of you in this race. I know he is some lengths ahead now, but it seems to me you mought pull up on him a little if you'll come down to your knittin right and untie your legs and use em for all they are worth. It's a race for blood, Ruf, it's a race for blood; and it would break your old mother's heart and bring your daddy's gray head in sorrow to the grave to see the distance flag flutter and flop down right in your face. You've got a head on your shoulders as long as a flour barrel, and if there aint some sense in it there ought to be. Brains runs in the Sanders family. Now I want you to brush up and go to college and let folks know there is somethin in you. You mustn't throw up your tail like a bellused horse before you reach the second quarter pole. Our family standin is at stake. Remember that, Ruf, and if you can't win the race you can make the race track devilish dusty for old Sol Simpkinses boy."

Father said he had about $300 saved up, and he was plum willing to spend every cent on me to hold up the family reputation. I told him if nothin else would suit him I was willin to stay in the race, but at the same time I was leanin to the opinion that he was placin his money on a short horse with mighty little show for haulin it in again. I knowed I had the stayin powers, but the trouble was I stayed in the same place too long. I didn't have any bursts of speed worth mentionin. And I knowed Tom Dick was runnin like a shot out of a cannon. He was speedy and it seems like he was going to show up considerable stayin qualities, too.

OFF TO COLLEGE

That fall the old folks fixed me and Tom Dick up and sent us off to college. I went away feelin like a 3-year-old, shod all around. But I didn't know anything about the lay of the land ahead of us. I was just goin it blind and trustin to my nigger luck to pull me through.

But it want long before I found out that things was not runnin to suit me at the college. The sundry and divers rules and regulations didn't set very well on the stomach of a plain, blunt country boy. We had to stay in most of the time and wear uniform coats and pants and brass buttons, and collars that stood up like a whitewashed fence around a country graveyard. We had to set up as straight as sticks, and rear back when we walked and come up clean and fresh and smilin every mornin. My collar was so blame high and hard till I had to go out and climb upon the back fence to spit. Tom Dick he took to sich things like a fish to water, but I didn't. I was too big and clumsy, and too fur behind the other boys. I couldn't learn my lessons for thinkin about my clothes and fancy fixments. I was too durn busy playing soldier. But it didnt take me more than a couple of weeks to learn somethin. I learned that I want built for college. My shape was dead agin me there. So, without wastin any time, I went to the president and told him that I had about made up my mind to throw down my hand and jump the game. I told him, moreover, that I didn't want to be fired out bodily, but like for him to give me a furlough for a few days. I wanted to go home and see father and have a talk with him, and if he insisted on my stayin in the race to the finish I would report for duty the next Monday. I felt like I was wastin a heap of good time and right smart of the old gentleman's money, and I wanted to see him face to face and tell him like an honest boy cxactly how the race was goin.

IT WAS A GO

The president of the college agreed with me in general and particular.

"Tell your father that I say it might be well enough for him to take your advice in this matter," says he. "I'm bound to think you've got some good material in you, Sanders, but it must be runnin in a sort of under current. It don't show up much on the surface. You are a well meanin honest boy, but ruther a slow team in books. Wisdom crieth aloud, she uttereth her voice in the streets, but it seems like you havent caught the step or got into the procession yet. You can make a first rate farmer out of yourself, and you may get to be justice of the peace in your beat. But you can do all that without a college education, which I fear, though it pains me to say it, would be quite too rich for your young and untamed blood. You may make a good judge of whisky and horses, but I dont think you will ever burn up anybody's mill pond, nor either go to congress."

I thanks the president for his kind and flatterin' words and boarded the next stage coach home.

ANOTHER FAMILY TALK

When I rounds up at home ruther sudden and onexpected like the old gentleman and mother was both astonished considerable, but seems like they were certain glad to see me. After supper the family circle was formed around the old fireplace, and I feels at home and glad enough to hug anything in sight. Father asked me how things was comin at the college, and then we had another family talk, wherein I done most of the talkin.

"Father," says I, "its no use. I felt like you was placin your money on a loser when we first went on the track and now I know it dead certain. I ain't been doin nothin at college but wastin my valuable time and your good money. I cant be a soldier and a scholar and a dude all at the same time. I wasnt built for the business. I'm no genius, as Tom Dick Simpkins is, but that ain't my fault. Maybe you wouldn't count me in as a slouch for straight, hard work and plain ploddin, but when it comes to these intellectual spurts and high flyin and fireworks I simply aint in it. I'm jest plain Rufus Sanders, with a big R and a big S, and that's all. I aint fit to be guvnor or a president or a general or a professor or a lawyer or a doctor, and we've got to brace up and look the sober, solemn truth right square in the face. The president of the college seems to think it would take a surgical operation to put a college education into my head, and if I got it there it wouldnt be of much use to me here on the old farm. Reckon he knows his game. Comin right down to business and brass tacks, father, it is all vanity for you to keep tryin to make somethin fine out of your onhappy boy. Jest give me say $200 and let me have some land and I'll buy a pair of good mules and go to work here on my native stompin ground. I want to play at a game wherein I knows all the pints. It aint much probable that you'll ever have a son in congress, but durn my buttons if I dont be a farmer from Farmersville."

Father said he reckons I was about three-thirds right, and it would have to be jest so, but it stuck in his craw powerful to think that old Sol Simpkinses boy had won the race in a canter as it were, when his first and only begotten and dearly beloved Rufus was among the entries. Mother she puts in there and said she'd lay that Simpkins boy want a bit smarter than me. But he had a heap more brass, and that was puttin him through. She lowed I was as good and promisin as anybody's son, and said how it wouldnt surprise her to see Tom Dick go to pieces and turn out bad yet. He was too snipshus and Smart Alecky, anyhow.

"I knows you to be a good, honest boy, peart and quick motioned, Ruf," father went on to say. "And I'm plum willin to let you play the game henceforwards to suit yourself. Pick your land and buy your mules and I'll foot the bill."

THE NATURAL RESULT

You can bet your whiskers I was about the proudest boy in the settlement then. I shucked my college clothes and spit on my hands and sails right into farmin on my own hook. I bought the handsomest pair of mules that ever came to these parts. The next year I made a good crop and had some money in the clear. Blamed if I haven't made more money most every year and now everything on the old farm belongs to Rufus Sanders in his own name.

So I say it don't take a college education to run a good average farm. I am getting along as well as the farmer that has been through college, and a heap sight better than lots of them.

No, Tom Dick never got to be a guvner, or a president, or a general, or any of them things. He was a genius, a regular jack at all trades and good at nothin. It makes me real sad to talk about it, but mother was dead right. Tom Dick won the race easy and then went all to smash. He shot up like a sky-rocket and then come down like a spent bullet. He wore fine clothes and read law and drunk whisky and made poetry and rolled high and spent his daddy's money like water runnin down hill. But he never did stack up any worth mentioning. He got away with all the money the old folks had saved up, and after they died he runs through with the old place like a dost of salts. When he got married he hit me for $50 to buy his weddin clothes, and got it, too. Poor Tom Dick, with all his weak pints, somehow I liked him.

The last time I saw him he was lookin tolerable sorry and seedy and shabby, and he told me he was still playin to mighty poor luck.

Tom Dick was always a likely lad, and smart as a steel trap, but it seems like the cards was cut straight agin him.

Genius is a very good thing, I reckon, for a man thats got plenty of money and time to keep it up, but it wont pay the feed bill nor buy a new frock for the baby.

5

LITERARY COMEDIANS

Charles Farrar Browne (1834–1867)

Artemus Ward

*T*HE CAREER of Charles Farrar Browne was marked as much by brevity as by spectacular success. It began in 1857 when Browne, a native of Maine, began contributing to the Cleveland *Plain Dealer* (a newspaper noted for its literary fare) a series of "Artemus Ward Sayings." It ended only ten years later with the death in England of Browne, the most popular humorist on two continents. Browne's major contribution was Artemus Ward himself. Not only a character on a printed page who wrote fictional accounts of his travelling tent show and wax museums, Artemus Ward was well known in the flesh as a platform speaker.

The physical presence of Ward on the lecture circuit did much to reinforce the mental picture created in the minds of his readers (though collections of his work were illustrated with his likeness). The living being was able to convey, as printed words could not, how timing, accentuation, gestures, and posture can enhance humor. The lessons to be learned from this demonstration were absorbed by at least two writers, Samuel L. Clemens and Henry Wheeler Shaw, and transferred to the humorous alter egos that each was to produce.

In the course of his platform appearances, Browne traveled across the United States. Many of the scenes and people he encountered found their way into Ward pieces, where the comic effect was enhanced by means of trick spelling and obvious punning. He writes of the Mormons and of seeing Edwin Forest in the role of Othello, but always atten-

---

The selections are from Charles F. Browne, *Artemus Ward, His Book* (New York: Carleton, 1862); and *Artemus Ward; His Travels* (New York: Carleton, 1865).

tion is drawn to the character of Ward, the travelling show-man.

Browne's career parallelled the years of the Civil War, and some of his material deals with its better-known aspects. However, Browne kept his comments on the war light for the most part, preferring apparently to be a professional funny man rather than the conscience of the country. He was one of several humorists who won the praise of President Lincoln. Salmon P. Chase, Secretary of the Treasury, tells of Lincoln reading Ward's sketch "High-Handed Outrage at Utica" at the same cabinet meeting at which he read the Emancipation Proclamation. One exception to this lightheartedness is his letter written from Richmond in May 1865. Here, with a rather heavy hand, he pours salt into the fresh wounds of the recently defeated Confederacy. Even though he attempts to make a plea for unity toward the end of the letter, the drubbing he gives the benighted Confederate capital constitutes the main thrust of the piece.

High-Handed Outrage at Utica

In the Faul of 1856, I showed my show in Utiky, a trooly grate sitty in the State of New York.

The people gave me a cordyal recepshun. The press was loud in her prases.

1 day as I was givin a descripshun of my Beests and Snaiks in my usual flowry stile what was my skorn & disgust to see a big burly feller walk up to the cage containin my wax figgers of the Lord's Last Supper, and cease Judas Iscarrot by the feet and drag him out on the ground. He then commenced fur to pound him as hard as he cood.

"What under the sun are you abowt?" cried I.

Sez he, "What did you bring this pussylanermus cuss here fur?" & he hit the wax figger another tremenjis blow on the hed.

Sez I, "You egrejus ass, that air's a wax figger—a represen-tashun of the false 'Postle."

Sez he, "That's all very well fur you to say but I tell you, old man, that Judas Iscarrot can't show hisself in Utiky with impunerty by a darn site!" with which observashun he kaved in Judassis hed. The young man belonged to 1 of the first famerlies in Utiky. I sood him, and the Joory brawt in a verdick of Arson in the 3d degree.

Artemus Ward in Richmond

Richmond, Va., May 18 & 65.

The old man finds hisself once more in a Sunny climb. I cum here a few days arter the city catterpillertulated.

My naburs seemed surprised & astonisht at this darin' bravery onto the part of a man at my time of life, but our family was never know'd to quale in danger's stormy hour.

My father was a sutler in the Revolootion War. My father once had a intervoo with Gin'ral La Fayette.

He asked La Fayette to lend him five dollars, promisin' to pay him in the Fall; but Lafy said "he couldn't see it in those lamps." Lafy was French, and his knowledge of our langwidge was a little shaky.

Immejutly on my 'rival here I perceeded to the Spotswood House, and callin' to my assistans a young man from our town who writes a good runnin' hand, I put my ortograph on the Register, and handin' my umbrella to a bald-heded man behind the counter, who I s'posed was Mr. Spotswood, I said, "Spotsy, how does she run?"

He called a cullud purson, and said, "Show the gen'lman to the cowyard, and giv' him cart number 1."

"Isn't Grant here?" I said. "Perhaps Ulyssis wouldn't mind my turnin' in with him."

"Do you know the Gin'ral?" inquired Mr. Spotswood.

"Wall, no, not 'zackly; but he'll remember me. His brother-in-law's Aunt bought her rye meal of my uncle Levi all one winter. My uncle Levi's rye meal was—"

"Pooh! pooh!" said Spotsy, "don't bother me," and he shuv'd my umbrella onto the floor. Obsarvin' to him not to be so keerless with that wepin, I accompanid the African to my lodgins.

"My brother," I sed, "air you aware that you've bin 'mancipated? Do you realise how glorus it is to be free? Tell me, my dear brother, does it not seem like some dreams, or do you realise the great fact in all its livin' and holy magnitood?"

He sed he would take some gin.

I was show'd to the cowyard and laid down under a one-mule cart. The Hotel was orful crowded, and I was sorry I hadn't gone to the Libby Prison. Tho' I should hav' slept comf'ble enuff if the bed-clothes hadn't bin pulled off me durin' the night, by a scoundrul who cum and hitched a mule to the cart and druv it off. I thus lost my cuverin' and my throat feels a little husky this mornin.

Gin'ral Hulleck offers me the hospitality of the city, givin' me my choice of hospitals.

He has also kindly placed at my disposal a small-pox ambool-ance.

UNION SENTIMENT

There is raly a great deal of Union sentiment in this city. I see it on ev'ry hand.

I met a man to-day—I am not at liberty to tell his name but he is a old and inflooentooial citizen of Richmond, and sez he, "Why! we've bin fightin' agin the Old Flag! Lor' bless me, how sing'lar!" He then borrer'd five dollars of me and bust into a flood of terrs.

Sed another (a man of standin and formerly a bitter rebuel), "Let us at once stop this effooshun of Blud! The Old Flag is good enuff for me. Sir," he added, "you air from the North! Have you a doughnut or a piece of custard pie about you?"

I told him no, but I knew a man from Vermont who had just organized a sort of restaurant, where he would go and make a very comfortable breakfast on New England rum and cheese. He bor-rowed fifty cents of me, and askin' me to send him Wm. Lloyd Garri-son's ambrotype as soon as I got home, he walked off.

Said another, "There's bin a trem'enduous Union feelin' here from the fust. But we was kept down by a rain of terror. Have you a dagerretype of Wendell Phillips about your person? and will you lend me four dollars for a few days till we air once more a happy and united people."

JEFF. DAVIS

Jeff. Davis is not pop'lar here. She is regarded as a Southern sympathiser. & yit I'm told he was kind to his Parents. She ran away from 'em many years ago, and has never bin back. This was show-in' 'em a good deal of consideration when we refleck what his con-duck has been. Her captur in female apparel confooses me in regard to his sex, & you see I speak of him as a her as frekent as otherwise, & I guess he feels so hisself.

R. LEE

Robert Lee is regarded as a noble feller.

He was opposed to the war at the fust, and draw'd his sword very reluctant. In fact, he wouldn't hav' drawd his sword at all, only he had a large stock of military clothes on hand, which he didn't want to waste. He sez the colored man is right, and he will at once go to New York and open a Sabbath School for negro minstrels.

THE CONFEDERATE ARMY

The surrender of R. Lee, J. Johnson and others leaves the Confedrit Army in a rather shattered state. That army now consists of Kirby Smith, four mules and a Bass drum, and is movin rapidly to'rds Texis.

A PROUD AND HAWTY SUTHENER

Feelin' a little peckish, I went into a eatin' house today, and encountered a young man with long black hair and slender frame. He didn't wear much clothes, and them as he did wear looked onhealthy. He frowned on me, and sed, kinder scornful, "So, Sir—you come here to taunt us in our hour of trouble, do you?"

"No," said I, "I cum here for hash!"

"Pish-haw!" he sed sneerinly, "I mean you air in this city for the purpuss of gloatin' over a fallen peple. Others may basely succumb, but as for me, I will never yield—never, never!"

"Hav' suthin' to eat!" I pleasantly suggested.

"Tripe and onions!" he sed furcely; then he added, "I eat with you, but I hate you. You're a low-lived Yankee!"

To which I pleasantly replied, "How'l you have your tripe?"

"Fried, mudsill! with plenty of ham-fat!"

He et very ravenus. Poor feller! He had lived on odds and ends for several days, eatin' crackers that had bin turned over by revelers in the bread-tray at the bar.

He got full at last, and his hart softened a little to'ards me. "After all," he sed, "you hav sum peple at the North who air not wholly loathsum beasts?"

"Well, yes," I sed, "we hav' now and then a man among us who isn't a cold-bluded scoundril. Young man," I mildly but gravely sed, "this crooil war is over, and you're lickt! It's rather necessary for sumbody to lick in a good square, lively fite, and in this 'ere case it happens to be the United States of America. You fit splendid, but we was too many for you. Then make the best of it, & let us all give in and put the Republic on a firmer basis nor ever.

"I don't gloat over your misfortins, my young fren'. Fur from it. I'm a old man now, & my hart is softer nor it once was. You see my spectacles is misten'd with suthin' very like tears. I'm thinkin' of the sea of good rich Blud that has been spilt on both sides in this dredful war! I'm thinkin' of our widders and orfuns North, and of your'n in the South. I kin cry for both. B'leeve me, my young fren' I kin place my old hands tenderly on the fair yung hed of the Virginny maid whose lover was laid low in the battle dust by a fed'ral bullet, and say, as fervently and piously as a vener'ble sinner like me kin say anythin' God be good to you, my poor dear, my poor dear."

I riz up to go, & takin' my yung Southern fren' kindly by the hand, I sed, "Yung man, adoo! You Southern fellers is probly my brothers, tho' you've occasionally had a cussed queer way of showin' it! It's over now. Let us all jine in and make a country on this continent that shall giv' all Europe the cramp in the stummuck ev'ry time they look at us! Adoo, adoo!"

And as I am through, I'll likewise say adoo to you, jentle reader, merely remarkin' that the Star Spangled Banner is wavin' round loose agin, and that there don't seem to be anything the matter with the Goddess of Liberty beyond a slite cold.

ARTEMUS WARD

David Ross Locke (1833–1888)

Petroleum Vesuvius Nasby

*T*HE PROGRESS of the American Civil War can be followed in the humorous writings of several fictional personalities, both Northern and Southern, whose offerings were often a welcome staple in newspapers of the period. Of these imaginary beings, none was better known than Petroleum V. Nasby, whose most famous aficionado was Abraham Lincoln. Senator Charles Sumner told of visiting the president just a few days before the close of the war and of being detained for some twenty minutes while Lincoln read him a collection of Nasby letters with great delight. All the while a large group of government officials were waiting in an anteroom. "For the genius to write these things I would gladly give up my office," Lincoln is reported to have said.

David Ross Locke, Nasby's creator, was a native of New York who migrated to Findlay, Ohio, and a small newspaper and printing business. From his initial appearance in Locke's Findlay *Jeffersonian* in March 1861, Nasby was a mask of biting, if obvious, irony. In pretending to denounce the shortcomings of blacks and extol the laudable qualities of Southerners, he underscores the fatuousness of such opinions. Thus, when supposedly writing from Richmond just after Lee's surrender, Nasby berates the Southern cause as weak and ridiculous while proclaiming it in glowing, heroic terms. In similar fashion, while pretending to write sympathetically of the incarceration of Jefferson Davis a few weeks later, he is really chiding those Northerners, such as

---

The selection is from David Ross Locke, *The Struggles (Social, Financial and Political) of Petroleum Vesuvius Nasby* (Boston: Lee and Shepard, 1888).

Horace Greeley, who befriended the former Confederate president in a spirit of humaneness.

Nasby's self-proclaimed positions of professor, "Postmaster at Confederate X Roads," and pastor of the "Church of the Noo Dispensashun" all suggest the bogus nature of the character and his statements. The style of the pieces, like the persona itself, was typical of American humor of the time. Nasby was a charlatan trying to sound educated and eloquent while exhibiting rank ignorance through his atrocious spelling and bigoted statements.

In 1865 Locke became editor of the *Toledo Blade* and continued to produce the still-popular Nasby letters until his death in 1888. Numerous collected editions appeared, which enhanced their popularity and durability.

The Fall of Richmond and Lee's Surrender

SAINT'S REST (wich is in the Stait uv Noo Jersey)
April the 10th, 1865.

I survived the defeat uv Breckinridge in 1860, becoz I knowd the Dimokrasy cood raise up in arms agin the unconstooshnality uv electin a seckshnal President, who wuz impregnatid with any seckshnal ijees that he got north uv Mason and Dixon's line.

I survived the defeat uv Micklellan (who wuz, trooly, the nashen's hope and pride likewise), becoz I felt ashoored that the rane uv the goriller Linkin wood be a short wun; that in a few months, at furthest, Ginral Lee wood capcher Washinton, depose the ape, and set up there a constooshnal guverment, based upon the great and immutable trooth that a white man is better than a nigger.

I survived the loss uv Atlanty, and Savanner, and Charleston, becoz, dependin on Suthern papers, I bleeved that them places wuz given up—mind, *given up*—becoz the Confedrits desired to concentrate for a crushin blow.

I survived the fall uv Richmond, tho it wuz a staggerer; becoz I still hed faith that that grate and good man, Lee, did it for stratejy, that he mite concentrate hisself sumwhere else; and when the Ablishnists jeered me, and sed "Richmond," and "Go up, bald head," to me, I shook my fist at em, and sed, "Wait, and you'll see."

I wuz a lookin for the blow that wuz to foller this concentratin. It cum!

But it wuz us who reseeved it, and a death blow it wuz. Ajacks defied the litenen; cood he hev bin a Northern Dimokrat, and stood this lick unmoved, he mite hev done it with perfect safety.

"Lee surrendered!"

Good hevins! Is this the end uv the concentratin? Is this the dyin in the last ditch? Is this the fightin till the last man wuz a inanimate corpse? Is this the bringin up the childrin to take their places, ez the old ones peg out under Yankee bullets?

"Lee surrendered!"

Why, this ends the biznis. Down goes the curtain. The South is conkered! CONKERED!! CONKERED!!! Linkin rides into Richmond! A Illinois rail-splitter, a buffoon, a ape, a goriller, a smutty joker, sets hisself down in president Davis's cheer, and rites despatches! Where are the matrons uv Virginia? Did they not bare their buzzums and rush onto the Yankee bayonets that guarded the monster? Did they not cut their childern's throtes, and wavin a Confedrit flag in one hand, plunge a meatknife into their throbbin buzzums with the tother, rather than see their city dishonored by the tread uv a conkerer's foot? Alars! not wunst.

Per contrary! I read in the papers that they did rush wildly thro the streets, with their childern in their arms.

But it wuz at the Yankee commissary trains, who give em bread and meat, wich they eat vociferously.

Their buzzums was bare.

But it wuz becoz their close hed worn out, and they didn't know how to weave cloth for new wuns.

In breef, they actid about ez mean ez a Northern Dimekrat ever did, and to go lower is unnessary.

This ends the chapter. The conféderasy hez at last concentratid its last concentrate. It's dead. It's gathered up its feet, sed its last words, and deceest. And with it the Dimokrasy hez likewise given up the ghost. It may survive this, but I can't see how. We staked our politikle fortune on it; we went our bottom dollar on it; it's gone up, and we ditto. Linkin will serve his term out—the tax on whiskey won't be repealed—our leaders will die off uv chagrin, and delirium tremens, and inability to live so long out uv offis, and the sheep will be scattered. Farewell, vane world. I'll embrace the Catholic faith and be a nun, and in a cloister find that rest that pollytics kin never give.

PETROLEUM V. NASBY,
Lait Paster uv the Church uv the
Noo Dispensashun.

Charles Henry Smith (1826–1903)

Bill Arp

*T*HE ADVENT of Bill Arp as a fictional newspaper personality was an unceremonious occurrence. At the beginning of the Civil War, Lincoln had appealed to the Southern states for volunteers, thus infuriating the sensibilities of the region. In Rome, Georgia, a local attorney named Charles Henry Smith wrote a biting satiric letter in retaliation, which he read to a group of citizens. One of these, a William Arp, suggested that his name be affixed to the bottom before publication. Thus was born "Bill Arp," who has been described as "a simple, strong, conservative Georgia cracker whose letters to the editor chronicle the successes and failures, hopes and frustrations, of an average Southerner during the War and Reconstruction."

During the war Arp was carried in the *Southern Confederacy* of Atlanta and was widely reprinted in regional newspapers. His popularity increased in the postwar years. Beginning in 1877, Smith gave up his law practice to devote full time to writing Arp letters and to lecturing. Though he wrote primarily for the *Atlanta Constitution,* syndication is said to have reached seven hundred newspapers. The letters, gradually altering in tone from the cracker voice to the more cultured tones of Smith, continued until 1903, the year Smith died. In the forty-two years that Smith was engaged in the Arp enterprise, he produced more than two thousand pieces, many of which were collected in volumes such as *Bill Arp, So Called* and *Bill Arp's Scrap Book.*

The selection is from Charles H. Smith, *Bill Arp, So Called* (New York: Metropolitan Record Office, 1866).

Bill Arp Philosophizes upon the War, Etc.

Mr. Editor—

Sir: If I could discern any thing gloomy in the political horizon, I would keep it to myself, and not go to putting my long face in the newspapers; but seeing things as I see 'em, I don't see any thing in the situation more distressing than usual.

My doctrine has always been, that if we was to fight and fight and fight until our army was played out, the biggest part of old Lincoln's job would be just begun. After he has whipped us, then he has got to subjugate us. He has got to hold us down, and he can't do it. I used to have a neighbor who was one of these mean, little, snarling, fic-dog sort of men, and I had him to whip about once a week for three months, but I didn't make a thing off of him. He would raise a new fuss with me in an hour after I had made him holler enough, and finally I sold him my land, and moved away just to get rid of him. Now the idea of old Lincoln taking possession of so many towns and cities, and so much territory, and holding it and keeping so many people down, is utter nonsense, and it can't be done. Besides, we are not whipped yet—not by three or four jug fulls. Suppose Sherman did walk right through the State. Suppose he did. Was anybody whipped? Didn't the rebellion just close right up on the ground behind him, just like shutting up a pair of waffle-irons? He parted the atmosphere as he went along, and it collapsed again in his rear immediately. He will have to go over that old ground several times yet, and then sell out and move away.

Well, they say that old Abe's Congress has finally and forever set free all the niggers, by amending the Constitution. How did that free 'em, or how did freeing 'em amend the Constitution? The darned old thing has been broke for forty years, and it is broke yet; but suppose they have freed 'em, it is no more than old Abe has done three or four times by his proclamations. What does it all amount to?—I want to buy a nigger, and I had just as lief buy a chunk of a *free* nigger as any other sort. I don't care a bobee about his being free, if I can subjugate him; and if he gets above his color, I will put thirty-nine whelks right under his shirt, and make him wish that old Lincoln stood in his shoes.

But, Mr. Editor, Sir: The way I see it is, that if we are to be whipped at all, then the infantry, which is to say the web-feet, are to be whipped first. After that, then comes the tug of war. Whipping the cavalry will be the devilishest undertaking of this or any preceding conflict. I tell you, sir, they can't be whipped until they are

An illustration from Charles H. Smith's Bill Arp's Scrap Book
(1884).

caught, and that event will never transpire. The truth is, that the
Confederate cavalry can fight 'em, and dog 'em, and dodge 'em, and
bushwhack 'em, and bedevil 'em, for a thousand years, and that is
as long as the most sanguine have calculated this war to last. The
Confederate cavalry are ubiquitous and everlasting. I have travelled
a heap of late, and had occasion to retire into some very sequestered
regions, but nary hill or holler, nary vale or valley, nary mountain
gorge or inaccessible ravine have I found, but what the cavalry had
been there, and *just left.* And that is the reason they can't be
whipped, for they have always *just left,* and took an odd horse or
two with 'em. For four years the Confederate Horse-Stealing
Cavalry have been pirooting around, preparing themselves for the
frightful struggle that is to come. By dodging around they have
completed their inspection of stock, and tried all its bottom, and
now it is reasonable to suppose they are ready to fight. The fact is,
Mr. Editor, stealing from our side is most played out, and I feel assured our enemies will suffer very soon. Such a crisis is, I reckon, a
blessing to the country, for when we have lost all of our property,
there won't be nothing to reconstruct, and we will all go to fighting.
Property in such a time is the bane of liberty. Old Blivins remarked,
that if we all had been as poor as him when the war begun, and had

held our own, the victory would have been won long ago. "How poor are you, Blivins?" said I. "Just four years ago," said he, "I was even with the world, which is to say I owed about as many as I didn't owe, and had nothing to boot, and that is the fix I want the Confederacy to get in."

We are that way in these parts, Mr. Editor, sure. What the Yankees didn't get in six months' continuous plunder, was brought out to enjoy when they left. Suddenly some friendly scouts appeared upon the arena, and made a general grab.

Every thing visible was appropriated without pay or ceremony. Our indignant citizens appealed for protection, and his Excellency the Governor sent up a major as the avenger of our wrongs, and the protector of our lives and property. The Major and his gallant boys appreciated our cause, and in order to prevent a recurrence of such robberies by the wandering scouts, they stole all the balance themselves and then run away. Such is war, Mr. Editor, but nevertheless, notwithstanding, I am for it as long as possible, and longer if necessary.

We are now trying the militia—Georgia militia luxuriating under their benign and peaceable rule. Slandered as they have been from the mountain to the sea, they are now the guardians of our sleeping liberties. Like a wall of fire they environ the outposts of Cherokee Georgia, and we will stand by 'em as long as they stand by us. Let their slanderers beware, and recollect the fate of Ike Johnson, that old veteran from the Virginia army. Ike was at home on a busting furlow, and he rode up to the militia and pulling out his repeater, exclaimed, with uncommon gravity, "*Lay down, meelish, I am going to bust this cap.*" Mr. Editor, Ike Johnson had to leave those parts prematurely.

And now, sir, will you allow us Romans to ask a favor of your wide-spreading paper? We desire you to intersperse in your columns some news of the Georgia Legislature. We understood they were powerfully scattered, and somewhat demoralized. Have they rallied yet, and did the Governor lose many of the public archives? I saw a member from Franklin the other day, and he had two pair of cotton cards in his hand. I asked him about the archives, and he said he understood the Governor got off about ten thousand pair of 'em, and that all the members got two pair apiece besides.

Do you suppose this is so?

Yours politely,
BILL ARP

Robert Henry Newell (1836–1901)

Orpheus C. Kerr

*T*HE VERY NAME "Orpheus C. Kerr" is an indication of the type of humor with which Robert Henry Newell endowed his well-known journalistic conception, as it contains an all-too-obvious pun. Kerr made his initial appearance in the New York *Sunday Mercury* in 1861, when the Lincoln administration was establishing itself in Washington. The usual drove of sycophants angling for government appointments was not far behind, except that in this case the number was perhaps greater than usual. Lincoln had come to the White House trailing clouds of legend—of the quick-witted country lawyer, the rail splitter, and birth in a log cabin. It is of such stuff that anecdote is easily fashioned, and Lincoln stories, most of them spurious, were rife among the office seekers. Newell's Kerr goes seeking an appointment along with the other hopefuls. In a series of letters to the editor, Kerr sent the *Mercury* pun-sprinkled accounts of life in Washington.

Humorous circumstances soon evolved into serious business, as the Civil War erupted only weeks after Lincoln's inauguration. However, the Orpheus C. Kerr papers continued throughout the hostilities and after. Although the subject matter of the letters changed, Kerr's humor was as well suited to one topic as another, for that humor was constructed of an opaque exterior shell of rhetorical bombast with an inner core of seriousness. Thus, Kerr talks of heroism, while in reality he is cowardly; he presents a funny parody of Poe's "Raven," ending each stanza with "Balti-

---

The selection is from Robert Henry Newell, *The Orpheus C. Kerr Papers* (New York: Blakemore & Mason, 1862).

more," rather than "nevermore," which really deplores the attack on the federal volunteers in that city in the spring of 1861. Parodying was to prove a favorite technique in the letters—sometimes humorous and irreverent, sometimes serious.

Because the letters follow the major events of 1861–1865, Newell is often considered primarily a Civil War humorist, and Kerr one of the humorous fictional voices who brought needed relief to the horrors of that conflict. But it is obvious from the underlying seriousness of the material that the author's sentiments were with the Union cause. Kerr, along with Artemus Ward and Petroleum V. Nasby, made a major contribution toward reassuring the partisans in whom he believed, while offering them comic relief.

Describing the South in Twelve Lines

Washington, D.C., April _____, 1861

The chivalrous South, my boy, has taken Fort Sumter, and only wants to be "let alone." Some things of a Southern sort I like, my boy; Southdown mutton is fit for the gods, and Southside particular is liquid sunshine for the heart; but the whole country was growing tired of new South wails before this, and my present comprehensive estimate of all there is of Dixie may be summed up in twelve straight lines, under the general heading of

REPUDIATION

Neath a ragged palmetto a Southerner sat,
A twisting the band of his Panama hat,
And trying to lighten his mind of a load
By humming the words of the following ode:
  Oh! for a nigger, and oh! for a whip;
  Oh! for a cocktail, and oh! for a nip;
  Oh! for a shot at old Greeley and Beecher;
  Oh! for a crack at a Yankee school-teacher;
  Oh! for a captain, and oh! for a ship;
  Oh! for a cargo of niggers each trip.
And so he kept oh-ing for all he had not,
Not contented with owing for all that he'd got.

In view of the impending conflict, it is the duty of every American citizen, who has nothing else to do, to take up his abode in the capital of this agonized Republic, and give the Cabinet the sanction of his presence. Some base child of treason may intimate that Washington is not quite large enough to hold every American citizen; but I'm satisfied that, if all the democrats could have one good washing, they would shrink so that you might put the whole blessed party into an ordinary custom house. Some of the republicans are pretty large chaps for their size, but Jeff Davis thinks they can be "taken in" easily enough; and I know that the new tariff will be enough to make them contract like sponges out of water. The city is full of Western chaps, at present, who look as if they had just walked out of a charity-hospital, and had not got beyond gruel diet yet. Every soul of them knew old Abe when he was a child, and one old boy can even remember going for a doctor when his mother was born. I met one of them the other day (he is after the Moosehicmagunticook post-office), and his anecdotes of the President's boyhood brought tears to my eyes, and several tumblers to my lips. He says, that when Abe was an infant of sixteen, he split so many rails that his whole county looked like a wholesale lumber-yard for a week; and that when he took to flat-boating, he was so tall and straight, that a fellow once took him for a smoke-stack on a steamboat, and didn't find out his mistake until he tried to kindle a fire under him. Once, while Abe was practicing as a lawyer, he defended a man for stealing a horse, and was so eloquent in proving that his client was an honest victim of false suspicion, that the deeply-affected victim made him a present of the horse as soon as he was acquitted. I tell you what, my boy, if Abe pays a post-office for every story of his childhood that's told, the mail department of this glorious nation will be so large that a letter smaller than a two-story house would get lost in it.

Of all the vile and damning deeds that ever rendered a city eternally infamous, my boy—of all the infernal sins of dark-browed treachery that ever made open-faced treason seem holy, the crime of Baltimore is the blackest and worst. All that April day we were waiting with bated breath and beating hearts for the devoted men who had pledged their lives to their country at the first call of the President, and were known to be marching to the defence of the nation's capital. That night was one of terror: at any moment the hosts of the rebels might pour upon the city from the mountains of guilty Virginia, and grasp the very throat of the Republic. And with the first dim light of morning came the news that our soldiers had been basely beset in the streets of Baltimore, and ruthlessly shot down by a treacherous mob! Those whom they had trusted as brothers, my boy—whose country they were marching to defend with their lives—assassinating them in cold blood!

I was sitting in my room at Willard's, when a serious chap from New Haven, who had just paused long enough at the door to send a waiter for the same that he had yesterday, came rushing into the apartment with a long, fluttering paper in his hand.

"Listen to this," says he, in wild agitation, and read:

BALTIMORE

Midnight shadows, dark, appalling, round the Capitol were falling,
    And its dome and pillars glimmered spectral from Potomac's shore;
All the great had gone to slumber, and of all the busy number
    That had moved the State by day within its walls, as erst before,
None there were but dreamed of heroes thither sent ere day was o'er
        Thither sent through BALTIMORE.

But within a chamber solemn, barred aloft with many a column,
    And with windows tow'rd Mount Vernon, windows tow'rd Potomac's shore
Sat a figure, stern and awful; Chief, but not the Chieftain lawful
    Of the land whose grateful millions Washington's great name adore—
Sat the form—a shade majestic of a Chieftain gone before,
        Thine to honor, Baltimore!

There he sat in silence, gazing, by a single planet's blazing,
    At a man outspread before him wide upon the marble floor;
And if 'twere for mortal proving that those reverend lips were moving,
    While the eyes were closely scanning one mapped city o'er and o'er—
While he saw but one great city on that map upon the floor—
        They were whispering—"BALTIMORE."

Thus he sat, nor word did utter, till there came a sudden flutter,
    And the sound of beating wings was heard upon the carved door.
In a trice the bolts were broken; by those lips no word was spoken,
    As an Eagle, torn and bloody, dim of eye, and wounded sore,
Fluttered down upon the map, and trailed a wing all wet with gore
        O'er the name of BALTIMORE!

Then that noble form uprising, with a gesture of surprising,
    Bent with look of keenest sorrow tow'rd the bird that drooped before
"Emblem of my country!" said he, "are thy pinions stained already
    In a tide whose blending waters never ran so red before?
Is it with the blood of kinsmen? Tell me quickly, I implore!"
        Croaked the eagle—"BALTIMORE!"

"Eagle," said the Shade, advancing, "tell me by what dread mischancing
    Thou, the symbol of my people, bear'st thy plumes erect no more?
Why dost thou desert mine army, sent against the foes that harm me,
    Through my country, with a Treason worlds to come shall e'er deplore?"
And the Eagle on the map, with bleeding wing, as just before,
        Blurred the name of BALTIMORE!

"Can it be?" the spectre muttered. "Can it be?" those pale lips uttered;
  "Is the blood Columbia treasures spilt upon its native shore?
Is there in the land so cherished, land for whom the great have perished,
  Men to shed a brother's blood as tyrant's blood was shed before?
Where are they who murder Peace before the breaking out of war?"
        Croaked the Eagle—"BALTIMORE."

At the word, of sound so mournful, came a frown, half sad, half scornful,
  O'er the grand, majestic face where frown had never been before;
And the hands to Heaven uplifted, with an awful pow'r seemed gifted
  To plant curses on a head, and hold them there forevermore—
To rain curses on a land, and bid thee grow forevermore—
        Woe art thou, O BALTIMORE!

Then the sacred spirit, fading, left upon the floor a shading,
  As of one with arms uplifted, from a distance bending o'er;
And the vail of night grew thicker, and the death-watch beat the quicker
  For a death within a death, and sadder than the death before!
And a whispering of woe was heard upon Potomac's shore—
        Hear it not, O BALTIMORE!

And the Eagle, never dying, still is trying, still is trying,
  With its wings upon the map to hide a city with its gore;
But the name is there forever, and it shall be hidden never,
  While the awful brand of murder points the Avenger to its shore;
While the blood of peaceful brothers God's dread vengeance doth implore,
        Thou art doomed, O BALTIMORE!

"There!" says the serious New Haven chap, as he finished reading, stirring something softly with a spoon, "What do you suppose Poe would think, if he were alive now and could read that?"

"I think," says I, striving to appear calm, "that he would be 'Raven' mad about it."

"Oh . . . ah . . . yes," says the serious chap, vaguely, "what will *you* take?"

Doubtless I shall become hardened to the horrors of war in time, my boy; but at present these things unhinge me.

                                Yours, unforgivingly,
                                ORPHEUS C. KERR

Henry Wheeler Shaw (1818–1885)

Josh Billings

*I*N MANY RESPECTS, Henry Wheeler Shaw can be seen as a protege of Charles Farrar Browne, the creator of Artemus Ward. Despite the fact that Shaw was sixteen years younger than Browne, he came to humorous journalism relatively late in life (at age 45), at a time when Artemus Ward dominated American humor. It is not surprising, therefore, that Shaw's humor looks to the Browne prototype for such devices as aphoristic structure and comic spelling. Moreover, in the guise of Josh Billings, Shaw became a popular lecturer, following the pattern set by Browne with Artemus Ward. Browne was also instrumental in helping Shaw find a publisher for the first collection of Billings's sayings and sketches.

Browne's is not the only influence to be found in Shaw's work, however. In writing sketches about various categories of people and animals, Shaw emulates the English character writers of the seventeenth century, whose standard mode was a short descriptive sketch of a subject, brought into sharp focus by means of a few salient details.

Like many creative journalists, Shaw came to the task after having tried other professions. A native of Massachusetts and for a time a student at Union College in New York, he worked at many jobs, including operating a steamboat on the Ohio River, auctioneering, and selling real estate. He contributed humorous sketches to several Massachusetts and New York newspapers beginning in 1859. He signed his work "Ephrem Billings," then "Si Sledlength," and finally "Josh

---

The selections are from Henry Wheeler Shaw, *The Complete Works of Josh Billings*, rev. ed. (New York: Dillingham, 1899).

Billings." At first Josh Billings was little more than a pseudonym. When Shaw published a sketch on the mule in the *Poughkeepsian* signed by Billings, it attracted little notice. But when he saw a piece on the same subject by Artemus Ward reprinted in virtually every American newspaper, he recognized that it was style and a comic persona that made the difference. Immediately he changed the spelling to a comic phonetic vein (the new title was "Essa on the Muel, bi Josh Billings"), and the essay—as well as the career of Josh Billings—were launched.

Much of the Billings material was subsequently published in the *New York Weekly* (which Shaw joined in 1867) and in the annual *Josh Billings' Farmer's Allminax,* which were issued from 1869 to 1880. The latter included many of the proverbs that enjoy frequent quotation even in the present day.

The Mule

The mule is haf hoss and haf Jackass, and then kums tu a full stop, natur diskovering her mistake.

Tha weigh more, akordin tu their heft, than enny other kreetur, except a crowbar.

Tha kant hear enny quicker, nor further than the hoss, yet their ears are big enuff for snow shoes.

You kan trust them with enny one whose life aint worth enny more than the mules. The only wa tu keep the mules into a paster, is tu turn them into a medder jineing, and let them jump out.

Tha are reddy for use, just as soon as they will du tu abuse.

Tha haint got enny friends, and will live on huckle berry brash, with an ockasional chanse at Kanada thistels.

Tha are a modern invenshun, i dont think the Bible deludes tu them at tall.

Tha sel for more money than enny other domestik animile. Yu kant tell their age by looking into their mouth, enny more than you kould a Mexican cannons. Tha never hav no dissease that a good club wont heal.

If tha ever die tha must kum rite tu life agin, for i never herd noboddy sa "ded mule."

Tha are like sum men, verry korrupt at harte; ive known them tu be good mules for 6 months, just tu git a good chanse to kick sumbody.

I never owned one, nor never mean to, unless thare is a United Staits law passed, requiring it.

The only reason why tha are pashunt, is bekause tha are ashamed ov themselfs.

I have seen eddikated mules in a sirkus.

Tha kould kick, and bite, tremenjis. I would not sa what I am forced tu sa again the mule, if his birth want an outrage, and man want tu blame for it.

Enny man who is willing tu drive a mule, ought to be exempt by law from running for the legislatur.

Tha are the strongest creeturs on earth, and heaviest ackording tu their sise; I herd tell ov one who fell oph from the tow path, on the Eri kanawl, and sunk as soon as he touched bottom, but he kept rite on towing the boat tu the nex stashun, breathing thru his ears, which stuck out ov the water about 2 feet 6 inches; i did'nt see this did, but an auctioneer told me ov it, and i never knew an auctioneer tu lie unless it was absolutely convenient.

The Flea

The smallest animal ov the brute creashun, and the most pesky, iz the Flea.

They are about the bigness ov an onion seed, and shine like a bran new shot.

They spring from low places, and kan spring further and faster than enny ov the bug-brutes.

They bite wuss than the musketoze, for they bite on a run; one flea will go aul over a man's subburbs in 2 minnitts, and leave him az freckled az the meazels.

It iz impossible to do ennything well with a flea on you, except sware, and fleas aint afraid ov that; the only way iz tew quit bizzness ov aul kinds and hunt for the flea, and when you have found him, he ain't thare. Thiz iz one ov the flea mysterys, the fackulty they hav ov being entirely lost jist as soon as you hav found them.

I don't suppose thare iz ever killed, on an average, during enny one year, more than 16 fleas, in the whole ov the United States ov America, unless thare iz a cazualty ov sum kind. Once in a while thare iz a dogg gits drowned sudden, and then thare may be a few fleas lost.

They are about az hard to kill az a flaxseed iz, and if you don't mash them up as fine az ground pepper they will start bizzness agin, on a smaller kapital, jist az pestiverous az ever.

Thare iz lots ov people who have never seen a flea, and it takes a pretty smart man tew see one ennyhow; they don't stay long in a place.

If you ever ketch a flea, kill him before you do ennything else; for if you put it oph 2 minnits, it may be too late.

Menny a flea haz past away forever in less than 2 minnits.

Singular Beings

THE POMPOUS MAN

The pompous man iz generally a snob at home and abroad. He fills himself up with an east wind and thinks he is grate just bekauze he happens tew feel big.

He talks loud and large, but deceives noboddy who will take the trubble tew meazzure him.

He iz a man ov small *caliber,* but a good deal ov bore.

His family looks upon him az the greatest man that the world haz had the honor to produce lately, and tho he gits snubbed often amungst folks, he rekompenses himself bi going home and snubbing hiz family.

THE HAPPY MAN

The happy man iz a poor judge of hiz own bliss, for he kant set down and deskribe it.

Happiness iz like health—thoze who hav the most ov it seem tew kno it the least.

Yu kant go out in the spring ov the year and gather happiness along the side ov the road just the same az you would dandylion—noboddy but a natral born phool kan do this they are alwus happy, ov course.

When i hear a man bragging how happy he iz, he dont cheat me, he only cheats himself.

THE HENPECKED MAN

The henpecked man iz most generally married; but thare are instances on reckord of single men being harrassed by the pullets.

Yu kan alwus tell one ov theze kind ov men, espeshily if they are in the company ov their wives. They look as humble and resighned tew their fate az a hen turkey in a wet day.

Thare aint nothing that will take the starch out ov a man like being pecked by a woman. It is wuss than a seven months' turn ov the fever and agy.

The wives ov hen-pecked husbands most alwus out liv their viktims, and I hav known them tew git marrid agin, and git hold ov a man that time (*thank the Lord!*) who understood all the hen-peck dodges.

One ov these kind ov husbands iz an honor tew his sex.

The hen-pecked man, when he gits out amungst men, puts on an air ov bravery and defiance, and once in a while will git a leetle drunk, and then go home with a firm resolve that he will be captain ov his household; but the old woman soon takes the glory out ov him, and handles him just az she would a haff-grown chicken, who had fell into the swill barrel, and had tew be jerked out dredful quick.

THE PHUNNY MAN

Thare iz hardly ennything that a man iz so vain ov az the humor that iz in him.

The phunny man iz seldum an humorist, and never a wit.

Hiz only pride iz tew make you laff; he seldum rizes abuv a jest, and very often iz the only one who kan see enny point even in that.

He iz generally the hero ov the ockashun in the rural distrikts, and kuntry bumbkins laff obstreprous whenever he opens his mouth.

The phunny man iz the clown at large, and hiz jests are sumtimes amuzing, but never remembered.

Thare iz seldum enny taint ov originality in him, and the quips and the quirks he deals in are old saws reset and refiled, and bad enuff done at that.

It iz a dredful unfortunit thing tew deal in cast oph jokes; for, like the old clothes bizzness, they will stick tew a man all thru life.

Samuel Langhorne Clemens (1835–1910)

Mark Twain

ALTHOUGH SAMUEL CLEMENS abandoned his journalistic career in the early 1870s, it served him well
in several important respects. It put him in contact
with other journalists and with the burgeoning American
West, both of which gave him impetus and material for his
earliest humorous stories. From an assignment to cover the
journey of some American tourists to Europe and the Near
East, he was afforded an expansive view of the great world
beyond the boundaries of the United States. And most importantly, in his early days as a reporter for the Virginia City,
Nevada, *Enterprise* he came to know Charles Farrar Browne,
from whom he learned the usefulness and effectiveness of an
alter ego or persona. From this realization Mark Twain ultimately emerged.

Today Mark Twain is recognized most readily from Clemens's fiction. It was not always so. The Mark Twain of popular
legend appeared for the first time on a San Francisco stage in
1866, where he delivered a lecture on Clemens's recent trip
to the Sandwich Islands—in actuality a journalistic assignment for the *California Alta.* Shortly thereafter, Clemens
joined a group of Americans traveling to Europe. In the guise
of Mark Twain, he sent back letters to the *Alta* and to the *New
York Tribune* and *Herald,* which were carried by those newspapers and were subsequently fashioned into *The Innocents
Abroad* (1869).

In these dispatches, Mark Twain's posture was usually
that of the skeptical American—culturally naive, yet pos-

The selection is from Samuel L. Clemens, *The Innocents Abroad* (Hartford: American Publishing, 1869).

sessed of penetrating common sense. Quick to unmask any semblance of sham or artifice presented by Europeans, he would occasionally belittle or scoff, much to their consternation. At times, however, he was genuinely moved. Being received by the Russian czar and his family and seeing the imposing cathedral of Milan were two such instances. On these occasions, irony and scoffing were forgotten, and even Mark Twain stood in awe.

Much has been made in recent years of the differences between Samuel Clemens and his famous alter ego. One of Clemens's biographers, DeLancey Ferguson, has summarized the relationship in a manner that also applies to many other authors who have indulged in similar creations:

> Humor, like lyric poetry, is a form of self-dramatization. The humorist, like the poet, does not express his whole nature, or the whole of his attitude toward life. He takes one aspect of himself and his relation to the world, and by projecting and magnifying that aspect achieves an expression which, while still personal, is sufficiently detached and concentrated to be communicable to other people through the impersonal medium of print. . . . But though all humor is thus dramatic in essence, its variety and success depend upon the variety and richness of the total personality of which one facet is thus projected. (Ferguson 1943, 107)

No other journalistic mask ever drew upon such variety and richness of personality.

The Gran Milan Cathedral

All day long we sped through a mountainous country whose peaks were bright with sunshine, whose hillsides were dotted with pretty villas sitting in the midst of gardens and shrubbery, and whose deep ravines were cool and shady, and looked ever so inviting from where we and the birds were winging our flight through the sultry upper air.

We had plenty of chilly tunnels wherein to check our perspiration, though. We timed one of them. We were twenty minutes passing through it, going at the rate of thirty to thirty-five miles an hour.

Beyond Alessandria we passed the battle-field of Marengo. Toward dusk we drew near Milan, and caught glimpses of the city and
the blue mountain peaks beyond. But we were not caring for these
things—they did not interest us in the least. We were in a fever of
impatience; we were dying to see the renowned Cathedral! We
watched—in this direction and that—all around—every where. We
needed no one to point it out—we did not wish any one to point it
out—we would recognize it, even in the desert of the great Sahara.

At last, a forest of graceful needles, shimmering in the amber
sunlight, rose slowly above the pigmy house-tops, as one sometimes
sees, in the far horizon, a gilded and pinnacled mass of cloud lift
itself above the waste of waves, at sea,—the Cathedral! We knew it
in a moment.

Half of that night, and all of the next day, this architectural
autocrat was our sole object of interest.

What a wonder it is! So grand, so solemn, so vast! And yet so
delicate, so airy, so graceful! A very world of solid weight, and yet it
seems in the soft moonlight only a fairy delusion of frost-work that
might vanish with a breath! How sharply its pinnacled angles and
its wilderness of spires were cut against the sky, and how richly
their shadows fell upon its snowy roof! It was a vision!—a miracle!—
an anthem sung in stone, a poem wrought in marble!

Howsoever you look at the great Cathedral, it is noble, it is
beautiful! Wherever you stand in Milan, or within seven miles of
Milan, it is visible—and when it is visible, no other object can chain
your whole attention. Leave your eyes unfettered by your will but a
single instant and they will surely turn to seek it. It is the first thing
you look for when you rise in the morning, and the last your linger-
ing gaze rests upon at night. Surely, it must be the princeliest creation that ever brain of man conceived.

At nine o'clock in the morning we went and stood before this
marble colossus. The central one of its five great doors is bordered
with a bas-relief of birds and fruits and beasts and insects, which
have been so ingeniously carved out of the marble that they seem
like living creatures—and the figures are so numerous and the design so complex, that one might study it a week without exhausting
its interest. On the great steeple—surmounting the myriad of
spires—inside of the spires—over the doors, the windows—in nooks
and corners—everywhere that a niche or a perch can be found
about the enormous building, from summit to base, there is a marble statue, and every statue is a study in itself! Raphael, Angelo,
Canova—giants like these gave birth to the designs, and their own
pupils carved them. Every face is eloquent with expression, and
every attitude is full of grace. Away above, on the lofty roof, rank on

rank of carved and fretted spires spring high in the air, and through their rich tracery one sees the sky beyond. In their midst the central steeple towers proudly up like the mainmast of some great Indiaman among a fleet of coasters.

We wished to go aloft. The sacristan showed us a marble stairway (of course it was marble, and of the purest and whitest—there is no other stone, no brick, no wood, among its building materials), and told us to go up one hundred and eighty-two steps and stop till he came. It was not necessary to say stop—we should have done that anyhow. We were tired by the time we got there. This was the roof. Here, springing from its broad marble flagstones, were the long files of spires, looking very tall close at hand, but diminishing in the distance like the pipes of an organ. We could see, now, that the statue on the top of each was the size of a large man, though they all looked like dolls from the street. We could see, also, that from the inside of each and every one of these hollow spires, from sixteen to thirty-one beautiful marble statues looked out upon the world below.

From the eaves to the comb of the roof stretched in endless succession great curved marble beams, like the fore-and-aft braces of a steamboat, and along each beam from end to end stood up a row of richly carved flowers and fruits—each separate and distinct in kind, and over 15,000 species represented. At a little distance these rows seem to close together like the ties of a railroad track, and then the mingling together of the buds and blossoms of this marble garden forms a picture that is very charming to the eye.

We descended and entered. Within the church, long rows of fluted columns, like huge monuments, divided the building into broad aisles, and on the figured pavement fell many a soft blush from the painted windows above. I knew the church was very large, but I could not fully appreciate its great size until I noticed that the men standing far down by the altar looked like boys, and seemed to glide, rather than walk. We loitered about gazing aloft at the monster windows all aglow with brilliantly colored scenes in the lives of the Saviour and his followers. Some of these pictures are mosaics, and so artistically are their thousand particles of tinted glass or stone put together that the work has all the smoothness and finish of a painting. We counted sixty panes of glass in one window, and each pane was adorned with one of these master achievements of genius and patience.

The guide showed us a coffee-colored piece of sculpture which he said was considered to have come from the hand of Phidias, since it was not possible that any other artist, of any epoch, could have copied nature with such faultless accuracy. The figure was that of a

man without a skin; with every vein, artery, muscle, every fibre and
tendon and tissue of the human frame, represented in minute detail. It looked natural, because somehow it looked as if it were in
pain. A skinned man would be likely to look that way, unless his
attention were occupied with some other matter. It was a hideous
thing, and yet there was a fascination about it somewhere. I am
very sorry I saw it, because I shall always see it, now. I shall dream
of it, sometimes. I shall dream that it is resting its corded arms on
the bed's head and looking down on me with its dead eyes; I shall
dream that it is stretched between the sheets with me and touching
me with its exposed muscles and its stringy cold legs.

It is hard to forget repulsive things. I remember yet how I ran off
from school once, when I was a boy, and then, pretty late at night,
concluded to climb into the window of my father's office and sleep
on a lounge, because I had a delicacy about going home and getting
thrashed. As I lay on the lounge and my eyes grew accustomed to
the darkness, I fancied I could see a long, dusky, shapeless thing
stretched upon the floor. A cold shiver went through me. I turned
my face to the wall. That did not answer. I was afraid that that thing
would creep over and seize me in the dark. I turned back and stared
at it for minutes and minutes—they seemed hours. It appeared to
me that the lagging moonlight never, never would get to it. I turned
to the wall and counted twenty, to pass the feverish time away. I
looked—the pale square was nearer. I turned again and counted
fifty—it was almost touching it. With desperate will I turned again
and counted one hundred, and faced about, all in a tremble. A white
human hand lay in the moonlight! Such an awful sinking at the
heart—such a sudden gasp for breath! I felt—I can not tell *what* I
felt. When I recovered strength enough, I faced the wall again. But
no boy could have remained so, with that mysterious hand behind
him. I counted again, and looked—the most of a naked arm was
exposed. I put my hands over my eyes and counted till I could stand
it no longer, and then—the pallid face of a man was there, with the
corners of the mouth drawn down, and the eyes fixed and glassy in
death! I raised to a sitting posture and glowered on that corpse till
the light crept down the bare breast,—line by line—inch by inch—
past the nipple,—and then it disclosed a ghastly stab!

I went away from there. I do not say that I went away in any sort
of a hurry, but I simply went—that is sufficient. I went out at the
window, and I carried the sash along with me. I did not need the
sash, but it was handier to take it than it was to leave it, and so I
took it.—I was not scared, but I was considerably agitated.

When I reached home, they whipped me, but I enjoyed it. It

seemed perfectly delightful. That man had been stabbed near the office that afternoon, and they carried him in there to doctor him, but he only lived an hour. I have slept in the same room with him often, since then—in my dreams.

Now we will descend into the crypt, under the grand altar of Milan Cathedral, and receive an impressive sermon from lips that have been silent and hands that have been gestureless for three hundred years.

The priest stopped in a small dungeon and held up his candle. This was the last resting-place of a good man, a warm-hearted, unselfish man; a man whose whole life was given to succoring the poor, encouraging the faint-hearted, visiting the sick; in relieving distress, whenever and wherever he found it. His heart, his hand and his purse were always open. With his story in one's mind he can almost see his benignant countenance moving calmly among the haggard faces of Milan in the days when the plague swept the city, brave where all others were cowards, full of compassion where pity had been crushed out of all other breasts by the instinct of self-preservation gone mad with terror, cheering all, praying with all, helping all, with hand and brain and purse, at a time when parents forsook their children, the friend deserted the friend, and the brother turned away from the sister while her pleadings were still wailing in his ears.

This was good St. Charles Borromeo, Bishop of Milan. The people idolized him; princes lavished uncounted treasures upon him. We stood in his tomb. Near by was the sarcophagus, lighted by the dripping candles. The walls were faced with bas-reliefs representing scenes in his life done in massive silver. The priest put on a short white lace garment over his black robe, crossed himself, bowed reverently, and began to turn a windlass slowly. The sarcophagus separated in two parts, lengthwise, and the lower part sank down and disclosed a coffin of rock crystal as clear as the atmosphere. Within lay the body, robed in costly habiliments covered with gold embroidery and starred with scintillating gems. The decaying head was black with age, the dry skin was drawn tight to the bones, the eyes were gone, there was a hole in the temple and another in the cheek, and the skinny lips were parted as in a ghastly smile! Over this dreadful face, its dust and decay, and its mocking grin, hung a crown sown thick with flashing brilliants; and upon the breast lay crosses and croziers of solid gold that were splendid with emeralds and diamonds.

How poor, and cheap, and trivial these gew-gaws seemed in presence of the solemnity, the grandeur, the awful majesty of Death!

Think of Milton, Shakespeare, Washington, standing before a reverent world tricked out in the glass beads, the brass ear-rings and tin trumpery of the savages of the plains!

Dead Bartoloméo preached his pregnant sermon, and its burden was: You that worship the vanities of earth—you that long for worldly honor, worldly wealth, worldly fame—behold their worth!

To us it seemed that so good a man, so kind a heart, so simple a nature, deserved rest and peace in a grave sacred from the intrusion of prying eyes, and believed that he himself would have preferred to have it so, but peradventure our wisdom was at fault in this regard.

As we came out upon the floor of the church again, another priest volunteered to show us the treasures of the church. What, more? The furniture of the narrow chamber of death we had just visited, weighed six millions of francs in ounces and carats alone, without a penny thrown into the account for the costly workmanship bestowed upon them! But we followed into a large room filled with tall wooden presses like wardrobes. He threw them open, and behold, the cargoes of "crude bullion" of the assay offices of Nevada faded out of my memory. There were Virgins and bishops there, above their natural size, made of solid silver, each worth, by weight, from eight hundred thousand to two millions of francs, and bearing gemmed books in their hands worth eighty thousand; there were bas-reliefs that weighed six hundred pounds, carved in solid silver; croziers and crosses, and candlesticks six and eight feet high, all of virgin gold, and brilliant with precious stones; and beside these were all manner of cups and vases, and such things, rich in proportion. It was an Aladdin's palace. The treasures here, by simple weight, without counting workmanship, were valued at fifty millions of francs! If I could get the custody of them for a while, I fear me the market price of silver bishops would advance shortly, on account of their exceeding scarcity in the Cathedral of Milan.

The priests showed us two of St. Paul's fingers, and one of St. Peter's; a bone of Judas Iscariot (it was black), and also bones of all the other disciples; a handkerchief in which the Saviour had left the impression of his face. Among the most precious of the relics were a stone from the Holy Sepulchre, part of the crown of thorns (they have a whole one at Notre Dame), a fragment of the purple robe worn by the Saviour, a nail from the Cross, and a picture of the Virgin and Child painted by the veritable hand of St. Luke. This is the second of St. Luke's Virgins we have seen. Once a year all these holy relics are carried in procession through the streets of Milan.

I like to revel in the dryest details of the great cathedral. The building is five hundred feet long by one hundred and eighty wide, and the principal steeple is in the neighborhood of four hundred feet high. It has 7,148 marble statues, and will have upwards of three thousand more when it is finished. In addition, it has one thousand five hundred bas-reliefs. It has one hundred and thirty-six spires— twenty-one more are to be added. Each spire is surmounted by a statue six and a half feet high. Everything about the church is marble, and all from the same quarry; it was bequeathed to the Archbishopric for this purpose centuries ago. So nothing but the mere workmanship costs; still that is expensive—the bill foots up six hundred and eighty-four millions of francs, thus far (considerably over a hundred millions of dollars), and it is estimated that it will take a hundred and twenty years yet to finish the cathedral. It looks complete, but is far from being so. We saw a new statue put in its niche yesterday, alongside of one which had been standing these four hundred years, they said. There are four staircases leading up to the main steeple, each of which cost a hundred thousand dollars, with the four hundred and eight statues which adorn them. Marco Compioni was the architect who designed the wonderful structure more than five hundred years ago, and it took him forty-six years to work out the plan and get it ready to hand over to the builders. He is dead now. The building was begun a little less than five hundred years ago, and the third generation hence will not see it completed.

The building looks best by moonlight, because the older portions of it being stained with age, contrast unpleasantly with the newer and whiter portions. It seems somewhat too broad for its height, but may be familiarity with it might dissipate this impression.

They say that the Cathedral of Milan is second only to St. Peter's at Rome. I can not understand how it can be second to any thing made by human hands.

We bid it good-bye, now—possibly for all time. How surely, in some future day, when the memory of it shall have lost its vividness, shall we half believe we have seen it in a wonderful dream, but never with waking eyes!

6

THE MELTING POT

George Wilbur Peck, creator of "Terence McGrant," and several of his characters. (from Peck's Sunshine, *1883)*

George Wilbur Peck (1840–1916)

Terence McGrant

*G*EORGE WILBUR PECK'S immense popularity—
which led to his becoming mayor of Milwaukee and
governor of Wisconsin—was derived almost en-
tirely from two of his colorful fictional creations. The better
known is "Peck's Bad Boy," whose exploits Peck recounted to
a national readership. This famous nemesis of the adult
world was, however, preceded by a character who, though
not so well known, demonstrates Peck's talent for political
satire.

The first administration of Republican President Ulysses
S. Grant was charged with nepotism almost as soon as it was
established in the spring of 1869. At this time Peck, a
staunch Democrat, was editing the *Representative* in Ripon,
Wisconsin. On St. Patrick's day, when the Grant administration was just two weeks old and was appointing its "first
regiment . . . of relatives to office," according to Peck, an old
Irishman named O'Reilly came to town. After consuming
prodigious amounts of "corn extract," he loudly proclaimed
that he was leaving for Washington to "get his regular post-
office."

Peck was moved to write the first letter from a similar,
though fictitious, kinsman for the pages of his *Representative*. This initial offering was seen by Peck's friend and fellow
editor Mark M. ("Brick") Pomeroy, who printed subsequent
McGrant letters in his New York weekly, *Pomeroy's Democrat*.

Though unabashedly partisan, the McGrant correspond-

The selection is from George Wilbur Peck, *Adventures of One Terence McGrant*
(New York: Lambert, 1871).

ence represents another installment in the canon of newspaper satire with an undeniable ethnic flavor. As a Hibernian speaking to readers of the 1870s, McGrant can be said to foreshadow the later and more enduring "Mr. Dooley" of Finley Peter Dunne.

Letter from New-York

GRANT HOUSE, BAXTER STREET,
(On the Ethiopian Plan,)
NEW-YORK, September 6, 1869.

MISHTER POMRY: I lift Soratoga to-day to take a look at New-York. We have been having a foine time at Soratoga, drinking wine and bathing, ye can bet. Me cousin has enjoyed it wid his usual presents of mind. There has been only two things to mar the happiness of meself and me cousin, since me lasht lether. The first was this, which marred me happiness. I was standing on the bache at Newport, watching the women stand on their heads, etc., when one of the most illigant famails thut ever wore a fig-leaf called me, and axed me would I bathe her. Ye may think it strange, but such is the custom there. Every woman of ony standing in society has a plebian engaged to howld them in the wather, and sandpaper them off wid a crash towel. This is what the woman wunted me to be afther doing till her. I was not well plazed to have her consider me a plebian; but then I didn't want the woman to suffer for the lack of assistance, so I rushed in till the raging deep, washed her and dried her, and let her go. She towld me to come again the nixt day at the same hour. I rather liked it, and as I found she was the daughter of a Boston banker, I, like an unlucky divil, went and towld me Cousin Ulisses. Now what do you think he is afther doing? May I fail to be confirmed be the Sinate as minister to Bug Gota, if he didn't make me change clothes wid him, and he tuck my place, and iver since the first day he washed that girl in my place, and she thinkin' it was me all the time. Now, is that ony good way for the President to treat his own second cousin, when there is plenty chances for him? You wouldn't take advantage of a man in that way, nor ony gintleman.

The sicond source of unpleasantness is to me Cousin Ulisses. He is very much displeased that Rawlins should so far forget his duty to his chief as to die just at this time. Me cousin had got tired of traveling, and had just got settled down at Soratoga for a little fun, when he is ordered back to the capital to attend a funeral. But he won't be afther laving that girl many days.

His going to Washington has furnished me an opportunity to visit New-York. I came as far as here on the same train wid me cousin; but, bless you! he didn't know it. Whether it was that he was too full for utterance, or that he was brooding over his sorrows, I don't know; but he didn't see me.

I called at your office to-day to see you, but your young man said that you were invisible. I wanted to tell you why I am here. I don't want it to get out, or I would have towld your young man. Ye remember I towld you about a girl that I thought of marrying afther I got a divorce from Bridget. Well, the girl couldn't wait so long; so, begorra, we have eloped, and are stopping at this house enjoying the honeymoon. O sir! I have been in many trying situations before, but this is the tryingest. I try to make belave that I am not happy, but there is a grin on me face all the day long. I have in me younger days stole paches, ravished melon patches, gone cooning, and been a week in the Treasury Department; but for rale solid comfort, give me a genuine elopement.

The way I was induced to quit the company of me lawful wife was this: Ye see Bridget has been carrying on the worst kind lately getting drunk, and disgusting even me cousin. We tried to break her of the habit; but ivery time me cousin took a drink, Bridget would take two, and you know there are few persons in America could stand that. She was simply disgusting, and narely broke our hairts. We put up wid it all until the night of the big dance here. O bless me sowl! I trimble wid indignation when I think of it. We had put Bridget to bed, and all of us had gone to the ball-room to dance wid the girls. When the second dance was about half through, the cry, "A ghost!" was heard to proceed from the hall. The women fainted, and the men poured wather down their necks to bring them out. I was dancing wid the girl that is now wid me here as me wife *pro tem*, and me cousin was twisting around the girl that he bathed in the salt wather. Afther all the breath had returned to the women, I looked till the door, and there, just as she had emerged from her virtuous couch, and drunk as the divil, was Bridget. Half a dozen men tried to stop her, but she gave them a welt over the eye and proceeded at once to me locality. I never was afther being scared of a women, but when they are under the influence of spirits, and in their nightclothes, they are dangerous. I tried to get out, but she tuck me by the ear and bate me. She had a bit of a stick, and she warmed me, and finally tuck me till our room. I didn't care for the bating; but to be misused in the prisence of ladies, and whin I was innocent of only forgery or ony thing of the kind wid the girl wid whom I was dancing, was moighty unpleasant. I see me cousin didn't like it, although he said nothing, in his usual eloquent manner.

Me experiences here, stopping at a foine hotel, in the most arishtocratic portion of the city, as me landlord informed me, are greater than I supposed they would be, or I would have made a draw on Bridget's stocking before I left; but niver you hade, I have an idea about me. You see, there is to be a dead-bate appointed as minister to China; and in consideration of me services to the President, in giving him me place at the say-side, I am to have the privilege of selecting the man to fill his position. I would go meself, but I don't understand the Chinese language, nor am I a success as a ratist. Me hair don't grow all in one place, nather, so I have concluded to set up in business. To that ind I have sint the following advertisement to the *Herald:*

> "PERSONAL.—Ony gintleman whose loyalty to the besht government on earth is inquestioned, and who wishes to serve his country as minister to China, can open negotiations wid a nare rilative of the President by calling at the Grant House, in Baxter street, New-York, and making the necessary deposit. The stable is in the rare of the house, in case parties should prefer to pay the first installment in horse-flesh. No editors nade apply. TERENCE Mc-GRANT."

You see I put in that lasht clause, because there are a large number of members of your profession who are so anxious to serve the government, and whose abilities are not the best. Now, before we lift Soratoga we had a lether of 300 pages from Grayley, and, though no one could rade it, we knew it was written in the Chinese language, and of course he wanted the appintment. No; my object is to get a gintleman to whom money is no object, but who is patriotic. Patriotism is the foundation-stone of all our success, and I am mighty short of money.

Be the way, is there ony law in New-York to prevent a man laving his wife if she proves unrasonable as a drinkist?

Yours, a brevet Mormon,
TERENCE McGRANT

P.S.—If Bridget calls at your office inquiring for me, till her I am drowned, and publish the obituary notice, if necessary, to convince her. I wouldn't have her catch me for tin dollars.

T. McG.

Samuel W. Small (1851–1931)

Old Si

WHEN SAMUEL W. SMALL'S modest contribution to American journalism is noted, it is in connection with the unwitting role it played in the creation of the celebrated Uncle Remus. Small left the *Atlanta Constitution* in 1878 to accept an appointment as United States Commissioner to Paris. His departure opened the way for Joel Chandler Harris to round out the character of Uncle Remus, who had been introduced to *Constitution* readers during Small's temporary absence from the paper in 1876–1877.

Small was a man of many accomplishments. In later life, as a well-known evangelist, he disclaimed his journalistic endeavors. The title page of a collected edition of Old Si pieces states that they were "written when [Small] was a wicked newspaperman." The sketches stand as a sort of dim memorial to Small's journalistic career. Although they contain frequent humorous turns of phrase and action, they lack the serious elements of the Uncle Remus sketches, and are thus to be seen primarily as evocations of caricature within an ethnic context.

Old Si Pilots a 'Possum Hunt

"Golly! hit wus cold 'nuff las' night ter freeze up a blas' furniss!" said Amos yesterday morning.

"Yes, but I like ter 'laff myself inter a ragin' feber, fer de bo'n trufe!" said Old Si.

The selection is from Samuel W. Small, *Old Si's Sayings* (Chicago: Revell, 1886).

"How was dat?"

"Well, some ob dese town gen'lmen, dey come arter me ter go wid dem ter hunt 'possum, an' I went."

"Dey moughter 'skused me!" put in Amos.

"Nebber mine, nigger, mebbe you kin be satisfide wid er or'nary cirkus, but ef yer want ter see de gran, hipperdrumedary an' moril caravangerie, you'se got ter go 'possum huntin' wid dat squad dat I wus in las' night!"

"What did dey do?"

"Dey went out in de woods an' prowled 'round dar whar de 'possums gin'rully gethers, an' dey hunted! Dey 'skivered mo' 'possum tracks an' seed mo' 'possum h'ar on de bark ob trees dan's bin in Georgy sence Stone Mountain was planted ter mark de norf-wes' corner ob de big survay!"

"Did dey ketch any, tho'?"

"Hol' on! De fust one dat dey treed wuz one dat dey foun' creepin' long de side ob a fence. When dey sicked de dog on hit an' hit cl'ared de fence at de fust bound dey lit out arter hit an' purty soon dey had hit up a tree. When de 'possum got up ter de fork hit turn'd 'round an' say: 'Sphit! me-ow-ow!' Good Mas'er, I jess tho't dat I would bus' right dar, fer dem boys hed done gone an' treed de bigges' ole gray cat dat ebber you see in yo' bo'n days!"

"Dey moughter kno'd dat warn't no 'possum when hit riz ober dat fence, es you prescribe!" said Amos.

"But sho'tly dey struck anudder trail, an' when de dog— one ob dese heah patent-breed fices—bark'd, one ob de boys say: 'By jings, fellers, we's got de re-prehensible trail wretch in de foallidge, at las'!' an' dey all helt a wah-dance onder de tree, but when dey flash'd de bull's-eye onter de right limb, a stray rooster shuck hissef an' say: 'tuck-awk-awk-awk': Den yer cood a heerd dem boys cussin' ober in de nex' county."

"Didn't dey ketch no 'possum at all, de whole night?"

"When I gits ter de 'possums I'll speak 'bout dem, but I wuz gwine on 'er say dat dey fizzled out on de fals' 'larms ob dat patent pup tell dey run agin a pole-cat—den dey all holler'd 'possum, an' hit wuz wuss dan holdin' a team ob young mules ober a ho'net's nes' ter keep dem boys fum bouncin' onter dat ole time centennial critter. But de dog went in—an' come out—but he warnt shuck hands with for his bravery, you bet! Arter dat skirmish dem boys opened de throttils ob dere canteens wide an' faus'd derserves inter er returnin' board respired wid de sperit ob sebenty-six!"

"An' no 'possum at las'!"

"Narry flicker ob a tail, but dar wuz laffin' 'nuff on my side ter mek a man fatter dan fo'ty possums briled!"

Joel Chandler Harris (1848–1908)

Uncle Remus

BY THE END OF 1876, the *Atlanta Constitution* was about to become one of the most prominent newspapers in the South, a fact indicated by its editorial staff. Its editor in chief was Evan P. Howell. Henry W. Grady and Joel Chandler Harris had recently become associate editors, though the achievements that would bring them lasting fame—and the *Constitution* widespread renown—lay ahead. Grady would become the leading advocate of the "New South," an economy built on trade rather than agriculture, and on national, as opposed to regional, commerce. Harris would become known as the author of beast fables narrated in the dialect of the Southern Negro by Uncle Remus, his universally loved raconteur.

The creation of Uncle Remus came about by accident. Within a few days after joining the *Constitution,* Harris was asked by Howell to produce a dialect column in which the narrator known as Uncle Remus gradually evolved. But the genial narrator of the stories of Br'er Rabbit and Br'er Fox did not appear until 1880. It has thus become customary to recognize two characters named Uncle Remus, the one attempting to make his way in an urban environment of the New South, the other back in "Putmon County," in the bosom of the family who had formerly owned him, spinning charming moral fables to their youngest scion.

One should ideally read Uncle Remus in both settings. In each, Harris has been faithful to his prototypes and especially to their dialect. Harris's beast stories deserve the close atten-

---

The selections are from Joel Chandler Harris, *Uncle Remus and His Friends* (Boston and New York: Houghton, Mifflin, 1892).

tion they have received. The fact that they are in the folkloristic tradition of the African slave gives them a sound basis. Though originally presented as articles in the *Atlanta Constitution*, they soon became a staple of American literature by appearing in numerous collected editions. Few journalistic masks have earned as secure a place in American letters.

Intimidation of a Colored Voter

"I hope you all young gentermens is well," said Uncle Remus, as he entered the editorial rooms of *The Constitution*, the other day. "I mighty po'ly myse'f, but dat ain't hender me from hopin' dat yuther folks is keepin' way from de doctor shops. Many is de po' creeter w'at done been ter doctor shops one time too much. Yit look at me. I bin dar mighty nigh much ez anybody, en Miss Sally say dey's lots er hard work in me yit, 'vidin' anybody kin git it out'n me. In my young days I use ter year talk dat de nighest road ter de buryin'-groun' wuz 'roun' by de doctor shop, but 'spite er dat I keeps on taking der truck, en I ain't see dat it do me no harm. Ef any you young gentermens gits ter feelin' low down in de sperets, en sorter 'quare in de naborhoods er de gizzard, you des rack 'roun' to Mars Dock Alexander en git some er dem ar quiernine en blue mast pills, en ef dey don't set you up, you kin des lay de blame onter me. When ole Miss was 'live, de doctor'd come 'roun' 'bout dis time er year, en all de niggers, little en big, 'ud hatter come up en git a dost er jollup en callymel; but deze days you gotter hunt de doctor up en git a piece er paper en beat 'roun' town twel you kin fine some un fer ter mix up de truck."

Uncle Remus paused, and then broke into a loud laugh. "W'at de name er goodness is I doin'? I des crope up yer fer ter ax you all young gentermens sump'n, en yet I is runnin' on like a cat-bird in a peach orchard. I dunner how you all is, but I ain't got no time fer ter be projickin'."

"Gracious heaven!" exclaimed one of the young men, "do you hear that? He says he hasn't got time! Won't somebody lead him out and ask him to call again and say one word—one little word—when he has got time?"

"En needer is I got time fer ter be runnin' on 'longer you all," Uncle Remus retorted indignantly. "You all kin take yo' shears an' split dem ar newspapers wide open, but ole Remus can't take no shears en cut truck outer t'er folks gyardin, kaze ef I did dey'd slap

de law on me. En ef I ain't got time ter stan' yer en talk, co'se I ain't
got no time fer ter be gwine ter law. Dat gyardin out dar at Wes' Een'
callin' me right now, en I ain't got a minnit ter spar'—dat I ain't."

"Suppose you go down in the fire-escape," some one suggested,
but Uncle Remus ignored the hint.

"Man down dar on de street ax how I gwine vote dis time, en I
des runned up yer fer ter ax you all gentermens ef deyer a gwinter
be n'er 'lection in de Nunited States er Georgy."

"Why, of course there is!"

"Now ain't dat too much!" exclaimed Uncle Remus with unmis-
takable bitterness. "Man go up en vote, en he ain't got time ter
change his cloze 'fo' he gotter rack up en vote ag'in."

"Why, have n't you heard about Boynton, Bacon, and the rest?"

"I year Miss Sally readin' out names en dates, en 'sputin'
'longer Mars John, but I tuck de idee dey wuz one er deze yer cake-
walks gwine on up dar."

"Up where?"

"Up dar whar de sleepin' kyars comes fum; some'rs up dar."

"He seems to be thoroughly familiar with the geography of our
common country," remarked one of the young men.

Uncle Remus grinned broadly.

"I lay dey don't fool me on de cake-walk, kaze dey wuz a nigger
man in one un um; but w'at pester me is deze yer 'lections follerin'
atter one er n'er des lak a drove er sheep. Eve'y time dey comes, ole
Remus gits in trouble wuss en wuss."

"Why so?"

"Des kaze. Mars John en Miss Sally gits ter 'sputin' 'bout w'ich
de bes' man, en den dey comes atter me. Hit's 'Remus, how you
gwine ter vote?' en 'No, you ain't,' en 'Yes you is,' ontwel I des na-
tally gits wo' out. Hit's pull en haul, pull en haul, day in en day out,
en I ain't got no peace er min' twel 'lection day done gone. Miss
Sally say vote dish year way, Mars John say vote dat ar way, en w'en
dat de case, w'at a ole nigger like me gwine do?"

"Well, how do you vote, after all?"

"Dat w'at I want to know: dat des zackly w'at I'm atter. Mars
John, he 'low he de boss; yit I notices dat w'en Miss Sally say I ain't
gwine to git no gravy on my grits, dey ain't no gravy dar, en de man
w'at kin eat grits widout gravy is got mo' strenk in his stummuck
dan w'at I is. Fum dis out twel atter de 'lection done good en gone,
you kin des put it down dat de rheumatiz done struck me in de
j'ints, en hit'll be dat servigrous dat I can't move skacely. En eve'y
time dey say vote, I'm a-gwine ter grunt en groan like one er deze
yer Wes' P'int ingines. But shoo! I ain't got time fer ter be runnin' on
yer wid you all."

Brother Rabbit Frightens Brother Tiger

"'T ain't de biggest en de strongest dat does de mostest in dis world," said Uncle Remus one day, when he and the little boy were talking over matters and things in general. The little boy had been talking about the elephant and the tiger which he had seen in a traveling menagerie, and he had asked the old man why the elephant was so strong and the tiger so fierce.

"No, honey, don't let nobody fool you 'bout dat. De cuckle-burr got needer life ner lim', yit when it git in de sheep wool it kin travel fast ez de sheep, you know dat yo'se'f. De elephen' may be strong; I speck he is; en de tiger maybe servigrous ez dey say he is; but Brer Rabbit done outdone bofe un um."

"How was that, Uncle Remus?" the little boy asked.

"Well, he done it so easy, honey, dat 't ain't skacely no tale. 'T ain't nothin' dat'll 'stonish you, en 't ain't nothin' dat'll make you laugh. Hit's des some er Brer Rabbit's eve'y-day doin's, des like you'd set down ter eat a plain dinner er pot-liquor en dumplin's wid no pie fer ter take de greasy tas'e out'n yo' mouf."

The youngster wanted to hear about it anyhow, and he said so. Whereupon Uncle Remus continued:

"One time, whiles Brer Rabbit wuz gwine 'long thoo de woods, he struck up wid Brer Tiger. 'T wan't nowhars 'bout here, honey," explained the old man, observing the child's look of astonishment. "'T was in some er de 'jinin' counties. Brer Rabbit struck up wid Brer Tiger, he did, en atter dey passed de time er day, dey went amblin' 'long tergedder. Brer Rabbit talk so big en walk so uppity dat Brer Tiger look at 'im sideways en grin. Bimeby dey come to whar dey wuz a creek, en dey want no foot-log in sight. Brer Tiger ain't want ter wet his feet no mo' dan a cat do, en needer do Brer Rabbit, en so dey went up de creek huntin' fer de foot-log. Dey go, en go, but dey ain't fin' none.

"Bimeby Brer Rabbit 'low he know how ter cross. Brer Tiger ax 'im how. Den Brer Rabbit grab a grape-vine hangin' fum de tree lim', en tuck a runnin' start en swung hisse'f on tudder side. When he tu'n de vine loose, it flew back ter whar Brer Tiger wuz, en Brer Tiger he cotch holt en made fer ter swing hisse'f 'cross. Time he done lef' de groun' good, de vine broke, en he come down on his back in de creek, *kersplash!*

"Co'se dis make 'im feel bad, en when he crawl'd out en shook hisse'f, en see Brer Rabbit settin' up dar, dry en clean, a-laughin' fit ter kill, hit make 'im feel wuss. He fetched er growl er two, en popped his mouf tergedder, but Brer Rabbit kep' one eye on 'im.

"Brer Tiger 'low, 'How come you ain't skeer'd er me, Brer Rabbit? All de yuther creeturs run when dey hear me comin'.'

"Brer Rabbit say, 'How come de fleas on you ain't skeer'd un you? Dey er lots littler dan what I is.'

"Brer Tiger 'low, 'Hit's mighty good fer you dat I done had my dinner, kaze ef I'd a-been hongry I'd a-snapped you up back dar at de creek.'

"Brer Rabbit say, 'Ef you'd done dat, you'd er had mo' sense in yo' hide dan what you got now.'

"Brer Tiger 'low, 'I gwine ter let you off dis time, but nex' time I see you, watch out!'

"Brer Rabbit say, 'Bein 's you so monst'us perlite, I'll let you off too, but keep yo' eye open nex' time you see me, kaze I'll git you sho'.'

"Brer Rabbit talk so biggity dat Brer Tiger put on his studyin' cap, en he make up his min' dat dey ain't room 'nuff in dat county fer bofe him en Brer Rabbit. Brer Tiger turn 'roun', he did, en watch Brer Rabbit go tippin' off, en he look so little en so sassy dat it make Brer Tiger mad. Hit make 'im so mad dat he kotch holt uv a tree en clawed mos' all de bark off'n it. Bless gracious! de furder he git fum Brer Rabbit, de mo' madder he got. He des declar' dat de nex' time he strike up wid Brer Rabbit he gwine ter gobble 'im up widout sayin' grace.

"So, den, dar 'twuz, Brer Tiger 'ginst Brer Rabbit, en Brer Rabbit 'ginst Brer Tiger: one big, en tudder one little; one servigrous fum de word go, en tudder one got needer tush ner claw. Hit look mighty bad fer Brer Rabbit! Well, I wish ter goodness you could er seed 'im 'bout dat time. He went 'long thoo de woods ez gay ez a colt in a barley-patch. He wunk at de trees, he shuck his fisties at de stumps, he make like he wuz quoilin' wid 'is shadder kaze it foller 'long atter 'im so close; en he went on scan'lous, mon!

"Brer Rabbit ain't gone so mighty fur 'fo' he hear a big noise in de bushes, en lo en beholes, dar wuz ole Brer Elephen trompin' 'roun' en th'ashin' out de tops er de saplin's. He look big ez a young house, but, bless yo' soul! dat ain't set Brer Rabbit back none. He des march up en ax ole Brer Elephen how he come on, en one word led to anudder, twel Brer Rabbit up'n tell ole Brer Elephen all 'bout de confab what he been had wid Brer Tiger. Den he 'low dat ef ole Brer Elephen will loan 'im a helpin' han' dey kin drive Brer Tiger bodaciously out'n de county. Ole Brer Elephen flop his years en shake his snout like he sorter jubious.

"He 'low, 'I ain't gwine ter git hurted, is I, Brer Rabbit?'

"Dis make Brer Rabbit roll his eyes en study.

"He ax, 'Who de name er goodness gwine hurt you, Brer Elephen?'

"Brer Elephen 'low, 'Brer Tiger got sharp claws en long tushes. I skeer'd he bite me en scratch me.'

"Brer Rabbit say, 'Cordin' ter dat I oughter be skeer'd uv a flea, kaze des ez I kin sqush a flea, des dat away you kin sqush Brer Tiger. Yit dey ain't gwine be no squshin' done. Ef you'll do what I tell you, we'll des take'n run Brer Tiger out'n de county. Goodness knows, ef my upper lip wuz long en limber like yone, I 'boun' I'd a done got rid er Brer Tiger long 'fo' now!'

"Brer Elephen, he 'gree ter do what Brer Rabbit say, but he flop his years en work his snout like he mighty restless in de min', en Brer Rabbit holp 'im up de best way he kin wid biggity talk.

"Soon nex' mornin' Brer Rabbit wuz up en a-movin'. He done had eve'ything fix, en he sot 'roun' in de bushes whar he kin see Brer Tiger long ways off. Bimeby he see Brer Tiger come sidlin' down de path, en no sooner is Brer Rabbit seed 'im dan he make a break en run te' whar Brer Elephen stannin'. Den Brer Rabbit tuck en wrop a long vine 'roun' one er ole Brer Elephen's behime legs, en den 'roun' a tree. He fix it so dat anybody passin' 'long would make sho' de leg tied hard en fas'. Den ole Brer Elephen kneel down, en Brer Rabbit tuck a runnin' start an' light up on his back. Dey done had all de 'rangements made, en when Brer Tiger come 'long, he seed a sight dat make him open his eyes. Dar wuz Brer Rabbit on top er ole Brer Elephen back, en dar wuz old Brer Elephen wid his behime leg ter de tree, a-swingin' backerds en forrerds, en a-rockin' fum side ter side.

"Brer Tiger look at um a little while, en de notion strike 'im dat Brer Rabbit was cotch up dar en can't get down. Dis make Brer Tiger laugh twel he show all his tushes. He walk 'roun', he did, en feel so good he run hisse'f 'ginst de saplin's des like you seen cats rub up 'ginst cheer-legs. Den he sot down flat er de groun' en grin at Brer Rabbit, en lick his chops. Ole Brer Elephen swing backerds and forrerds en rock fum side to side.

"Brer Tiger 'low, 'I tole you I'd git you, Brer Rabbit, en now I done come atter you.'

"Brer Elephen swing backerds en forrerds, en rock fum side ter side.

"Brer Rabbit say, 'You done come, is you? Well, des wait a min- ute twel I get thoo skinnin this creetur what I des cotch. Stay dar twel I git good en ready fer you.'

"Den Brer Rabbit dip down his head by ole Brer Elephen's year en whisper, 'Squall when my nose on yo' neck. Don't be skeer'd. Des squall.'

"Den old Brer Elephen squeal thoo dat snout er his'n; you mought er heard him a mile er mo'.

"Brer Rabbit holler out, 'Des wait, Brer Tiger. Yo' turn 'll come terreckly. It'll go mighty hard wid you ef I hatter run atter you.'

"Ole Brer Elephen swing backerds en forrerds, en rock fum side ter side. Eve'y time Brer Rabbit'd nibble behime his years, he'd squall out en tromple de groun'.

"When he first seed Brer Rabbit up dar on ole Brer Elephen's back, Brer Tiger sorter sot hisse'f on de groun' fer ter make a jump at 'im, but time he see how ole Brer Elephen hollerin' en prancin', Brer Tiger riz en 'gutter back off. A hick'y nut fell off'n a tree en hit de groun', en Brer Tiger jump like somebody shot at 'im. When Brer Rabbit see dis it tickle 'im so dat he come mighty nigh laughin' out loud. But he dip his head down, en make like he gnawin' ole Brer Elephen on de neck, en ole Brer Elephen, he squall loud ez he kin.

"Brer Rabbit prance up en down on Brer Elephen back like he huntin' fer a mo' tender place, en he holler out:

" 'Don't go 'way, Brer Tiger. Des wait; I'll be ready fer you terreckly.'

"Brer Tiger, he back off, en Brer Elephen swing backerds en forrerds, Brer Rabbit holler out, 'No use ter git weak-kneed, Brer Tiger. Gi' me time. Dis Elephen blood taste salty. It make me dry. You won't have long to wait.'

"Brer Tiger, he back off en back off. Brer Rabbit, he make out he bitin' ole Brer Elephen on de year. Ole Brer Elephen swing backerds en forrerds en rock fum side ter side, en snort en tromple de grass.

"'Bout dat time Brer Rabbit make like he gwine ter come down. He make like he huntin' fer a saft place ter jump, en when Brer Tiger see dat, he made a break en des fell over hisse'f tryin' ter get out'n reach. Brer Rabbit holler at 'im, but he ain't stop; he des keep a-runnin', en 't wuz many a long day 'fo' de creeturs seed 'im back dar in dat settlement.

"Elephen skeer'd er tiger," Uncle Remus went on, by way of explanation. "En all de time dat Brer Rabbit wuz talkin' ter Brer Tiger, Brer Elephen wuz so skeer'd dat a little mo 'n he'd 'a' went tarin' thoo de woods like a harrycane. Ez 't wuz, des ez soon ez Brer Tiger got out'n sight, old Brer Elephen retched up wid his snout en wrung de top off'n er saplin' en 'gun ter fan hisse'f wid it."

"Uncle Remus," said the little boy, when the old man had brought the story to a close, "did you ever see an elephant?"

"Well, suh," said Uncle Remus, after a long pause, "you tetch me in a tender place, you sho'ly does. I seed um, en I ain't seed um. Now, how kin you make dat out?"

"How could that be?" asked the child, laughing.

"I tell you now, dey ain't no fun in it," continued the old negro, trying to frown. "I done hear talk dat dey wuz a show gwine ter come 'long de road, on de way ter town, but it drapt out'n my min', twel one day I wuz ridin' dat ar roan mule, takin' a letter over ter Marse Bill Little's. I went on, I did, en tuck de note en start back wid de answer. Marse Bill Little had done gi' me a dram fer ole 'quaintance sake, en I wuz warm in my feelin's. Dat ar roan mule des paced 'long free en easy, en dey want no happier nigger dan what I wuz.

"Well, suh, I heard a little fuss in front er me, en I raise my head, en right dar at me, right spang 'pon topper me, wuz a great big elephen. I des got a glimpse un 'im, kaze de roan mule seed 'im time I did, en he des give a squat en a flutter, en de nex' thing I know'd my head wuz driv in de groun' in about up ter my neck. I dunner how long I laid dar, but time I got de mud en grit out'n my eyes de elephen wuz done gone. You may say I seed de elephen, er you may say I ain't seed 'im; I ain't gwine ter 'spute 'bout it. But dat ar roan mule seed 'im."

Charles Bertrand Lewis (1842–1924)

Brother Gardner

O F THE MANY HUMOROUS WRITERS who published in the *Detroit Free Press,* few were as successful as Charles Bertrand Lewis, who frequently wrote under the pseudonym "M. Quad." For much of the twenty-two years that he wrote for the paper, Lewis was part owner. The sketches delivered by his persona Brother Gardner appeared during the final quarter of the nineteenth century when verbal caricature, often in the form of colorful characters speaking in dialect, was much in vogue. This was the climate in which Uncle Remus, Old Si, Terence McGrant, and Yawcob Strauss flourished.

These characters were of course created for many different purposes, but Lewis seems to have intended for Brother Gardner simply to entertain. The philosophical social leader is at times a bit pompous, but is generally agreeable to the tastes of his readers. Having him preside over the Lime-Kiln Club is a variation on the much-used convention of grouping characters in an organization, which is traceable to the *Spectator* of Addison and Steele. But the over-all perspective is one of caricature—the presentation of Negro life in America as perceived through the stereotypes and clichés developed by many whites. There is, nonetheless, an innocence about the pieces. They contain a gentle form of satire, and are apparently not meant to bespeak racial consciousness.

Such sketches as "The Revised" and "De Good Ole Days" appealed to the widely accepted Judaeo-Christian ethic as perceived in Lewis's day. Brother Gardner's plea for

---

The selections are from M. Quad and Brother Gardner [Charles Bertrand Lewis], *Brother Gardner's Lime Kiln Club* (Chicago: Belford, Clark, 1882).

such virtues as forthrightness and plainness in behavior and dress had an obvious appeal to the instincts of the average American, regardless of race.

The Revised

"I take pleasure an' satisfaction," said the President, as he held up a parcel, "in informin' you a worthy citizen of Detroit, who does not car to hab his name menshun'd, has presented dis revised edishun of de Bible to de Lime-Kiln Club. We do not open our meetins wid prayer, nor do we close by singin' de Doxology, but, neberdeless I am suah dis gift will be highly appreshiated by all. Dar has bin considuble talk in dis Club about dis revised edishun. Some of you hab got de ideah dat purgatory has all been wiped out, an' heben enlarged twice ober, an' I have heard odders assert dat it didn't forbid lyin', stealin', an' passin' off bad money. My frens, you am sadly mistaken. Hell is jist as hot as eber, an' Heben has'nt got any mo' room. In lookin' ober some of de changes, las' night, I selected out a few paragraphs which have a gineral b'arin. Fur instance, it am jist as wicked to steal water mellyons as it was las y'ar or de y'ar befo', an' de skeercer de crap, de bigger de wickedness.

"No change has bin made in regard to loafin' aroun' de streets. De loafer am considered jist as mean an' low as eber he was, an' I want to add my belief dat he will grow meaner in public estimashun all de time.

"De ten commandments am all down heah widout change. Stealin', an' lyin', an' covetin', an' runnin' out nights am considered jist as bad as eber.

"I can't find any paragraph in which men am excused for payin' deir honest debts, an' supportin' deir fam'lies.

"I can't fin' whar a poo' man or a poo' man's wife—white or black—am 'spected to sling on any pertickler style.

"Dog fights, chicken liftin', polyticks, playin' keerds fur money, an' hangin' aroun' fur drinks, an' all sich low bizness am considered meaner dan eber. Fact is, I can't fin' any change whateber which lets up on a man from bein plumb up an' down squar', an hones wid de world. Dey have changed de word 'Hell' to 'Hades', but at de same time added to de strength of de brimstun an' de size of de pit, an' we want to keep right on in de straight path if we would avoid it. Doan' let any white man make you believe dat we's lost any Gospel by dis revision, or dat Peter, or Paul, or Moses hab undergone any change ob speerit regardin' de ways ob libin' respectably an' dyin' honorably."

De Good Ole Days

"What I am longin' arter," said Brother Gardner as Trustee Pullback ceased coughing and Samuel Shin finally got a rest for his feet, "what I am longin' arter am a sight of a good, old-fashioned man or woman—sich as we could find in ebery house thirty y'ars ago, but sich as cannot be found now in a week's hunt. It makes me lonesome when I realize dat our old-fashioned men an women are no mo'. In de days gone by, if I fell sick, one woman would run in wid catnip, anoder wid horseradish leaves, anoder wid a bowl o' gruel, an' tears would be shed, an' kind words spoken, an' one couldn't stay sick to save him. In dose good ole days de kaliker dress an' white apron abounded. An honest woman wasn't afeard to wash her face on account of de powder. Ebery woman wore her own ha'r, an' she wore it to please herself instead of fashun. Thick hoes kept her feet dry, thick clothes kept her body warm, an' dar was no winkin' an' wobblin' an' talkin' frew de teef. Dar was goodness in de land in dem good ole days. Dar was prayin' to God, an' de hearts meant it. De woman who wore a No. 6 shoe was as good as a woman wid a foot all pinched out of shape an' kivered wid co'ns. You didn't h'ar much 'bout beach o' promise cases n' odder deviltry. De man who parts his ha'r in de middle, an' believes he mashes his wictims by de score wasn't bo'n den. People didn't let deir nayburs die under deir noses widout eben knowin' dat sickness had come to de family. Men workded hard an' put in full time, an' women foun' sunthin' to do besides gaddin' de streets to show off a small foot or a new bonnet.

"De world calls it progress. We must shut our hearts against our naybur, sacrifice all fur fashun, conceal our limps an' pains, appear what we am not, an' when we go to de grave fur rest we am forgotten in a week. Whar one woman looks to Heaben a dozen looks to fashun. Whar one man helps de poo' from kindness of heart a dozen chip in because de list of names will be published in de paper. When I sot down of an evenin' an' fink dese fings ober it makes me sad. I doan' know jist how wicked Sodom was, nor what deviltry dey was up to in Gomorrah, but if either town had mo' wanity, wickedness, frivolity an' deceit dan Detroit, Chicago, Buffalo, or any odder city in dis kentry, rents mus' have bin awful high."

Edward W. Townsend (1855–1942)

Chimmie Fadden

OVER THE COURSE of some thirty years, the *New York Sun* became a showcase for interesting fictional characters. One of the earliest was the creation of Edward Waterman Townsend. Jimmy ("Chimmie") Fadden narrated his stories in the colloquial style of the Bowery district of New York City at roughly the same time (the mid-1890s) that George Ade's famous "Fables in Slang" were appearing in the *Chicago News* and in wide syndication.

The narratives have a keen bite, in that Townsend has placed Fadden in the midst of the New York haut monde, as butler-valet for the wealthy Burton family. Fadden's entourage is fleshed out by such characters as Mr. Burton, Miss Fanny (Burton's wife), Whiskers (Fanny Burton's father) and Duchess (Fanny Burton's French maid). The sketches recreate satirically the familiar situation of the commoner in the halls of the exalted, which is as old as satire itself. Though occasionally dated by contemporary references, the Fadden pieces retain a certain freshness after almost a century. Several dozen were collected into such volumes as *Chimmie Fadden Explains* (1895) and *Chimmie Fadden and Mr. Paul* (1902).

The selection is from Edward W. Townsend, *Chimmie Fadden Explains, Major Max Expounds* (New York: U.S. Book Company, 1895).

The Duchess Plays Even

"P'raps, de Duchess will get me turned down so hard one of dese days I'll never get de wrinkles took outter me. Sure, I'd get dead sore on de Duchess if it wasn't dat she's de boss jollier you ever seed, and you can't keep mad wid her long. We is all down at Mr. Burton's place in de country yet, and I'm up in de city to-day tendin to sendin some tings down dere what dose fool servants didn't pack up when we went down. I has t' do all dose tings now, de Duchess and me has to, cause Miss Fannie won't let no one else do em for her, and I guess dey'd all starve t' deat and not have no close t' wear if it wasn't for me takin care of em.

"We went t' de country just before de lection cause his Whiskers and Mr. Burton and Mr. Paul used t' jaw and jaw so much bout politics and bosses and Mugwumps and dinky tings like dose dat Miss Fannie she just bundled de whole gang off t' de country, where dey'd have someting else t' jaw bout and couldn't vote. We is goin t' stay over Tanksgiven Day, what's a day de President makes at Albany when folks don't have t' make no excuse for gettin a load. Dat's right.

"Well, as I was tellin you, we was all down in de country de time when dey had de horse show at de Madison Square Garden. One day Miss Fannie tells me and de Duchess t' chase ourselves up t' town t' get some tings from de house what she wanted, and de Duchess she gives me a wink and tells me t' sneak me dress suit along wid me what Mr. Burton give me, and we'd have some fun.

" 'What t'ell?' I says to her. 'What's your game?' I says, like dat. See?

"She tells me t' saw wood and say nottin till we was up in town; so I says nottin, but just sneaks me clawhammer wid us, and we come away lookin as pious as a parson.

"Say, what do you tink? Dat Duchess had pinched de tickets t' Miss Fannie's box at de horse show. Sure! I treatened t' give her a good lickin for it, but she just laughed and says dat Miss Fannie and none of our folks was goin t' use de tickets and what de harm of our usin dem so as t' give de horse show some style.

"Say, what do you tink of dat goil? She's a angel—I don't tink!

"Well, when we packed up de tings at de house what was wanted, and went t' de candy shop and de flower store for some dude tings Mr. Paul wanted for Miss Fannie—it's always Mr. Paul and not Mr. Burton what orders dose dude tings for Miss Fannie, which I tink is queer and de Duchess doesn't—well, when we done all our errants and had dinner, de Duchess tells me to put on me harness, me clawhammer, and she skipped t' Miss Fannie's room.

"Say, dat goil would make a actor lady out on top of de stage. Sure. You never seed de like of her when she waltzes out of Miss Fannie's room. I was paralyzed. I taut I was off me base and that it was Miss Fannie for a minute. She was all made up in Miss Fannie's close and hat and gloves and had dose dinky glasses what you looks tru at de teeater, and she was out of sight till she opened her mout t' talk, and den she was de Duchess, straight.

"She looked me over, and den made me part me hair in de middle and plaster it down each side, and put on a collar dat was so high it chucked me chin back so far I looked I was smellin something bad, and den she said I was 'oh fay', what's dago for 'fit', and we chases ourselves to der show.

"Before we chases ourselves I told de Duchess dat she couldn't go till she swore dat she wasn't up t' no game what would queer Miss Fannie.

"Say, den she told me de greatest song and dance you ever heard, what was so mixed up dat I couldn't tumble to all of it, but de game as near as I could get on was someting like dis: Miss Fannie was in England wid his Whiskers onct, which you has to go furder dan Sandy Hook t' get to, where she met a mug what you has to say 'Sir' to before you says his name. De Duchess knows all dis, cause she was wid Miss Fannie, you see, and she knowed dat his Whiskers had blowed off de mug at his house here, and his club, when Miss Fannie was in school, before dey went t' England. But in England de mug never blowed off his Whiskers, but only just called on him and Miss Fannie onct, for a minute, what's de way dose mugs do, de Duchess says.

"Say, dis is an awful long yarn and nearly makes me crazy t' remember it all. Tanks, I wouldn't mind. Here's lookin at you.

"Well, as I was tellin you, de mug comes over t' dis country again and chases himself up to our house, and when he finds dat Miss Fannie is at de country place, what do you tink he does? He must be a real gent—I don't tink. He writes t' Miss Fannie, and, holly dee! he makes a bluff dat he's waitin for t' be invited t' de country place. Dat's straight, for de Duchess saw his letter after Miss Fannie trun it away. De Duchess seed dat Miss Fannie was mad at de mug's cheek, after de way he turned em down in England, and so de Duchess she puts up de job I'm tellin you bout.

"Well, we goes t' de horse show, and sits in de box, and pretty soon de Duchess seed de very mug we was layin for walkin along lookin at a paper where was printed de names of de folks what owned boxes, and den lookin at de folks in de box. When he seed us he looks at his paper, and den at us again, and den he hoists his dicer, and de Duchess she bowed, and I hoists me dicer and I bows, and de mug chases up to our box.

"De Duchess she whispers t' me t' do most of de gabbing, for, says she, 'He'll tink your Bowery patwah is Yankee brogue.'

"Dem's her very langwudge, 'Me Bowery patwah!' I'd like t' know what t'ell, dat's what I'd like t' know.

"I didn't have no time t' give her a roast, for de mug comes into de box like he owned it and begins tellin de Duchess dat he heered of her marriage, tinkin she was Miss Fannie, see? and turns to me and says, 'Mr. Burton, I spose,' and de Duchess nearly stamps me foot off t' keep me mout shut.

"Say, I never knowed de Duchess was such a dead game sport. De mug never called her down onct, cause stid of talkin she just mostly smiled and answered wid her shoulders and hands and eyes, like dose French forners can, and only spoke de few American words what she can speak like me.

"I chipped in whenever de Duchess give me de wink, but it was a hard game, and I was glad when de Duchess said we must go.

"De mug says he'd see us to our carriage, and I says dat de carriages was in de country, and we'd walk home. Den he says could he walk along? And when we was opposite Del's he says what's de matter wid glass of wine and a little supper? Say, I never taut de Duchess would run de bluff dat far; but she was out for blood, and her eyes was just dancin wid de fun she was havin wid de mug.

"Well, we went into Del's and de mug ast de Duchess wouldn't she order. Would she! holly gee! Say, you'd died t' hear her rattle off de order t' de waiter what understood her forn langwudge. I guess de mug didn't understand, cause he looked easy until de waiter began bringin on de wine and grub and den he near fell in a fit. I don't tink dere was much left in de pantry nor de wine cellar when dey'd brought de Duchess's order. Sure.

"I tink de mug began t' tumble before we'd finished dat supper, for de Duchess began talkin as fast as a quarter-horse after she'd tackled de second cold bot. He began t' look at bote of us a little queer, and den he ast, eyin de Duchess pretty hard, when was he expected up t' de country place. De Duchess looked at him harder dan he looked at her, and den she made her eyes bigger dan silver dollars, and says, like she was paralyzed wid sprise, says she, 'Who do you take us for?'

"'For Mr. and Mrs. Burton,' says de mug, kinder wite round de gills.

"Den de Duchess give me de wink to trow him down, and I says, says I, like I was a actor. I says: 'What t'ell!' I says. 'Dis is Mrs.

Burton's maid, and I'm Mr. Burton's man. See?' I says like dat, 'See?' says I.

"Say, I don't tink he did see, for he shut his eyes like he was knocked out, while de folks at de odder table near died laughin, lots of dem being swell mugs what knowed us by sight, and bein onto our game from de start. Den we chased ourselves, haughty like, while de gilly we'd done was hypnoitized."

Charles Follen Adams (1842–1918)

Yawcob Strauss

*A*LTHOUGH COMIC STRIPS did not appear in American newspapers until 1889 (the *New York World* introduced the first examples late that year), earlier readers were not without the kinds of characters and exploits that would later be given graphic treatment in the new medium. Of these forerunners, few enjoyed the popularity of leedle Yawcob Strauss, whose childish pranks suggest a lovable Teutonic Dennis the Menace.

Charles Follen Adams, a Boston dry goods merchant, had begun writing dialect verse about 1870, when the "Hans Breitmann" dialect poems of Charles G. Leland were enjoying considerable vogue. Adams's interests ran naturally to the German dialect, as he had served with both Pennsylvania Dutch and German immigrant soldiers during the Civil War and had found their "scrapple English" amusing. His poem "Leedle Yawcob Strauss," first published in the *Detroit Free Press* in 1876, became a national favorite almost immediately. Not only was it widely reprinted; it became the showpiece of the popular readings that Adams gave in the Boston area. One of its most distinguished admirers was Dr. Oliver Wendell Holmes, who observed that the poem "moistened thousands of eyes—these old ones of mine among the rest."

The selection is from Charles Follen Adams, *Leedle Yawcob Strauss and Other Poems* (Boston: Lee and Shepard, 1878).

Leedle Yawcob Strauss

I haf von funny leedle poy,
    Vot gomes schust to mine knee;
Der queerest schap, der createst rogue,
    As efer you dit see.

He runs, und schumps, und schmashes dings
    In all barts off der house:
But vot off dot? he vas mine son,
    Mine leedle Yawcob Strauss.

He get der measles und der mumbs,
    Und eferyding dot's oudt;
He sbills mine glass off lager bier,
    Poots schnuff indo mine kraut.

He fills mine pipe mit Limburg cheese,
    Dot vas der roughest chouse:
I'd dake dot vrom no oder poy
    But leedle Yawcob Strauss.

He dakes der milk-ban for a dhrum,
    Und cuts mine cane in dwo,
To make der schticks to beat it mit,
    Mine cracious, dot vas drue!

I dinks mine hed vas schplit abart
    He kicks oup sooch a touse:
But nefer mind; der poys vas few
    Like dot young Yawcob Strauss.

He asks me questions sooch as dese:
    Who baints mine nose so red?
Who vas it cuts dot schmoodth blace oudt
    Vrom der hair ubon mine hed?

Und vhere der plaze goes vrom der lamp
    Vene'er der glim I douse.
How gan I all dose dings eggsblain
    To dot schmall Yawcob Strauss?

I somedimes dink I schall go vild
　　Mit sooch a grazy poy,
Und vish vonce more I gould haf rest,
　　Und beaceful dimes enshoy;

But ven he vas ashleep in ped,
　　So guiet as a mouse,
I prays der Lord, "Dake anyding,
　　But leaf dot Yawcob Strauss."

7

COLYUMNISTS

Finley Peter Dunne, creator of "Mr. Dooley." (caricature by "Spy"; photo from A Book of American Humor in Prose and Verse, *1925)*

Finley Peter Dunne (1867–1936)

Mr. Dooley

*B*Y THE TIME Finley Peter Dunne began to write dialect columns for the *Chicago Post* in December 1892, such writings were already a well-established component of American feature pages. At the outset, Dunne apparently saw his own attempts as nothing more than light, amusing anecdotes. But some of this humorous grist was gleaned from his frequenting of the public house run by one James McGarry, an Irish immigrant from County Roscommon. Dunne began quoting the colorful publican in his *Post* column, but attributed his words to an imaginary character called "Colonel McNeary." As the McNeary columns became more frequent and increasingly popular, and as McGarry came to be identified by more and more readers, Dunne was forced to change the name of his colorful narrator, as well as the location of his establishment. Thus was born, on 7 October 1893, Martin Dooley—like McGarry, a Roscommon man and proprietor of a gin mill, but removed from the central city. Dooley dispensed his friendly spirits far out on Archer ("Archey") Road, the domain of Hibernians, most of whom would never approach the status of the dignified McGarry. But whatever the relative prominence of McGarry and Dooley, both were part of the Irish subculture of Chicago, of which Finley Peter Dunne was also a scion. As Dunne's biographer Elmer Ellis put it, Dunne "reduced all questions to the unique terms of Archey Road, and provided the needed balance to keep a measure of sanity in his readers."

The selections are from Finley Peter Dunne, *Dissertations by Mr. Dooley* (London and New York: Harper, 1906); and *Mr. Dooley in Peace and War* (Boston: Small, Maynard, 1898).

Through the mid-1890s, the Dooley pieces (for which Dunne was usually paid ten dollars above his regular salary) became popular ornaments of the *Chicago Post*. Although various reprints appeared it was not until 1898, when America was celebrating Admiral George Dewey's victory over the Spanish naval squadron in Manila Bay, that Dooley's essays on the new national hero made him an American institution in his own right. Perhaps the best known of these pieces was "On His Cousin George," in which the publican claims kinship with the admiral. For more than a decade thereafter, Dooley enjoyed an international following, as he wrote regularly about important people of the time such as William McKinley, Theodore Roosevelt, William Jennings Bryan, and Queen Victoria. Interspersed among these writings are essays on less-dated topics that have helped to give the Dooley material a more timeless aspect.

Like many of the journalistic masks fashioned before his time, Dooley represents the point of view of the commoner who sees the pretentious as fair game. His wry common sense appeals to the least experienced reader, while his adept turn of phrase and occasional epigrammatical lines exhibit a wit that is appreciated by the most sophisticated audiences. For instance, in 1901 the Supreme Court ruled on the famous Insular Cases, the resolution of which determined that citizens of territories such as Puerto Rico, which were obtained through American expansionism, were not automatically citizens of the United States, and thus could exact tariff duties. In other words, as the current phrase had it, the Constitution did not follow the Flag. In discussing this and other recent Supreme Court decisions with his friend and straight man, Hennessy, Dooley translates the puzzling workings of the Court into language understandable to any and all: "No matter whether th' constitution follows the flag or not, th' supreme court follows th'iliction returns."

On His Cousin George

"Niver fear," said Mr. Dooley, calmly. "Cousin George is all r-right."

"Cousin George?" Mr. Hennessy exclaimed.

"Sure," said Mr. Dooley. "Dewey or Dooley, 'tis all th' same. We dhrop a letter here an' there, except th' haitches,—we niver dhrop thim,—but we're th' same breed iv fightin' men. Georgy has th' thraits iv th' fam'ly. Me uncle Mike, that was a handy man, was tol' wanst he'd be sint to hell f'r his manny sins, an' he desarved it; f'r, lavin' out th' wan sin iv runnin' away fr'm annywan, he was booked f'r ivrything from murdher to missin' mass. 'Well,' he says, 'anny place I can get into,' he says, 'I can get out iv,' he says. 'Ye bet on that,' he says.

"So it is with Cousin George. He knew th' way in, an' it's th' same way out. He didn't go in be th' fam'ly inthrance, sneakin' along with th' can undher his coat. He left Ding Dong,[1] or whativer 'tis ye call it, an' says he, 'Thank Gawd,' he says, 'I'm where no man can give me his idees iv how to r-run a quiltin' party, an' call it war,' he says. An' so he sint a man down in a divin' shute, an' cut th' cables, so's Mack cudden't chat with him. Thin he prances up to th' Spanish forts, an' hands thim a few oranges. Tosses thim out like a man throwin' handbills f'r a circus. 'Take that,' he says, 'an' ray-mimber th' Maine,' he says. An' he goes into th' harbor, where Ad-miral What-th'-'ell is, an', says he, 'Surrinder,' he says. 'Niver,' says th' Dago. 'Well,' says Cousin George, 'I'll just have to push ye ar-round,' he says. An' he tosses a few slugs at th' Spanyards. Th' Spanish admiral shoots at him with a bow an' arrow, an' goes over an' writes a cable. 'This mornin' we was attackted,' he says. 'An,' he says, 'we fought the inimy with great courage,' he says. 'Our victhry is complete,' he says. 'We have lost ivrything we had,' he says. 'Th' threachrous foe,' he says, 'afther destroyin' us, sought refuge be-hind a mud- scow,' he says; 'but nawthin' daunted us. What boats we cudden't r'run ashore we surrindered,' he says. 'I cannot write no more,' he says, 'as me coat-tails are afire,' he says; 'an' I am bravely but rapidly leapin' fr'm wan vessel to another,' followed be he says. 'If I can save me coat-tails,' he says, 'they'll be no kick comin',' he says. 'Long live Spain, long live mesilf.'

"Well, sir, in twenty-eight minyits be th' clock Dewey he had all th' Spanish boats sunk, an' that there harbor lookin' like a Spanish stew. Thin he r-run down th' bay, an' handed a few war-rm wans into th' town. He set it on fire, an' thin wint ashore to war-rm his poor hands an' feet. It chills th' blood not to have annything to do f'r an hour or more."

"Thin why don't he write something?" Mr. Hennessy de-manded.

"Write?" echoed Mr. Dooley. "Write? Why shud he write? D'ye

---

1. Admiral Dewey had sailed from China to the Philippines.

think Cousin George ain't got nawthin' to do but to set down with a fountain pen, an' write: 'Dear Mack,[2]—At 8 o'clock I begun a peaceful blockade iv this town. Ye can see th' pieces ivrywhere. I hope ye're injyin' th' same gr-reat blessin'. So no more at prisint. Fr'm ye'ers thruly, George Dooley.' He ain't that kind. 'Tis a nice day, an' he's there smokin' a good tin-cint see-gar, an' throwin' dice f'r th' dhrinks. He don't care whether we know what he's done or not. I'll bet ye, whin we come to find out about him, we'll hear he's ilicted himself king iv th' F'lip-ine Islands. Dooley th' Wanst. He'll be settin' up there undher a pa'm-three with naygurs fannin' him an' a dhrop iv licker in th' hollow iv his ar-rm, an' hootchy-kootchy girls dancin' befure him, an' ivry tin or twinty minyits some wan bringin' a prisoner in. 'Who's this?' says King Dooley. 'A Spanish gin'ral,' says th' copper. 'Give him a typewriter an' set him to wurruk,' says th' king. 'On with th' dance,' he says. An' afther awhile, whin he gits tired iv th' game, he'll write home an' say he's got the islands; an' he'll tur'rn thim over to th' gover'mint an' go back to his ship, an' Mark Hanna'll organize th' F'lip-ine Islands Jute an' Cider Comp'ny, an' th' rivolutchinists'll wish they hadn't. That's what'll happen. Mark me wurrud."

Oats as a Food

"What's a breakfast food?" asked Mr. Hennessy.

"It depinds on who ye ar-re," said Mr. Dooley. "In ye're case it's annything to ate that ye're not goin' to have f'r dinner or supper. But in th' case iv th' rest iv this impeeryal raypublic, 'tis th' on'y amusement they have. 'Tis most iv th' advertisin' in th' pa-apers. 'Tis what ye see on th' bill-boords. 'Tis th' inspiration iv pothry an' art. In a wurrd, it's oats.

"I wint over to have breakfast New Year's mornin' at Joyce's. Th' air was sharp, an' though I'm not much given to reflectin' on vittles, regardin' thim more as a meedjum f'r what dhrink I take with thim thin annything else, be th' time I got to th' dure I was runnin' over in me mind a bill iv fare an' kind iv wondhrin' whether I wud have ham an' eggs or liver an' bacon, an' hopin' I cud have both. Well, we set down at the table, an' I tucked me napkin into me collar so that I wudden't have to chase it down in me shoe if I got

---

2. President William McKinley

laughin' at annything funny durin' an egg, an' squared away. 'Ar-re ye hungry?' says Joyce. 'Not now,' says I. 'I've on'y been up two hours, an' I don't think I cud ate more thin a couple iv kerosene-lamps an' a bur-rd-cage,' says I. 'But I'm li'ble to be hungry in a few minyits, an',' says I, 'p'raps 'twud be just as well to lock up th' small childher,' I says, 'where they'll be safe,' I says, thinkin' to start th' breakfast with a flow iv spirits, though th' rosy Gawd iv Day sildom finds me much betther natured thin a mustard plasther.

" 'What's ye'er fav'rite breakfast dish?' says Joyce. 'My what?' says I. 'Ye'er fav'rite breakfast dish?' says he. 'Whativer ye've got,' says I, not to be thrapped into givin' me suffrage to annything he didn't have in th' house. 'Anny kind iv food, so long as it's hot an' hurrid. Thank Hiven I have a mind above vittles, an' don't know half th' time what I'm atin',' says I. 'But I mane prepared food,' says he. 'I like it fried,' says I; 'but I don't mind it broiled, roasted, stewed, or fricasseed. In a minyit or two I'll waive th' cookin' an' ate it off th' hoof,' I says. 'Well,' says he, 'me fav'rite is Guff,' he says. 'P'raps ye've seen th' advertisemint: "Out iv th' house wint Luck Joe; Guff was th' food that made him go." Mother prefers Almost-food, a scientific preparation iv burlaps. I used to take Sawd Ust, which I found too rich, an' later I had a peeroyd iv Hungareen, a chimically pure dish, made iv th' exterryor iv bath towels. We all have our little tastes an' enthusyasms in th' matther iv breakfast foods, depindin' on what pa-apers we read an' what billboords we've seen iv late. I believe Sunny Jim cud jump higher on Guff thin on Almostfood, but mother says she see a sign down on Halsted Sthreet that convinces her she has th' most stimylatin' tuck-in. An-nyhow,' he says, 'I take gr-reat pains to see that nawthin' is sarved f'r breakfast that ain't well advertised an' guaranteed pure fr'm th' facthry, an' put up in blue or green pa-aper boxes,' he says. 'Well,' says I, 'give me a tub iv Guff,' I says. 'I'll cloe me eyes an' think iv an egg.'

"What d'ye suppose they give me, Hinnissy? Mush! Mush, be Hivens! 'What kind iv mush is this?' says I, takin' a mouthful. 'It ain't mush,' says Joyce. 'It's a kind iv scientific oatmeal,' says he. 'Science,' says I, 'has exthracted th' meal. Pass th' ink,' says I. 'What d'ye want ink f'r?' says he. 'Who iver heerd iv atin' blottin' pa-aper without ink?' says I. 'Ate it,' says he. 'Give me me hat,' I says. 'Where ar-re ye goin'?' he says. 'I f'rgot me nose-bag,' I says. 'I can't ate this off a plate. Give it to me an' I'll harness mesilf up in Cavin's buggy, have mesilf hitched to a post in front iv th' city hall, an' injye me breakfast,' I says. 'Ye have a delightful home here,' says I. 'Some day I'm goin' to ask ye to take me up in th' kitchen an' lave me fork down some hay f'r th' childher. But now I must lave ye to ye'er prepared oats,' I says. An' I wint out to Mulligan's resthrant an' wrapped mesilf around buckwheat cakes an' sausages till th' cook got buckwheat cake-makers'-paralysis.

"I don't know how people come to have this mad passion f'r oats. Whin I was a boy they was on'y et be horses, an' good horses rayfused thim. But some wan discovered that th' more ye did to oats th' less they tasted, an' that th' less annything tastes th' betther food it is f'r th' race. So all over th' counthry countless machines is at wurruk removin' th' flavor fr'm oats an' turnin' thim into break-fast food. Breakfast food is all ye see in th' cars an' on th' billbooards. In th' small cities it's th' principal spoort iv th' people. Where childher wanst looked on th' boords to see whin th' minsthrel show was comin' to town, they now watch f'r th' an-nouncement iv th' new breakfast food. Hogan tol' me he was out in Decatur th' other day an' they was eighty-siven kinds iv oats on th' bill iv fare. 'Is they annything goin' on in this town?' he ast a dhrummer. 'Nawthin' ontil th' eight, whin Oatoono opens,' says th' man. People talk about breakfast food as they used to talk about bicycles. They compare an' they thrade. A man with th' 1906 model iv high-gear oats is th' invy iv th' neighborhood. All th' saw-mills has been turned into breakfastfood facthries, an' th' rip-saw has took th' place iv th' miller.

"Does it do anny harm, says ye? Ne'er a bit. A counthry that's goin' to be kilt be food is on its last legs, annyhow. Ivry race has its pecoolyarity. With th' Rooshyans it's 'pass th' tallow candles'; with th' Chinese a plate iv rice an' a shark's fin. Th' German sets down to a breakfast iv viggytable soup, Hungaryan goolash, an' beer. Th' Frinchman is satisfied with a rose in his buttonhole an' tin minyits at th' pianny. An Irishman gets sthrong on potatoes, an' an English-man dilicate on a sound breakfast iv roast beef, ham, mutton pie, eggs, bacon, an' 'alf-an'-'alf. Th' docthors bothers us too much about what we put into that mighty tough ol' man-iv-all-wurruk, th' human stomach. Hiven sint most iv us good digistions, but th' doc-tors won't let thim wurruk. Th' sthrongest race iv rough-an'-tumble Americans that iver robbed a neighbor was raised on pie. I'm f'r pie mesilf at anny time an' at all meals. If food makes anny diff'rence to people, how do I know that all our boasted prosperity ain't based on pie? Says I, lave well enough alone. It may be that if we sarched f'r th' corner-stone iv American liberty an' pro-gress, we'd find it was apple-pie with a piece iv toasted cheese.

"People don't have anny throuble with their digistions fr'm atin'. 'Tis thinkin' makes dyspepsy; worryin' about th' rent is twinty times worse f'r a man's stomach thin plum-puddin'. What's worse still, is worryin' about digistion. Whin a man gets to doin' that all th' oats between here an' Council Bluffs won't save him."

"Joyce tells me his breakfast food has made him as sthrong as a horse," said Mr. Hennessy.

"It ought to," said Mr. Dooley. "Him an' a horse have th' same food."

Donald Robert Perry Marquis (1878–1937)

Hermione

The Old Soak

archy and mehitabel

*O*F THE MYRIAD SATIRIC GUISES that have graced American news sheets, few have enjoyed the popularity or durability of those created by Don Marquis. Although he had worked on newspapers in Washington, D.C., and Atlanta, he made his reputation on the *New York Sun* with his "Sun Dial" column and, beginning in 1922, on the *New York Tribune* with "The Lantern." It was in these feature columns that Marquis assumed the masks that have delighted millions of American readers.

The significance of these personages exists on two levels: First, they afford the means for Marquis to speak to contemporary audiences with his characteristic irony, incisiveness, and occasional acerbity. Perhaps more important, however, each character represents one or more important aspects of its zeitgeist. Hermione, the featherbrained socialite, was constantly championing people (such as the revolutionary poet, Fothergil Finch) and causes with which she had little in common, but with which it was fashionable to become "involved." She was a composite portrait of the many pseudointellectuals encountered by Marquis during the 1910s on prowls through Greenwich Village—"New York's Cognos-

The selections are from Don Marquis, *Hermione and Her Little Group of Serious Thinkers* (New York and London: Appleton, 1916); *The Old Soak and Hail and Farewell* (Garden City, N.Y. and Toronto: Doubleday, Page, 1921); *archy and mehitabel* (Garden City, N.Y.: Doubleday, Doran, 1927); *archy s life of mehitabel* (Garden City, N.Y.: Doubleday, Doran, 1933).

what have i done to deserve all these kittens

Don Marquis's popular "archy and mehitabel" and "Old Soak."
(the archy and mehitabel drawings are by George Herriman,
perhaps the most famous of Marquis's illustrators; The Old Soak,
1921)

cente Center," as he wryly characterized it.

Clem Hawley, the "Old Soak," proclaimed the benefits of pre-Prohibition America, with its saloons and ready availability of potable spirits. His bibulous monologues expose both the oppressive piety as well as the hypocrisy of the crusaders against Demon Rum. In virtually all respects he was perceived as far more lovable and sympathetic than the Puritans who had ruined his former way of life. The affectionate esteem in which Hawley was held by his public can be gauged by his adaptation to the stage (423 Broadway performances) and motion pictures (one silent version and one with sound).

Archy and mehitabel, created in 1916, became Marquis's two best-known newspaper personae and ranged over a broad spectrum of crazes and fads of the time. For instance, archy the cockroach wrote in vers libre, a fashionable poetic mode of the 1920s. Reincarnation, a popular belief of the time, was reflected in archy's claim that he and the alley cat, mehitabel, were both reembodiments: he of a vers libre poet, she of Cleopatra. The cat's devil-may-care philosophy of "toujours gai" evidenced the hedonism of the era.

The earthiness and basic realism of both characters may be said to reflect the essential beliefs and attitudes of Marquis himself. Despite his accomplishments and the fame that resulted from them, he endured such devastating personal tragedies as the deaths of two children and of two wives, prolonged impairment of his own health, and perpetual financial strife.

The fictional creations of Marquis spoke to their times in voices fashioned from those times. Their statements are as much gleanings from social history as they are well-wrought satiric literature. Thus, the columns have both a timely and a timeless appeal. Many have consistently remained in print and are still available in collected editions.

Fothergil Finch, the Poet of Revolt

Isn't it odd how some of the most radical and advanced and virile of the leaders in the New Art and the New Thought don't look it at all? There's Fothergil Finch, for instance. Nobody could be more virile than Fothy is in his Soul. Fothy's Inner Ego, if you get what I mean, is a Giant in Revolt all the time.

And yet to look at Fothy you wouldn't think he was a Modern Cave Man. Not that he looks like a weakling, you know. But—well, if you get what I mean—you'd think Fothy might write about violets instead of thunderbolts.

Dear Papa is *entirely* mistaken about him.

Only yesterday dear Papa said to me, "Hermione, if you don't keep that damned little *vers libre* runt away from here I'll put him to work, and he'll die of it."

But you couldn't expect Papa to appreciate Fothy. Papa is *so* reactionary and conservative.

And Fothy's life is one long, grim, desperate struggle against Conventionality, and Social Injustice, and Smugness, and the Established Order, and Complacence. He is forever being a martyr to the New and True in Art and Life.

Last night he read me his latest poem—one of his greatest, he says—in which he tries to tell just what his Real Self is. It goes:

Look at Me!
Behold, I am founding a New Movement!
Observe me. . . . I am in Revolt!
I revolt!
Now persecute me, persecute me, damn you, persecute me, curse you, perse-
    cute me!
Philistine,
Bourgeois,
Slave,
Serf,
Capitalist,
Respectabilities that you are,
Persecute me!
Bah!
You ask me, do you, what I am in revolt against?
Against you, fool, dolt, idiot, against you, against everything!
Against Heaven, Hell and punctuation . . . against Life, Death, rhyme and
    rhythm . . .
Persecute me, now, persecute me, curse you, persecute me!
Slave that you are . . . what do Marriage, Toothbrushes, Nail-files, the Deca-
    logue, Handkerchiefs, Newton's Law of Gravity, Capital, Barbers, Prop-
    erty, Publishers, Courts, Rhyming Dictionaries, Clothes, Dollars, mean
    to Me?
I am a Giant, I am a Titan, I am a Hercules of Liberty, I am Prometheus, I am
    the Jess Willard of the New Cerebral Pugilism, I am the Modern Cave
    Man, I am the Comrade of the Cosmic Urge, I have kicked off the Boots of
    Superstition, and I run wild along the Milky Way without ingrowing
    toenails, I am I!

Curse you, what are You?
You are only You!
Nothing more!
Ha!

Bah! . . . persecute me, now persecute me!

Fothy always gets excited and trembles and chokes when he reads his own poetry, and while he was reading it Papa came into the room and disgraced himself by asking him if there was any *Money* in that kind of poetry, and Fothy was so agitated that he fairly screamed when he said:

"Money . . . money . . . curse money! Money is one of the things I am in revolt against. . . . Money is death and damnation to the free spirit!"

Papa said he was sorry to hear that; he said one of his companies needed an ad writer, and he didn't have any objection to hiring a free spirit with a punch, but he couldn't consider getting anyone to write ads that hated money, for there was a salary attached to the job.

And Fothy said: "You are trying to bribe me! Capitalism is casting its net over me! You are trying to make me a serf: trying to silence a Free Voice! But I will resist! I will not be enslaved! I will not write ads. I will not have a job!"

And then Papa said he was glad to hear Fothy's sentiments. He had been afraid, he said, that Fothy had matrimonial designs upon me. And the man who married *his* daughter would probably have to stand for possessing a good deal of wealth, too, for he had always intended doing something very handsome for his son-in-law. So if Fothy didn't want money, he wouldn't want me, for an enormous amount of it would go with me.

Papa, you know, thinks he can be awfully sarcastic.

So many Earth Persons pride themselves on their sarcasm, don't you think?

And Papa is an Earth Person entirely. I've got his horoscope. He isn't *at all* spiritual.

But you can imagine that the whole scene was *frightfully* embarrassing to me—I will *never* forgive Papa!

And I haven't made up my mind *at all* about Fothy. But what I do know is this: once I get my mind made up, I *will not* stand for opposition from any source.

One must be an Individualist, or perish!

Preparing for Christmas

"Christmas," said the Old Soak, "will soon be here. But me, I ain't going to look at it. I ain't got the heart to face it. I'm going to crawl off and make arrangements to go to sleep on the twenty-third of December and not wake up until the second of January.

"Them that is in favour of a denaturized Christmas won't be interfered with by me. I got no grudge against them. But I won't intrude any on them, either. They can pass through the holidays in an orgy of sobriety, and I'll be all alone in my own little room, with my memories and a case of Bourbon to bear me up.

"I never could look on Christmas with the naked eye. It makes me so darned sad, Christmas does. There's the kids . . . I used to give 'em presents, and my tendency was to weep as I give them. 'Poor little rascals,' I said to myself, 'they think life is going to be just one Christmas tree after another, but it ain't.' And then I'd think of all the Christmases past I had spent with good friends, and how they was all gone, or on their way. And I'd think of all the poor folks on Christmas, and how the efforts made for them at that season was only a drop in the bucket to what they'd need the year around. And along about December twenty-third I always got so downhearted and sentimental and discouraged about the whole darned universe I nearly died with melancholy.

"In years past, the remedy was at hand. A few drinks and I could look even Christmas in the face. A few more and I'd stand under the mistletoe and sing. 'God rest ye merry, gentlemen.' And by the night of Christmas day I had kidded myself into thinking I liked it, and wanted to keep it up for a week.

"But this Christmas there ain't going to be any general iniquity used to season the grand religious festival with, except among a few of us Old Soaks that has it laid away. I ain't got the heart to look on all the melancholy critters that will be remembering the drinks they had last year. And I ain't going to trot my own feelings out and make 'em public, neither. No, sir. Me, I'm going to hibernate like a bear that goes to sleep with his thumb in his mouth. Only it won't be a thumb I have in my mouth. My house will be full of children and grandchildren, and there will be a passel of my wife's relations that has always boosted for Prohibition, but any of 'em ain't going to see the old man. I won't mingle in any of them debilitated festivi- tics. I ain't any Old Scrooge, but I respect the memory of the old- time Christmas, and I'm going to have mine all by myself, the mel- ancholy part of it that comes first, and the cure for the melancholy.

This country ain't worthy to share in my kind of a Christmas, and I ain't so much as going to stick my head out of the window and let it smell my breath till after the holidays is over. I got presents for all of 'em, but none of 'em is to be allowed to open the old man's door and poke any presents into his room for him. They ain't worthy to give me presents, the people in general in this country ain't, and I won't take none from them. They might 'a' got together and stopped this Prohibition thing before it got such a start, but they didn't have the gumption. I've seceded, I have. And if any of my wife's Prohibition relations comes sniffin' and smellin' around my door, where I've locked myself in, I'll put a bullet through the door. You hear me! And I'll know who's sniffin' too, for I can tell a Prohibitionist sniff as fur as I can hear it.

"I got a bar of my own all fixed up in my bedroom and there's going to be a hot water kettle near by it and a bowl of this here Tom and Jerry setting onto it as big as life.

"And every time I wake up I'll crawl out of bed and say to myself: 'Better have just one more.'

" 'Well, now,' myself will say to me, 'just one! I really hadn't orter have that one; I've had so many—but just one goes.'

"And then we'll mix it right solemn and pour in the hot water, standing there in front of the bar, with our foot onto the railing, me and myself together, and myself will say to me:

" 'Well, old scout, you better have another afore you go. It's gettin' right like holiday weather outside.'

" 'I hadn't really orter,' I will say to myself again, 'but it's a long time to next holidays, ain't it, old scout? And here's all the appurtenances of the season to you, and may it sing through your digestive ornaments like a Christmas carol. Another one, Ed.'

"And then I'll skip around behind the bar and play I was Ed, the bartender, and say, 'Are they too sweet for you, sir?'

"And then I'll play I was myself again and say, 'No, they ain't, Ed. They're just right. Ask that feller down by the end of the bar, Ed, to join us. I know him, but I forget his name.'

"And then I'll play I was the feller and say I hadn't orter have another but I will, for it's always fair weather when good fellows gets together.

"And then me and myself and that other feller will have three more, because each one of us wants to buy one, and then Ed the bartender will say to have one on the house. And then I'll go to sleep again and hibernate some more. And don't you call me out of that there room till along about noon on the second day of January. I'll be alone in there with my joy and my grief and all them memories."

The Old Brass Railing

TO CHARLEY STILL

Our minds are schooled to grief and dearth,
　　Our lips, too, are aware,
But our feet still seek a railing
　　When a railing isn't there.

I went into a druggist's shop
　　To get some stamps and soap,—
My feet rose up in spite of me
　　And pawed the air with hope.

I know that neither East nor West,
　　And neither North nor South,
Shall rise a cloud of joy to shed
　　Its dampness on my drouth,—

I know that neither here nor there,
　　When winds blow to and fro,
Shall any friendly odours find
　　The nose they used to know,—

No stein shall greet my straining eyes,
　　No matter how they blink,
Mine ears shall never hear again
　　The highball glasses clink,—

There is not anywhere a jug
　　To cuddle with my wrist,—
But my habituated foot
　　Remains an optimist!

It lifts itself, it curls itself,
　　It feels the empty air,
It seeks a long brass railing,
　　And the railing isn't there!

I do not seek for sympathy
　　For stomach nor for throat,
I never liked my liver much—
　　'T is such a sulky goat!—

I do not seek your pity for
    My writhen tongue and wried,
I do not ask your tears because
    My lips are shrunk and dried,—

But, oh! my foot! My cheated foot!
    My foot that lives in hope!
It is a piteous sight to see
    It lift itself and grope!

I look at it, I talk to it,
    I lesson it and plead,
But with a humble cheerfulness,
    That makes my heart to bleed,

It lifts itself, it curls itself,
    It searches through the air,
It seeks a long brass railing,
    And the railing isn't there!

I carried it to church one day—
    O foot so fond and frail!
I had to drag it forth in haste:
    It grabbed the chancel rail.

My heart is all resigned and calm,
    So, likewise, is my soul,
But my habituated foot
    Is quite beyond control!

An escalator on the Ell
    Began its upward trip,
My foot reached up and clutched the rail
    And crushed it in its grip.

It grabs the headboard of my bed
    With such determined clasp
That I'm compelled to scald the thing
    To make it loose its grasp.

Sometimes it leaps to clutch the curb
    When I walk down the street—
Oh, how I suffer for the hope
    That lives within my feet!

Myself, I can endure the drouth
  With stoic calm, and prayer.
But my feet still seek a railing
  When a railing isn't there.

                    —THE OLD SOAK

archy s autobiography

if all the verse what i have wrote
were boiled together in a kettle
twould make a meal for every goat
from nome to popocatapetl
mexico

and all the prose what i have penned
if laid together end to end
would reach from russia to south bend
indiana

but all the money what i saved
from all them works at which i slaved
is not enough to get me shaved
every morning

and all the dams which i care
if heaped together in the air
would not reach much of anywhere
they wouldnt

because i dont shave every day
and i write for arts sake anyway
and always hate to take my pay
i loathe it

and all of you who credit that
could sit down on an opera hat
and never crush the darn thing flat
you skeptics

                    —ARCHY

the song of mehitabel

this is the song of mehitabel
of mehitabel the alley cat
as i wrote you before boss
mehitabel is a believer
in the pythagorean
theory of the transmigration
of the soul and she claims
that formerly her spirit
was incarnated in the body
of cleopatra
that was a long time ago
and one must not be
surprised if mehitabel
has forgotten some of her
more regal manners

i have had my ups and downs
but wotthehell wotthehell
yesterday sceptres and crowns
fried oysters and velvet gowns
and today i herd with bums
but wotthehell wotthehell

i wake the world from sleep
as i caper and sing and leap
when i sing my wild free tune
wotthehell wotthehell
under the blear eyed moon
i am pelted with cast off shoon
but wotthehell wotthehell

do you think that i would change
my present freedom to range
for a castle or moated grange
wotthehell wotthehell
cage me and i d go frantic
my life is so romantic
capricious and corybantic
and i m toujours gai toujours gai

i know that i am bound
for a journey down the sound
in the midst of a refuse mound
but wotthehell wotthehell
oh i should worry and fret
death and i will coquette
there s a dance in the old dame yet
toujours gai toujours gai

i once was an innocent kit
wotthehell wotthehell
with a ribbon my neck to fit
and bells tied onto it
o wotthehell wotthehell
but a maltese cat came by
with a come hither look in his eye
and a song that soared to the sky
and wotthehell wotthehell
and i followed adown the street
the pad of his rhythmical feet
o permit me again to repeat
wotthehell wotthehell

my youth i shall never forget
but there s nothing i really regret
wotthehell wotthehell
there s a dance in the old dame yet
toujours gai toujours gai
the things that i had not ought to
i do because i ve gotto
wotthehell wotthehell
and i end with my favorite motto
toujours gai toujours gai

boss sometimes i think
that our friend mehitabel
is a trifle too gay

—ARCHY

mehitabel joins the navy

expenses going up
and income going down
but wotthehell do i care
the sailors are in town

a tom cat off a cruiser
was seeing of the city
says he between his whiskers
hello my pretty kitty

oh i am pure and careful
in manner well instructed
i ve seldom spoke to strangers
and seldom been abducted

so i replied discreetly
ain t you the nervy guy
how dare you brace a lady
so innocent and shy

oh look he said our warships
have all their flags unfurled
oh come and join the navy
and we will see the world

but the first place that he took me
was not a ship at all
it was a dive in harlem
where they hailed him admiral

a loud shebeen in harlem
which flowed with song and cheer
and we danced upon the tables
for oysters stewed in beer

the second place he took me
he had been there before
we danced for smelt and fishballs
and they called him commodore

twas down in coney island
they named me puss cafe
as we danced among the bottles
for cream and gin frappe

my room rent keeps a mounting
and credit going down
but wotthehell do i care
the sailors are in town

the next place that we landed
he done a noble deed
he sliced the eye from a fresh wharf cat
who tried to make my speed

avast you swabs and lubbers
when a sailor says ahoy
tis a patriotic duty
to give the navy joy

oh i always am the lady
discreet as well as gay
but the next place that he took me
the devil was to pay

for we seen the icebox open
and tried to raid the loot
and the next we knew we was out in the street
ahead of the barkeep s boot

but wotthehell do i care
i neither whine nor fret
what though my spine is out of line
there s a dance in the old dame yet

i would not desert the navy
nor leave it in the lurch
though each place that he took me
was less and less like a church

and now the fleet is sailing
with all its flags unfurled
and five little kittens with anchor marks
are tagging me round through the alleys and parks
but i have seen the world

oh my maternal instinct
has proved to be my curse
it started when i was an ingenue
and went from bad to worse

but wotthehell do i care
whether it s tom or bill
for any sailor off of the fleet
there s a dance in the old dame still

—MEHITABEL THE CAT

the lesson of the moth

i was talking to a moth
the other evening
he was trying to break into an electric light bulb
and fry himself on the wires

why do you fellows
pull this stunt i asked him
because it is the conventional
thing for moths or why
if that had been an uncovered
candle instead of an electric
light bulb you would
now be a small unsightly cinder
have you no sense?

plenty of it he answered
but at times we get tired
of using it
we get bored with the routine
and crave beauty
and excitement
fire is beautiful
and we know that if we get
too close it will kill us

but what does that matter
it is better to be happy
for a moment
and be burned up with beauty
than to live a long time
and be bored all the while
so we wad all our life up
into one little roll
and then we shoot the roll
that is what life is for
it is better to be a part of beauty
for one instant and then cease to
exist than to exist forever
and never be a part of beauty
our attitude toward life
is come easy go easy
we are like human beings
used to be before they became
too civilized to enjoy themselves

and before i could argue him
out of his philosophy
he went and immolated himself
on a patent cigar lighter
i do not agree with him
myself i would rather have
half the happiness and twice
the longevity
but at the same time i wish
there was something i wanted
as badly as he wanted to fry himself

—ARCHY

8

CRACKER-BARREL PHILOSOPHERS

Actions speak louder'n flags.

One of Kin Hubbard's many "Abe Martin" illustrations. (from Abe Martin's Back Country Sayings, 1917)

Frank McKinney Hubbard (1868–1930)

Abe Martin

Miss Fawn Lippincut

KIN HUBBARD was a journalist of multiple talents. He was master of the well-turned quip; he illustrated his work with adroit pen-and-ink drawings; and he infused his humorous writings with a homespun philosophy that endeared him to his multitudes of readers. A native Hoosier, he wrote primarily of the rural Indiana ambiance that he had known from youth. Speaking most often as "Abe Martin," Hubbard evoked the past of America's heartland—the good simple existence centering upon the family and the village, and undergirded by the virtues of common sense.

In the years that he wrote for the *Indianapolis News* (1891–1930), Hubbard witnessed many changes in his pastoral world and the values embodied in it. Although the setting for most of his work is Brown County, a rural area in central Indiana, Hubbard projects the world at large against this backdrop.

Abe Martin is Hubbard's most familiar guise, though occasionally another fictional personage, such as Miss Fawn Lippincut, is employed for the sake of variety. Rather than calling the prevailing point of view conservative, it would be fairer to say that change is viewed warily. Many of Martin's epigrammatic remarks are directed to the automobile ("It's gittin' so it don't make much difference how we conduct ourselves in society if we've got good road manners") and many

The selections are from Frank McKinney Hubbard, *Abe Martin's Broadcast* (Indianapolis: Bobbs-Merrill, 1930); and *Abe Martin's Primer* (Indianapolis: Abe Martin Publishing Company, 1914).

toward politicians ("It seems like th' less a statesman amounts to th' more he loves th' flag").

Along with Don Marquis and Will Rogers, Kin Hubbard's journalistic alter ego enjoyed a center-stage position during perhaps the finest period for the fictional persona in the history of American journalism, the 1920s. The Abe Martin pieces were syndicated in numerous newspapers, and a number of collections (e.g., *Abe Martin's Primer, Abe Martin's Broadcast, Abe Martin: Hoss Sense and Nonsense*) enjoyed wide distribution and sales. His friend Will Rogers wrote in a "daily telegram" that Hubbard's death in 1930 was to humorists "just like Edison's would be to the world of invention."

An example of Kin Hubbard's innovative marketing of the popular "Abe Martin." (from Abe Martin's Back Country Sayings, *1917)*

The Country Newspaper

"Well, well, Lile Kite's cow died last evenin' after a brief illness. Suppose you run over after you git your work out an' see if ther hain't somethin' you kin do," said Lester Plum to his wife, as he laid aside the local family newspaper. If ther's one thing more'n another that's essential to a good, well-ordered country town it's a live, gossipy newspaper, an' I hope I never live to see the day when it's crowded out of existence or takes on any city airs. The big city dailies, filled with all the news o' the outlyin' world, Ramsay Macdonald's speeches, highbrow scandals, endurance flights, torso mysteries, gangland feuds, Washington gossip, school bus horrors, demoralizin' divorces, rum plots, an' women's views, are all right fer big noisy, bustlin' squirmin' centers o' population, where ever' buddy's all right till he's put in jail, but in the decent, quieter, an' more resigned settlements, fer removed from disturbin' influences an' artificiality, the country newspaper, with its pages crowded with wholesome, homey news, is the thing. Ther's enough gown' on right under the very nose o' the general run o' humanity to keep it upset without havin' to read about all the unhappy an' disquietin' things which are continually besettin' the universe, such as sensational impeachments, acquitted murderesses, Calcutta riots, beer wars, missin' girls an' cashiers, family wipeouts, farm sufferers, fliers long overdue, books suppressed, an' Democratic plans for 1932. How much finer it is, how much more upliftin' to quietly set down at the close of the day an' open up an eight-page home newspaper an' read, "Gran'maw Pash is not so well today." We've known Gran'maw Pash all our lives an' we want to know how she's gittin' on. We read with pleasure that Wesley Plum has decided not to make the race fer township clerk, an' we're really glad. He's too fine a feller to mix in politics. An' here's a full account of a council meetin' to consider doin' away with the town pump. All the speeches are printed word fer word, an' here's our name printed right in with the rest. "Avery Moots is holdin' a fine heifer fer the owner, who may have the same by provin' ownership an' payin' fer this ad." This item'll catch the eye o' somebuddy that's lost the heifer an'll be the means o' unitin' 'em. But ther's not a word in the whole newspaper about the arrest o' Art Lark. I reckon the editur thinks poor ole Mrs. Lark has had her share o' trials an' tribulations an' that ther's nothin' to be gained by addin' to the load that is already breakin' her heart. Country editurs are nearly allus human. Hello, here's the weddin' notice o' Bib Kite an' Hester Bentley, givin' the names of all the guests, what they had on, what the presents wuz an' everything. O' course the editur knows this weddin' hain't gown' to hold, but he's been fair, an' started the young couple off the best he knowed how. An' here's a blunder: "Miss Edith Purviance has accepted a lucrative position in one of the largest millinery establishments in the east." Jest wait till she sees they didn' spell it "Edythe."

Our Appallin' Literary Output

When we look at th' great mass o' literature that tests th' capacity o' bookstores an' news-stands we can't help thinkin' what a scramble ther must be fer even standin' room in th' field o' literature. Most anybuddy roundin' forty kin easily remember th' day when two or three family story papers, a couple o' magazines, a stock o' Ned Buntline's yeller backs, an illustrated pink weekly devoted t' crime an' th' prize ring an' "Lovell's Library" constituted what wuz regarded at th' time as a first class book an' news depot. "Lovell's Library" wuz made up of paper backed novels—thrillin' stories of adventure an' heart meltin' tales o' love—by such celebrated writers as Wilkie Collins, Clark Russell, Mrs. Henry Wood, Ouida, Hugh Conway, Charlotte Braeme, Robert Buchanan an' Th' Duchess. Th' great popularity o' *Adam Bede, Th' Mill on th' Floss, Black Beauty, Lena Rivers, Uncle Tom's Cabin, Robinson Crusoe* an' *Enoch Arden* had dwindled t' a fair demand, but were t' be found among th' others.

Jest think o' th' apallin' literary output o' t' day. It would require an abandoned skatin' rink t' carry a full line o' current literature. In th' average home th' cartin' away o' th' accumulated literature has come t' be as much of a problem as th' removal o' ashes an' garbage. A literary disposal plant is one o' th' urgent needs o' th' times. On returnin' from a week's vacation one has t' tunnel thro' th' great drifts o' papers an' magazines t' reach th' front door.

Ther's no longer any mystery about how th' other half o' th' world lives. It writes. Fer ever' mail box ther's an amateur writer. As th' day draws t' a close he may be seen skulkin' along thro' th' shadows t' a mail box bearin' a thick reel o' manuscript addressed t' some magazine publisher. He knows some magazine needs it t' balance up its advertisin'. When a magazine editur returns a manuscript it's because he hain't got room fer it. It's no sign he has read it. Writers know that. They jest remail it t' some other editor. Th' great difficulty in contributin' t' th' magazines is knowin' which magazine needs your stuff. When a magazine editur rips open a story he counts th' pages an' calls t' his assistant: "George, kin we use about twenty-eight hundred words next month?" an' George answers right off th' bat (bein' thoroughly familiar with th' number o' ads): "Yes, it'll jest balance up th' ads."

Th' amateur author never gits discouraged. Sometimes he drys up fer a week or ten days, but he's soon at it agin. He knows that ther must be somewhere some editur that's holdin' his forms open fer his story an' he mails it an' remails it till he hits th' right editur.

Writin' looks awful easy, an' most of it must be awful easy. That's th' reason so many neglect ther personal appearance an' become writers. I've often thought I'd lay off some afternoon an' write a novel. But writin' fer magazines is th' best sport. It's as lazy an' fascinatin' as fishin'. You're your own master. You don't even have t' be available. Jest so your story is long enough or short enough—jest so th' editor has room fer it.

When we reflect that *Pilgrim's Progress* wuz writt'n in jail, that Silvio Pellico an' Tasso did ther best writin' behind th' bars, that Sir Walter Raleigh's admirable history o' th' world wuz written with his hands handcuffed behind him in th' Tower o' London, that Leigh Hunt wuz layin' out a fine when *Rimini* wuz written, an' that Daniel Defoe laid th' plans fer *Robinson Crusoe* while he wuz in a lock-up we must confess that th' world t'day is lenient indeed.

—Miss Fawn Lippincut

William Penn Adair Rogers (1879–1935)

Will Rogers

*A*LTHOUGH **WILL ROGERS** was known and loved as a personality by mainstream America, his image of a common man possessed of horse sense and natural wit was carefully developed and cultivated. Rogers, like most creators of public masks, was a complex man who avoided burdening his readers with his own problems or fears. He expressed opinions on disaster and tragedy, to be sure, but he did so in a manner that relieved, rather than underscored, such burdens. Given the findings of certain of his biographers (Alworth 1974; Ketchum 1973), a case can be made for identifying the Will Rogers of the newspaper columns and the electronic media as a masterful and consistent creation in the tradition of the American journalistic mask. The public man—the lasso-twirling, gum-chewing philosopher of the Ziegfeld Follies, the personality of the newspaper column, the down-home voice on the radio—was apparently very different from the private one, who could be short-tempered, irascible, tense, and far from humorous.

His writings fall mainly into the categories of weekly articles (approximately the length of an editorial or short feature) and the much shorter daily telegrams, which number in the thousands. Both types of article were broadly syndicated and probably attracted more readers, both nationally and internationally, than the work of any single print journalist before or since.

Rogers's newspaper years (he was also featured on the

The selections are from *The Writings of Will Rogers*, edited by Joseph A. Stout et al., vol. 2, *Convention Articles* (1976); ser. 3, vols. 1–3, *Daily Telegrams* (1978–1979); ser. 4, vols. 1 and 3, *Weekly Articles* (1980) (Stillwater: Oklahoma Univ. Press).

vaudeville stage, on radio, and in motion pictures) extended from the early 1920s until his untimely death in an airplane crash in 1935: in other words, from the twilight years of Harding's administration to the first Franklin D. Roosevelt administration. It is appropriate that his writings be defined by means of such political parameters because, above all else, Rogers was a political commentator, who maintained that "America has the best politicians money can buy." Yet, while he was quick to point a playfully accusing finger at the foibles of politicians and their politics, he generously gave credit when it was deserved—often to the very individuals who had been the butt of his jokes (an excellent example being Calvin Coolidge).

Politics was only one of Rogers's favorite topics, however. The many subjects addressed in his newspaper pieces reveal a man closely attuned to the full spectrum of his times. To read his articles in chronological order is to follow the course of the events of those times. To read his brief, telegraphic comments on Lindbergh's solo flight, the 1929 stock market crash, the ensuing Great Depression, or the Lindbergh kidnapping is to view an abbreviated social history, crystallized into short, clear gems of homely wit and humor.

Aviation Is 20 Years Old but Congress Never Heard of It

As I am writing this 2 blocks away the body of Samuel Gompers, the great labor leader, is being viewed and wept over by hundreds of big strong men, who are appreciative of what he had spent his life in doing for them.[1] He was a good friend of mine. Just a few weeks ago he come to see our show and as is customary with any notable in the audience, I introduced him, with: "Our notable guest has been 40 years at the head of the largest organization of men in this country. He has done more for the working man than any man living. The reason the Federation of Labor has been so successful is because when they found a good man they kept him. They didn't go

---

1. Samuel Gompers, American labor leader who helped found the American Federation of Labor in 1886. He served as its president almost continuously from 1865 until his death on December 13, 1924. [Ed. note]

off electing some new fellow every 4 years, and the smartest thing that he ever did for them was to keep his organization out of Politics. He makes them work his way, but vote like they want to."

Well, that introduction seemed to please the old fellow, and I then tried this one on him for a laugh: "Mr. Gompers has spent his life trying to keep Labor from working too hard, and he has succeeded beyond his own dreams."

I have before me here in the dressing room a Picture Post Card mailed in Mexico from him, just before he took sick: "Am going to bring you back a new lariat and some new jokes." He will be missed, and that's saying a lot in these times. All labor stops for two minutes today as a tribute to him. I suppose Capital will take it out of their salary at the end of the week.

And while we are on the subject of labor, I see a lot in the papers about this 20th or Child Labor Amendment, and I have been asked how I stand on that. If Congress or the States would just pass one law, as follows, they wouldn't need any 20th Amendment: "EVERY CHILD, REGARDLESS OF AGE SHALL RECEIVE THE SAME WAGE AS A GROWN PERSON." That will stop your child labor. They only hire them because they pay them less for the same work than they would have to pay a man. If children don't do more for less money, why is it that they want to use them? No factory or farmer or anybody else hires a child because he is so big hearted he wants to do something for the child. He hires him because he wants to save a man's salary. It's become a habit and a custom that if a child does something for us, no matter how good and prompt they do it, to not give them as much as we would a grown person, because I suppose, people think they would just spend it foolishly if they had too much.

There is no use getting excited over a little thing like an Amendment to our Constitution nowadays, because if you don't like this one wait till the next day and they will have some more. I think I will miss a few weeks in voting and wait till they get up in the thirties on their Amendments, and then start voting again with them. It's pitiful when you think how ignorant the founders of our Constitution must have been. Just think what a Country we would have if men in those days had the brains and forethought of our men today!

Well, yesterday was the 20th Anniversary of the first Flying Machine flight by the Wright Brothers.[2] People wouldn't believe that

---

2. Orville and Wilbur Wright, American aeronautical pioneers who made the first successful flights in a motor-powered airplane. They conducted the flights at Kitty Hawk, North Carolina, in 1903. [Ed. note]

a man could fly, AND CONGRESS DON'T BELIEVE IT YET.

The anniversary of the Wrights' flight was celebrated all over the World yesterday. France launched their 54th Flying Squadron (Squadron, I said; not airship. But a whole Squadron! 54th!). England turned out two gross. Japan hatched out a batch. Americans celebrated the occasion by letting one Aviator out, and deciding to keep up the other three. Our Air Service is waiting for Congress to make an appropriation to have the valves ground and carbon removed from the engines.

Of course this year was a kinder slow year for us because our Aviators were gone around the world.[3] If a war ever breaks out while our Air Force is off on a trip like that we are going to be up against it. Of course we hold all the records in doing everything that an Aviator ever did, and of course Congress figures that in case of a War we would just show the enemy these records and the enemy would call off their Air part of the war.

We are improving though. We have two Dirigibles now, the Los Angeles, which holds 20 million feet of gas, (somebody with a sense of humor named that) and we have The Shenandoah. So in case we get one shot down we will have another one in reserve.

Of course we will have to notify the enemy that they will do us a great favor by shooting one of them down near where the other one is, because we have to use the same air in both of them. We have two Airships but only one set of air, so they will have to give us time to change.

The Germans had some of that helium gas in one airship when they brought it over here, but their Contract only called for delivery of the Ship, and nothing was said about the Air. So some Dutchman opened the gate and let it all out.

Congress, by the way, is going to make an appropriation to get some more of this gas, as soon as some one tells them that they use it in the navigation of this ship. They will perhaps compromise on only appropriating enough money to get half enough gas. And then tell the Air Service: "Well, use what you got there and take it up as high as you can, and when we meet next year we will see what can be done about getting enough to get you on up."

America invents everything, but the trouble is we get tired of it the minute the new is wore off.

Well, I see where the Holiday Booze has started in on its Spring Drive. It's getting so Xmas kills more people than it makes happy. I used to think it was the Bootleggers that were the ones responsible

---

3. Four United States Army airplanes, each carrying a two-man crew, made the first complete air flight around the world in 1924. [Ed. note]

for Prohibition, but I think the Undertakers are behind it stronger than the Bootleggers.

New Jersey had a big 50 million dollar Booze Scandal and they tried to bring it into Court but they couldn't do anything because they couldn't find anybody in the State to try the case, because everybody was mixed up in it. A Catholic Priest was the one who discovered the Gang, and now I see where the Ku Klux have offered to make him a member. That will be a Cosmopolitan organization yet.

I see a good deal of talk from Washington about lowering the Taxes. I hope they do get 'em lowered down enough so people can afford to pay 'em. Well, of all the fool things, the prize one goes to a troop of Society Women here in New York who for the last couple of weeks have been entertaining some woman who was supposed to be the Czarina of Russia, of course, that was in case Russia decided to have a Czar and a Czarina.[4] It would be about like me announcing that I had decided to be King of Oklahoma (in case, of course, Oklahoma ever decided to have a King).

Well, the Monday Opera Club, an organization that just can't stand Opera unless it is served on Monday, (Monday, by the way in any Theatrical business is an off night and you can get a Party Rate). Well, these people had lost out on the Prince of Wales' visit, so they decided to dig 'em up some Royalty of their own. This Czarina didn't have anything booked, (not even a Country) so she offered to come for expenses Plus 10 Percent of the gross.

It seems, according to press reports, the Social standing of the Monday Opera Corporation was not just what the members desired, so it was figured a Cook's Tour of Homes of the Elite of Park and Fifth Avenue personally conducted by the Monday Opera Club with a possible but not probable Czarina, would just about put the Monday Opera Club up among the Six Best Sellers.

Mind you, this Opera troop couldn't lose anything. They got the French Line to transport Exhibit A, over free. It's the off season on our best Oceans, and the Waldorf had about run out of Democrats since (and even a little before) election. Nobody was occupying their Royal Suite, (Oscar had gone to Europe) so in exchange for Press Notices that was arranged for Gratis a Rolls Royce in exchange for Photos in its weeklies did the taxi-ing.[5] On the last night at a big

---

4. Cyril, grand duchess of Russia and the wife of the leading pretender to the Russian throne. She visited the United States in late 1921 to raise money for her husband's campaign to gain the throne. [Ed. note]

5. Oscar Tschirky, known as "Oscar of the Waldorf," famous Swiss-born maître d'hôtel of the Waldorf-Astoria and its successor, the Waldorf, from 1893 to 1943. [Ed. note]

farewell reception, the ladies bended the knee to Royalty, and then kissed the hand and wished her God speed on her journey to the Throne. Now can you see some big bohunk American stooping over kissing the hand of somebody who wanted to be Czar of all the Russias? In the first place he would do it about as gracefully as a Cub Bear trying to play Mahjong, because we all know he is only a half generation removed from a dinner pail. And these Monday Opera Women—they would have jumped off the Palisades if they had been sure of the first mention in the Society Casualty list. The attempted Czarina has returned to Europe with enough quiet laughs tucked away to last a Russian a lifetime.

Then we wonder why we are funny to Europeans. We are funny to ourselves if we just get a mirror. One thing, the Monday Opera Club was not a hooded organization. They allowed, even welcomed, the publication of names.

Daily Telegrams

WILL ROGERS WIRES AN OPINION ON THE SACCO-VANZETTI CASE

BOSTON, Mass., May 12 [1927].—I am the only person in Boston who has not expressed an opinion on the Sacco-Vanzetti case. All I know is that it should not take a nation or a State seven years to decide whether anyone committed a crime or not. It's a good thing they were young men when the crime was committed, otherwise they wouldn't live long enough for justice to make up its mind.

The Mayor in the cradle of liberty.

Will.

THE MORAL WILL ROGERS DRAWS
FROM LINDBERGH'S GREAT FEAT

NEW YORK, N.Y., May 22 [1927].—Of all things that Lindbergh's great feat demonstrated, the greatest was to show us that a person could still get the entire front pages without murdering anybody.

Nobody knows what he will do now, but he has had an invitation to return to America and address the regular weekly luncheon of the Kiwanis Club of Claremore, Okla.

Boy, that Prince of Wales better not appear in the same crowd as this bird and expect anybody to look at him.

One of his ardent admirers,

Will Rogers

THOUGHTS OF WILL ROGERS
ON THE LATE SLUMP IN STOCKS

LOS ANGELES, Cal., Oct. 31 [1929].—Sure must be a great consolation to the poor people who lost their stock in the late crash to know that it has fallen in the hands of Mr. Rockefeller, who will take care of it and see that it has a good home and never be allowed to wander around unprotected again.

There is one rule that works in every calamity. Be it pestilence, war or famine, the rich get richer and the poor get poorer. The poor even help arrange it. But it's just as Mr. Brisbane and I have been constantly telling you. "Don't gamble"; take all your savings and buy some good stock, and hold it till it goes up, then sell it.

If it don't go up, don't buy it.

Yours,
WILL ROGERS

WILL ROGERS PAYS TRIBUTE
TO HUBBARD AND HIS HUMOR

HOLLYWOOD, Cal., Dec. 26 [1930].—Kin Hubbard is dead. To us folks that attempt to write a little humor his death is just like Edison's would be to the world of invention. No man in our generation was within a mile of him, and I am so glad that I didn't wait for him to go to send flowers. I have said it from the stage and in print for twenty years.

My dressing room when I play Indianapolis won't be the same without Kin sitting in there. I loved his work and I loved him.

Just think—just two lines a day, yet he expressed more original philosophy in 'em than all the rest of the paper combined. What a kick Twain and all that old gang will get out of Kin.

Yours,
WILL ROGERS

ROGERS HAILS SOUSA'S TUNES
AS HIS ENDURING MONUMENT

BEVERLY HILLS, Cal., March 8 [1932].—He was in life rather small of stature. Not particularly impressive, very modest and unassuming. Yet he produced something that any hour of the day or night can quicken the blood and thrill the nerves of every American man, woman or child. His tunes were the Lincoln's Gettysburg address of music.

"El Capitan," "Washington Post" and "Stars and Stripes

Forever" is a monument that needs no concrete. It's for the soul, and not for the eye.

Our little March King is dead, but his marches will be marched-to down through the ages.

Yours,
WILL ROGERS.

WILL ROGERS EXPRESSES
SORROW OF THE COUNTRY

BEVERLY HILLS, Cal., May 13 [1932].—One hundred and twenty million people lost a baby, 120,000,000 people cry one minute and swear vengeance the next. A father who never did a thing that didn't make us proud of him. A mother who, only the wife of a hero, has proven one herself. At home or abroad they have always been a credit to their country. They have never fallen down. Is their country going to be a credit to them? Will it make him still proud that he did it for them? Or in his loneliness will it allow a thought to creep into his mind that it might have been different if he had flown the ocean under somebody's colors with a real obligation to law and order?

America goes further into debt, and the debt is to the Lindberghs.

Yours,
WILL ROGERS.

WILL ROGERS PAYS TRIBUTE
IN HIS OWN WAY TO COOLIDGE

BEVERLY HILLS, Cal., Jan. 5 [1933].—Mr. Coolidge, you didn't have to die for me to throw flowers on your grave. I have told a million jokes about you, but every one was based on some of your splendid qualities. You had a hold on the American people regardless of politics. They knew you were honest, economical and had a native common sense.

History generally records a place for a man that is ahead of his time. But we that lived with you will always remember you because you was WITH your time.

By, golly, you little, red-headed New Englander, I like you. You put horse sense into statesmanship and Mrs. Coolidge's admiration for you is an American trait.

Yours,
WILL ROGERS

Philander Chase Johnson (1866–1939)

Senator Sorghum

Uncle Eben

OR FORTY-SEVEN YEARS, Philander Johnson was a staff writer for the *Washington Star*, though his readers identified less with Johnson himself than with Senator Sorghum, Uncle Eben, and several other characters who made frequent appearances in Johnson's "Shooting Stars" column. Johnson's thirty-first anniversary on the *Star* was celebrated in 1922 with a gala party, complete with persons dressed in the manner of a number of his characters and a congratulatory letter from President Warren G. Harding (addressed to Senator Sorghum).

If Johnson's fictional creations are little noted today, the same cannot be said for some of their utterances. Johnson was a master of the journalistic epigram, which is often as timely as it is brief. A number of Johnson's have endured, even if their provenance is not usually acknowledged. For instance, he is credited with such phrases as "Cheer up, the worst is yet to come" and "Don't throw a monkey wrench into the machinery." Such remarks have been emulated by such later journalistic guises as the modern-day "Senator Soaper."

Johnson was also a playwright and a folksy poet in the manner of Eugene Field and James Whitcomb Riley. The poem "A Symphony," narrated by Uncle Eben, is a represent-ative example of his verse, which was described by a contem-

The selections are from Philander Chase Johnson, *Sayings of Uncle Eben* (Washington, D.C.: Bauble, 1896); and *Senator Sorghum's Primer of Politics* (Philadelphia: Henry Altemus, 1906).

porary reviewer as containing "the instinct for the earth, for natural beauty, for simple things, for people unspoiled." The character of Uncle Eben is, of course, reminiscent of Brother Gardner and Uncle Remus, who established the black dialect and character in feature writing.

From Senator Sorghum's Primer of Politics

I am not worrying about what posterity will say of me. The historians do not make nearly so much trouble for men in my position as the newspaper reporters.

Some men remind me of our old parrot. It had so little sense that it earned a heap of credit and admiration for learning anything at all.

Occasionally a reputation for great wisdom is obtained by doing absolutely nothing and thereby avoiding mistakes.

The man who goes into politics because he needs the money isn't likely to do as much harm as the man who goes into it merely because he has money to burn.

The reformer is a man who gets pushed off the band-wagon and has to start a procession of his own.

Going behind the returns of an election is like a post-mortem. It may afford information, but it never cures anything.

A man who hasn't judgment enough to keep the cow out of the garden, will sit on the top rail of the fence and tell exactly how to guard the United States Treasury.

Some candidates are too honest to use money in an election. Others are too economical.

In practical politics, it is foolish to make a mistake; but it is twice as foolish to own up to it.

A really great political speech is one during which the audience stops long enough between cheers to get the exact sense of what you are saying.

When a man is first elected to office the compliment makes such a great impression on his mind that there is danger of his wanting everything complimentary the rest of his life.

A Symphony

I's done let down the fiddle's strings
    An' I's hung 'im on de wall
Foh I doan hab use foh no sich things
    When de Souf'-win' comes ter call.
Foh de cloud he res' by de ribber bank
    Ter hahk ter de chorus whah de weeds grow rank,
An' de small birds whistle an' de yaller jackets hum
    An' de bull-frog hammer on 'is big bass drum.

Yoh's got ter eddycate yer ear
    Or yoh can't appreciate
De compositions dat yoh hear
    When er wahm day's growin' late;
But when yoh's in de frame ob mind
    Yoh want's no better dan what yoh find
When de small birds whistle an' de yaller jackets hum
    An' de bull-frog hammer on 'is big bass drum.

—UNCLE EBEN

Sayings of Uncle Eben

When er man talks 'bout whut er good fren' ob yourn he am, listen ter him but doan' trade hosses wif him.

De wu'kman dat tu'ns out er po' job am better dan de man dat doan' do nuffin' but look on an' make remahks.

Some men would stahtle de worl' ef dey wus ez industrious wu'kin' ez dey is in makin' 'scuses.

Lots er men woldn' hate wu'k nigh so much ef dey'd only take de trouble ter git 'quainted wif it.

Idleness meks er man talkative. Seems like it's onpossible ter do nuffin' an' say nuffin' simultuously.

De canerdate dat gits defeated am hahd ter convince dat dis worl' am pergressin'.

De difficulty 'bout bein er statesman out'n a job am de trouble yoh's li'ble ter 'sperience gittin' er recomend f'um yoh las' place.

Sometimes de big words git de mos' applause but dey doan mek nigh so many people change dah min's.

Er man am intitled ter his own opinions. Hit am only when he tries ter mek somebody er present ob 'em dat he gits dis'gree'ble.

Ez soon ez er man begins ter t'ink de worl' kain't git erlong wifout him, he meks it unpossible foh anybody ter git erlong wif him.

Some men seems ter fink dat talkin' at de top er yoh voice kin take de place ob speakin' f'um de bottom ob yoh h'aht.

Dah's too much time wasted in tryin' ter 'lect er Congress dat'll legislate de mawgidges off' de fahms.

Hit am mahvellous how much easier some men fin's hit ter pay off de national debt dan ter settle de grocery bill.

Cuhcumstances alter cases. De man dat likes ter hyah hisse'f holler in er ahgyment doan 'pear ter git no satisfaction 'tall f'um 'is voice drivin' cows.

9

NOSTALGISTS

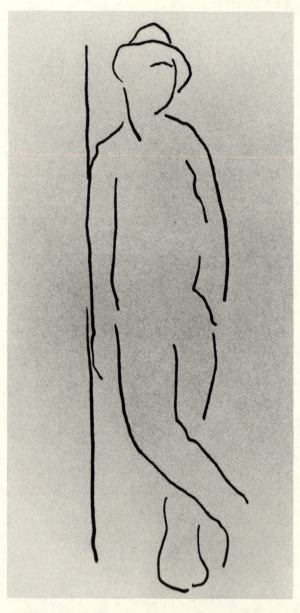

One of Wharton Esherick's two line drawings of Sherwood Ander-son's "Buck Fever." (from the collection of Welford D. Taylor)

Sherwood Anderson (1876–1941)

Buck Fever

WHEN SHERWOOD ANDERSON bought his two country weeklies, the *Marion Democrat* and the *Smyth
County News,* in the late summer of 1927, he had
had virtually no experience either running or writing for
newspapers. Within three weeks, however, a fictional reporter named Buck Fever was introduced into his pages.
Though bearing the trappings of the Virginia highlander,
Buck represented a time-honored tradition in American
journalism. And during the four years that he appeared in
Anderson's newspapers, Buck Fever grew in stature, familiarity, and popularity. He appeared most frequently in the
"Buck Fever Says" column, which became a staple in both
newspapers.

One of the most practical uses made of Buck's talents
was to point out the foibles of Anderson himself—his stinginess, his tendency toward self-importance, his laziness.
Thus, in the columns containing byplay between the two,
Buck served as a kind of mirror to Anderson, reducing him
from a writer of serious literature to simply a fellow Mar-
ionite.

Although Buck Fever comments most often upon Anderson or some aspect of life in Marion, he is at his best when
taking a commonplace incident and developing it into an
amusing story or anecdote—as in "The Three Hens." Collectively, the Buck Fever articles form the largest body of humorous writing done by Anderson.

The selections are from Sherwood Anderson, *The Buck Fever Papers,* edited by
Welford Dunaway Taylor (Charlottesville: Univ. Press of Virginia, 1971).

Buck Fever Says

Seems to us, for a quiet man who pretends, as he does, to be an author, S. A. is jazzing up this paper a good deal.

The boys down at Curtis barber shop are out practicing with boxing gloves in the back yard when there isn't any haircutting to do. Pretty soon we'll get a prize fighter in this town and that will be any amount better for putting us on the map than a author.

The *Ben Hur* show at the Marion Theater was good. Miss Smith who works at the General Francis Marion eat shoppe told us, when we were eating our pie the other day, it made her cry. I wish I had been with her. I like to be with girls when they get tender like that.

What do you suppose they want to call it a "Shoppe," for? They tell us the New Ford is a jim dandy and doesn't cost too much. It costs too much for a reporter on this enlightened paper. Mr. S. A. got braggy the other day and showed me a letter he got from the *New York World*. A man named Mr. Louis Weitzenkorn wrote it. He asked Mr. S. A. to write a piece for the *World Sunday Paper* about his running a paper in Marion. Mr. S. A. thinking if he could not make any money any other way he would try to make it on them, wrote this Mr. Weitzenkorn a letter, the nerviest I ever see, asking him to give $300 dollars for writing the piece. In his letter Mr. S. A. said he did not know much about journalism and this Mr. Weitzenkorn came right back at him and said, "I guess you don't if you think you can get $300 out of us." I would have wrote it myself for a two dollar bill.

—Buck Fever

The Three Hens

Here is how it is. Mrs. Handy moved down—or up—or over from Troutdale to the St. Clair country. She had several hens. Mrs. Handy has had, as she herself says, heaps and heaps of trouble. Life has been in short a troublous voyage for her. I neglected to say that she has also a rooster to attend her hens—being I fancy a fair minded woman.

What are hens without a rooster, or for that matter what is a rooster without his hens?

Three of Mrs. Handy's hens were stolen. This was at night. In the morning Mrs. Handy got up and listened for the glad morning cry of her rooster. He was sad and silent. His hens were gone. A sad morning it was for him. Well do I know how he felt—or if I don't know I guess my Paw does. I have heard him lots of times, when he had been scrapping with Maw. "I wish I was a rooster," he said.

Mrs. Handy claimed, or at least she heard, that some boys had stolen her hens. For plain and fancy "he said" and "she said," the St. Clair District is the best in the world. You can just about hear anything you want to hear down there and a lot you don't want to hear.

Mrs. Handy went to see the parents of the boys. They claim they said to her, "No our boys did not steal your hens but you are a woman who has had her troubles. We will just give you three hens. But you must not start any trouble."

But Mrs. Handy did start trouble. The boys were arrested and tried in Justice Dickinson's Juvenile Court, the whole countryside coming in for the trial. One of the boys was convicted and sent to the reform farm, the other was let go.

"But what about our three hens?" the parents said to Mrs. Handy and to Justice Dickinson, "Do we get them back?"

Mrs. Handy shook her head. Justice Dickinson shook his head. "I don't see how that could be," he said.

And there was something else to this matter. We don't know whether or not it should be mentioned in a family Journal but here goes. Truth will out. Mrs. Handy's rooster had really become attached to the three strange hens in the yard. Never had he crowed more cheerfully. Joyfully did he greet each coming day, etc., etc.

And then up comes the parents and relatives of the boys and gets the hens—as one might say, "off" Mrs. Handy.

There is a moral question involved. Were the hens given Mrs. Handy on the understanding that she would keep quiet about the whole matter? One of the hens was about to become a mother. That complicates matters too. There is always a complicated situation.

The St. Clair District is shaken to its roots. Who do those hens belong to? Where is the right and wrong of this matter? If the hens belong to those who have recently got them off Mrs. Handy should they be separated from the rooster? Can families and family life be ruthlessly broken up in this way?

It is a serious question. Three other hens might be found for Mrs. Handy but what about the rooster? Does anyone know that a rooster will take up family life with just any hen?

Mrs. Handy's rooster is said to be sad. He is to droop and waste away. Something ought to be done. But where is the right and wrong of this matter?

(Written for this paper by Buck Fever. All poultry paper rights reserved.)

Bill Breck's representation of Edward Streeter's "Bill." (from That's Me All Over, Mable, *1919)*

Edward Streeter (1891–1976)

Bill

ASIDE FROM A BRIEF STINT as a reporter on the *Buffalo Express* at the beginning of his career (1914–1916), Edward Streeter had little professional connection with newspapers. He was, rather, a banker and a writer of humorous books such as *Father of the Bride* and *Mr. Hobbs' Vacation.* His enduring contribution to journalism occurred in a most unusual manner. While serving as a first lieutenant in the 27th (New York) Division during World War I, he contributed to his division newspaper, *The Gas Attack,* a sequence of loosely connected letters, which were signed simply "Bill." Bill Smith, the letters indicated, was a typical doughboy, in that he represented small-town America and was very much a novice at military affairs. His correspondence was addressed to Mable, the girl back home.

Soldiers who read the letters doubtlessly saw themselves reflected in the simple style, the malapropisms, the frequent misspellings, the repeated accounts of awkwardness in becoming acclimated to life in uniform. What had started as a modest attempt at creation soon spread beyond the compound of the 27th New York. Before Streeter shipped out for France in 1918, a number of the letters had been collected into a volume, *Dere Mable,* illustrated by G. William Breck, a corporal in the same division. By the time the division returned the next year, *Dere Mable* and a successor, *That's Me All Over, Mable,* had sold more than three-quarters of a million copies.

The selections are from Edward Streeter, *Dere Mable* (New York: Dodd, Mead, 1941).

Just over twenty years after these two volumes appeared, they were reprinted by popular demand, as once again young Americans prepared to enter another war. Apparently the new generation of soldier (Bill introduces the volume with a letter to his son, who has just been drafted) recognized in the letters the possibility of comfort in the shared experience. Bill Smith is a small-town boy with little education or sophistication, plunged into a turmoil that he has not created, yet out of which he must help to effect a successful issue. Unlike the satiric masks in American journalism, Bill poses no superior ideas or solutions. Indeed, the innocent candor with which he speaks often results in dramatic irony, as his readers are presumed to be much more sophisticated than he. Bill Smith, therefore, represents the average American newly enlisted into the trenches because he *is* that average American, trying as best he can to maintain balance in an atmosphere growing increasingly precarious.

Dere Mable: Love Letters of a Rookie

Camp Wadsworth S.C.
Sep. the 27 1917

Dere Mable:

I guess you thought I was dead. Youll never know how near you was to right. We got the tents up at last, though, so I got a minit to rite. I guess they choose these camps by mail order. The only place there flat is on the map. Where our tents is would make a good place for a Rocky Mountin goat if he didnt break his neck. The first day the Captin came out an says "Pitch your tents here." Then he went to look for someone quick before anyone could ask him how. I wish I was a Captin. I guess he thought we was Alpine Chasers. Eh, Mable? But you probably dont know what those are.

Honest, Mable, if Id put in the work I done last week on the Panamah Canal it would have been workin long before it was. Of course there was a lot of fellos there with me but it seemed like all they did was to stand round and hand me shovels when I wore em out.

The Captin appresheates me though. The other day he watched

me work awhile and then he says "Smith." He calls me Smith now. We got very friendly since I been nice to him. I noticed none of the other fellos had much to say to him. I felt kind of sorry for him. Hes a human bein even if he is a Captin, Mable. So every time I saw him I used to stop him and talk to him. Democratic. Thats me all over, Mable. "Smith" he says "If they was all like you round here war would be hell, no joke." By which he meant that we would make it hot for the Boshes.

I been feelin awful sorry for you, Mable. What with missin me and your fathers liver gone back on him again things must have been awful lonesome for you. It isnt as if you was a girl what had a lot of fellos hangin round all the time. Not that you couldnt have em, Mable, but you dont an theres no use makin no bones about it. If it hadnt been for me I guess things would have been pretty stupid though I dont begrudge you a sent. You know how I am with my money. I guess you ought to anyway. Eh, Mable? Never talk of money matters in connexun with a woman. Thats me all over.

Now I got started an found a fountin pen an the Y.M.C.A. givin away paper like it does Im goin to rite you regular. They say there goin to charge three sents for a letter pretty soon. That aint goin to stop me though, Mable. There aint no power in heavin or earth, as the poets say, as can come between you and me, Mable. You mite send a few three sent stamps when you rite. That is if your fathers able to work yet. And willin, I should add. Of course it aint nothin to me but Id keep these letters what you get from me as a record of the war. Some day you can read em to your gran-children an say "Your Granfather Bill did all these things." Aint I the worst, Mable? Serious though I havnt found noone so far what has thought of doin this except the newspapers. I guess Ill get a lot of inside stuff that theyll never see. So this may be the only one of its kind. But it doesnt matter to me what you do with them, Mable.

Later Ill tell you all about everything but I guess you wont understand much cause its tecknickle. Lots of the fellos are gettin nitted things and candy and stuff right along. Dont pay no attenshun to that, though, or take it for a hint cause it aint. I just say it as a matter of rekord. Independent if nothin. Thats me all over.

Yours till the war ends

BILL

On the range
May the 1 1918

Dere Mable:

I am bustin into society up here at the range. Last Sunday while I was takin a bath in a little town near here the minister ast me to dinner. Not while I was in the tub, of course, Mable. He ast Joe Loomis to. He had to really cause he was with me. Hes not a regular minister. Hes got a lot of money and pointed shoes an is down in the mountins for cronik azmuth. Their highbrow people, Mable. The kind that changes the needle after every record.

The minister has two daughters, both girls, an a wife. One of the girls is good lookin. The other is more like youd expeck. Joe was ast for her while I amused the good looker. Anybody but Joe could have seen that. Not him. He kept buttin in an makin an ass of hisself.

We was ast for dinner at hapast one. Joe thought it would be politer not to run in an eat an run out like it was a canteen. So we went a little early. About noon. They played highbrow pieces on the phoneygraph. The kind that has only one tune on em an cost so much everybody has to lissen. Joe dont know nothin about music of course. While some big shot was carryin on like nobodys business he says if theyll speed it up hed like to dance.

The minit we sat down to dinner Joe started tellin one of his stories about how he almost got killed one time. They was all waitin for him to shut up sos the minister could say grace before the soup got cold. Joe thought they were lissenen to him. Thats somethin never happened to him before. He kept draggin it out. The only thing finally stopped him was he forgot the point. Then the minister put his nose in his soup and began sayin grace. Joe thought he was talkin to him and kep askin "Hows that and what say" all the time he was prayin.

I aint never goin out with that fello again. All durin dinner he kept sayin, "My gawd I hate to make such a hog of myself." Then the minister would look like hed lost some money and my girl would giggle. The ministers wife passed him some stuff she said was real old spider corn cake. Joe said he didnt care how old it was. Since hed been in the army hed got sos he could eat anything. Then he thought a while an says he guessed it must have been a relief to the spiders to get rid of em. Nobody said nothin. Just to show his poyse Joe took his fork out of his mouth and speered four pieces of bread across the table.

He was all for keepin the same plate through dinner and gettin up an helpin. Said he knew what it was like to be in the kitchen on Sunday. They forgot the coffee till dinner was over. They didn't like to waste it bein war times so the ministers wife ast us if wed like to go into the drawin room an have it. Joe said he wasnt much at drawin but My gawd if he sat round makin a hog of hisself any longer theyd have to give it to him ina bed room. They gave us coffee in egg cups. Seein I wasnt payin for it I didnt say nothin. Manners. Thats me all over, Mable. We got talkin about one thing and another. I was tellin them about the war and when it was goin to end. Joe was sittin on the sofa with the other daughter pickin the sole of his shoe. I felt sorry for him. I knew hed be lookin at fotygraphs pretty soon if he didnt buck up.

The ministers wife asked me what I thought of wimmins sufrage. I said I thought it was a good thing but you couldnt tell. Thats the beauty of always keepin read up on things. If you happen to go out an meet some inteligent people you can talk on pretty near anything. Then she turned to Joe and ast how he felt. Joe jumped like somebody sprung at him an says "A little sick to my stummick thanks but it will be all right as soon as things set a bit."

The good lookin one said she thought our officers was awful cute. I guess she never seen our Lootenant. She said she just couldnt resist them. I says, quick without thinkin it up "Of course, its against the law to resist an officer." That got em all laffin an they forgot Joe for a while.

Both the daughters sang a duette. Joe says that was the best thing about it. They got through twice as quick. We got laffin so hard I says I guess wed have to go sos to be in time for mess. Then Joe got awful polite and backed over a rubber plant an says "My gawd excuse me." He wont never be ast again.

I guess were goin to begin shootin again pretty soon. The Lootenant says the artillery is goin to have a Brigade problem. The infantry is comin up from camp for it. I guess well all take a lot more interest in the shootin if theres somethin worth while to fire at.

yours in spite of better things
Bill.

P.S. Joe Loomis just got a letter that smelt and what do you suppose, Mable? It was from the goodlookin daughter askin him to come over to dinner next Sunday. I guess there not as high brow as I thought.

Richard E. Yates (1910–   )

Horace P. Hardscrabble

*B*ETWEEN 1952 AND 1974, the pages of the *Arkansas Gazette* of Little Rock carried a series of letters to the editor signed by a mythical yet typical Arkansan named Horace P. Hardscrabble. These were important years for American politics in general and for Arkansas politics in particular. The period includes the gubernatorial terms of the controversial Democrat Orville Faubus (1955–1967) and the antidesegregation policies he imposed on the Little Rock schools. Moreover, they conclude with the embattled Republican president, Richard M. Nixon, in the year that he resigned the presidency in the wake of the Watergate scandal. True to his name, Hardscrabble makes a hard-won living from a modest farming operation; his comments are peppered with colloquialisms typical of the type and the region. But Hardscrabble's point of view is ironic rather than literal. In the words of his creator, "He pretends to be a faithful Republican. He 'defends' Republicans and 'attacks' Democrats and liberals in such a way that Republicans and conservatives, he hopes, could do without such a defender." It is obvious in the Faubus pieces, however, that the satire cuts in both directions.

Although never revealed to the readers of the *Arkansas Gazette*, the author of the Hardscrabble pieces was long presumed to be Richard E. Yates, a professor of history at Hendrix College in Conway, Arkansas. In a letter accompanying the sketches he selected for this volume, Professor Yates admitted that he had "just about abandoned silent smiles and

---

The selections are supplied courtesy of Richard E. Yates.

230

evasive answers" and that he thought the time had come "to make a clean breast of the whole business."

The letters chosen by Professor Yates reveal the typical "situation" of the series: Hardscrabble being prodded into action by his straight man, Timothy Peckworthy (proprietor of a feed store and a patient listener). The letters thus reflect several time-honored strains of their tradition: the plain man commenting upon the exploits of the mighty; the setting reflecting America's lost days of innocence; the indulgent straight man and the naturally fluent orator.

Letters to the Editor of the Arkansas Gazette

June 17, 1960

To the Editor of the *Gazette:*

Timothy Peckworthy threw his newspaper into the wood box and tossed a mild profanity after it.

"I do wish," he said, "that Faubus would stick to the truth."

"It seems to me," I replied, "that the governor has already made enough sacrifices."

"Sacrifices!" he exploded. "Are you out of your mind?"

"Now, Timothy," I said, "let's give the devil his due. You know very well that Faubus has done more sacrificing than any governor we've had since the Civil War. When you add up all these sacrifices, it's enough to scare a man. It's scared him. That's why he's been so nervous lately.

"Towards the shag end of 1957, the governor figured it this way: 'I can't get a third term without making sacrifices, but a fellow can't advance himself without cost. That's a law of life.'

"So he gritted his teeth, squared his shoulders, tightened his belt, and began to sacrifice. First, he sacrificed the good name of the state of Arkansas. Up to that time, we had a pretty fair reputation as a poor but progressive little state, not given to jerky hysterics over the race question and not having more than the regulation number of holes in our head. We have a different reputation now.

"Next, the governor sacrificed Little Rock. The capital city wasn't known all over the world then, but its name didn't give offense where it was known. Now its name is a by-word and a reproach in all languages, including the Scandinavian. In far-off Rangoon and in nearby Havana, men clinch political arguments by scornfully spitting out the name 'Little Rock!' just as we Republicans used to hit a Democrat over the head with 'Yalta!'

"Then with a third term assured, the governor's eye fell upon the children of the Little Rock high schools. 'My!' he said, 'what tender, juicy little sacrifices these would make!' So he slammed the school doors shut and told the kids their sacrifices would pay handsome dividends in state rights, local self-government, racial purity, and other such coin."

"If you don't mind my butting in," Timothy said, "will you tell me what sacrifice the governor, himself, has made—personally and out of his own hide?"

"Now, you'll have to ask Mr. Faubus about that," I replied.

"Better wait and ask him twenty years from now, when Arkansas' reputation has been restored and when he'll begin to wonder what kind of name he's going to send kicking down the corridors of time."

HARDSCRABBLE.

Conway.

                                                                May 1, 1973

To the Editor of the *Gazette:*

"Did you hear the President talk about Watergate last night?" Timothy Peckworthy asked.

"I sure did," I told him. "I wouldn't have missed it for the world. Whenever Nixon spends the morning heaving out three White House aides, trusty and loyal friends, and then makes a dessert out of polishing off a cabinet member, I've just got to hear him talk about it.

"It did seem to me he was a little vague in describing just what these fellows had done. I somehow got the impression, though, that Kleindienst had been keeping bad company and that the others had pulled the wool over Nixon's eyes. You see, he had asked the White House aides to investigate themselves and see whether they were mixed up in the Watergate affair, fore or aft. They looked high and low, but couldn't find a single scrap of evidence against themselves. So they gave themselves a clean bill of health. Nixon believed and trusted them. He's a very trusting person and has been so for the last three or four months.

"The high point of the speech—a real record in presidential

drama—was Nixon's acceptance of full responsibility for Watergate. When he had worked himself up to that point, I said to myself: 'He's in for it now. When a man's responsible, he's got to pay. I wonder how hard he'll be on himself.' It turned out, though, that Nixon didn't offer to serve any part of the sentences slapped on the Watergate burglars. He didn't offer to pay any part of their fines. He didn't even apologize for being responsible for the whole mess.

"This has been a good lesson to me, and I'm thankful that Nixon taught it to me. For years I've been trying to duck responsibility for the devilment I've gotten into, believing that when a man's responsible somebody's entitled to take a whack at him. Hereafter, when Abigail asks what heavy-footed clown trampled down the plants in her flower bed, I'm not going to lie out of it by blaming the dog or a visiting cow. I'm going to look her right straight in the eye and say: 'I accept full responsibility'."

"I wonder," Timothy said, "what Nixon will do if the investigations show that he knew about Watergate from the very beginning and then later tried to cover it up."

"That's easy," I said. "He'll say: 'I accept full responsibility,' and then he'll say: 'Let us turn our minds and hearts to the really serious problems of our country, the world, the universe, and points beyond—foreign affairs, domestic problems, mother, and apple pie. God bless America. God bless you one and all'."

HARDSCRABBLE.

Conway.

Charles R. McDowell, Jr. (1926–   )

Aunt Gertrude

*I*N HIS SYNDICATED NEWSPAPER COLUMN Charles R. McDowell, Jr., frequently carries on dialogues with his friend "Reliable Source" and with his Thurberesque neighbor, "Mr. Bumbleton." But when his "Aunt Gertrude" sends him a letter from her farm in rural Virginia, he allows her wryly humorous words to flow uninterrupted. McDowell is one of the last American journalists to employ a well-realized fictional mask, and the epistolary form of these communications is as firmly rooted in our journalistic heritage as the masks themselves.

Like many such creations before her, Aunt Gertrude is fashioned from materials generally recognizable to her readers, but not specifically identifiable. She lives in a farming community in rural Virginia, obviously not too distant from Richmond, the capital city. Long the bastion of the Democratic Byrd organization, much of the population in such areas has changed to the Republican column since the mid-1960s, when the Democratic party became increasingly identified with liberal policies and the Republicans seemed to offer a safe haven for those with more conservative leanings. Aunt Gertrude, who might be classed as a "teacher's college liberal," and her husband, Uncle Frazier, have remained within the Democratic fold without making any great issue of the fact until Uncle Frazier and his friend Fred Cagle (a staunch Republican) begin "discussing" politics. Still, the columns are in no sense partisan. Rather, the community of Aunt Gertrude and Uncle Frazier affords a window on a number of larger worlds—the Commonwealth of Virginia as a

---

The selections are supplied courtesy of Charles R. McDowell, Jr.

whole; Washington, D.C. (where nephew Charlie is based); the national and even international scenes.

Fictional journalists have consistently represented the point of view of the common person in America. In so doing, they have always attempted to deflate the pompous and unmask the pretentious. Aunt Gertrude is no exception, but she performs these offices with a charm and a seemingly innocent humor that is uncommon in the tradition.

Aunt Gertrude Drops a Line

December 2, 1979
Washington

My dear nephew,

Well, after a couple of false starts, winter is finally here, I guess. We welcome it on the farm. Now comes our chance to sleep later. The only thing that absolutely has to be done in the morning is the milking, and if you shift the cows gradually to a winter schedule, there's no need to get out there before 5:30. We stay up later at night, too. I see Johnny Carson is still on the "Tonight" show, and still pretty good. The 11 o'clock news is worse than ever, but that's just the nature of news these days.

As you know, I've always stayed up late on Saturday night. When I was younger there was usually a square dance somewhere around the county. Sometimes your Uncle Frazier and I would go over to Fred and Elsie Cagle's, or they'd come over here, and play cards until the men started to argue over politics. Once, after we were snowed in over there all night, your Uncle Frazier said he'd rather go to the Happy Hour Roadhouse on a Saturday night, and take his chances on a fistfight with somebody from up in Filleman's Hollow, than to play cards with his friend Fred Cagle. So there was a period when we stayed home and played Scrabble. That ran down after a few years because one of us was winning all the time. Your Uncle Frazier is a fine man and I've always tried to make him happy, but I simply will not throw a game of Scrabble. Now on Saturday night we have people to supper, or we play cards with non-Republicans, or we just stay home and read to each other out of the farm magazines and *The New Yorker.* And no matter what, I watch "Saturday Night Live." It almost always gives me something to shock people with after church on Sunday morning. If Miss Philleulah Murkley hasn't told 'em first, that is.

Anyhow, we're glad winter is here. That recent spell of warm weather was no joy for us. There was a lot of rain mixed into that non-glorious Indian Summer, and the fields were deep mud, and we didn't have all the corn in, and I needed cold weather, anyway, because I was canning and I couldn't do it fast enough to keep up with the last stuff coming out of the garden and the orchard.

Everything is all right now. Your Uncle Frazier has relaxed the last few days by splitting four cords of wood. He did three cords with Fred Cagle's mechanical splitter and one with a maul and wedge to leave himself feeling manly for the rest of the winter. We needed the wood for the heat stove in the back parlor. That stove has been in this house forever. I can remember my mother-in-law sitting by that little stove, sewing, before I married into this family, and I can remember her resisting her children's complaints that it was old-fashioned and embarrassing for them when they brought friends home.

Your Uncle Frazier and I decided to keep the stove, with its twisty old stovepipe and all, when we put in central heating. Then our own children began to protest constantly that the stove was embarrassing to have in the house in the modern age. At Martha's wedding, I had to close off the back parlor to keep her city friends from being offended by the sight of a little iron stove. Now all my children are putting wood-burning stoves into their homes. It's the modern thing to do.

It's the same with pickup trucks. I remember Martha asking her father to park the pickup out by the barn instead of in front of the house because it was so "country." Now she and her husband, a stockbroker, live in a fancy suburb and have a pickup truck for a second car.

I mentioned watching television, which we don't do a lot except in winter. Well, we saw a great show the other night. "A Tribute to Mother Maybelle Carter" with Johnny Cash and June, of course, and Waylon Jennings, Willie Nelson, Emmylou Harris, Lynn Anderson, Linda Ronstadt, people like that. On prime time, mind you.

Two of the children called long-distance, separately, to remind us to watch the show. Country music is "in" with bright young people these days, you see. I told 'em, I'm your mother—remember?—and I'm the one who had to turn off the "Grand Old Opry" when you had your sophisticated friends in the house.

Redneck music, they used to call it. Now it's on prime time. And you'd think the younger generation invented Willie and Waylon.

I really liked Ray Charles on that show, by the way. What a joyful man! My kind of redneck musician! There he was, Ray Charles in his tweeds, bobbing and swaying and taking his turn on

"Will the Circle Be Unbroken?" With Willie and Waylon and the rest, all in honor of Mother Maybelle.

The circle is unbroken, all right, and ever wider.

Well, I must close now. I've got to clean up the house and polish the stove in the back parlor. Martha and her husband are coming for the weekend. And they're taking us out square-dancing Saturday night! It's the "in" thing. They've had lessons.

Yours for progress,
AUNT GERTRUDE

Aunt Gertrude on World News

WASHINGTON—Aunt Gertrude, who keeps me informed about the view of world affairs from her rural community, has written another letter.

December 3, 1989

My dear nephew,

Miss Philleulah Murkley and Wade Fernley have not agreed on anything really significant since Miss Philly taught Wade in school and held the upper hand. The upper hand held a ruler. Since Wade grew up, their relationship has stabilized into a steady, grumpy, competitive standoff.

I have seen Miss Philly win a few rounds from Wade over the years, at public meetings and in debates at Frowzer's Grocery, but her best argument has always been her threat to go after him with her rolled-up umbrella. Wade never actually gives in, although he does shut up sometimes.

Their fiercest disagreements are about politics. Wade is conservative. He is so conservative that he could barely tolerate Ronald Reagan. His main gripe was Reagan's picking a "moderate Republican," George Bush, for vice president. Wade says a moderate Republican is worse than an outright Democrat, and some day he might even vote for a Democrat to prove he means it.

Miss Philly is our community's leading liberal, although she denies she's a Democrat. She just votes that way, she says, because the Republicans don't give her any choice. The last acceptable Republican on the national scene, she says, was Teddy Roosevelt. When Miss Philly was a little girl, her father took her into the booth with him while he voted for Teddy for president, and she has regarded herself as a moderate Republican ever since.

Naturally that just feeds Wade Fernley's prejudice, and that delights her, and that enrages him, and so they go along not getting along and making a point of it.

With that background, you will understand how stunned some of us were the other day when Miss Philly and Wade came into Frowzer's Grocery together and stood there together smiling at the group gathered around the checkout counter. It was such a sight that nobody said anything.

After a minute, Miss Philly elbowed Wade (elbowed him very gently, I remember thinking at the time), and he said he wanted to make an announcement, a "joint announcement" for the two of them. You could have heard a pin drop.

Wade said he and Miss Philly had agreed that events in Eastern Europe were "encouraging almost beyond belief," that Presidents Gorbachev and Bush were "doing a good job, even if we do have certain reservations," and that "everyone should wake up and realize that we are living through a time of historic change and new hope for the world."

Everyone in the grocery applauded and tried to focus on historic change in the world rather than on Wade and Miss Philly.

Then she spoke. Miss Philly said events still had to play themselves out and doubtless there were "dicey times ahead." Tom Frowzer asked if that applied to her and Wade. She told Tom he had a trivial mind with absolutely no sense of proportion, and she would thank him to let her finish her part of the joint announcement.

Miss Philly said she and Wade had agreed to suspend their animosity one day each week—Friday—and to meet on that day for an hour or so to "discuss and appreciate" what's going on in the world. The first meeting would be next week in the board room of Wade's bank and everyone was invited to join in. Everyone nodded and made assenting noises.

She went on to say that the meetings might have to be moved to the back room of the feed store, even to the volunteer fire department, if democratic reform in Eastern Europe and the Soviet Union continued apace and public interest picked up. Anyone who isn't avid about world events these days, she added, is a dope.

Miss Philly yielded the floor back to Wade. He said, speaking only for himself, that he thought everyone should stay away from the news in any form on the day of the meeting, at least until the meeting is over. There was some grumbling from news fans.

But Wade said changes in the communist world were coming so fast, new concessions, new government, new freedoms, along with summit meetings and meetings of Gorbachev and the pope and the like, that nobody had a chance to comprehend one day's astonishments before the next day's astonishments piled in on top of them.

So one period a week of no news at all would allow everybody to catch up. What did Miss Philly think of that?

Her first reaction, she said, was to call it one of the dumbest ideas she ever heard. But because this was the day of suspended animosity between her and Wade, she would call it one of the best ideas Wade ever had.

I won't tell you which side of the argument I took because it would only make a news guy mad.

Sincerely,
AUNT GERTRUDE

Selected Bibliography

Adams, Charles Follen. *Leedle Yawcob Strauss and Other Poems*. Boston: Lee and Shepard, 1878.

Alworth, E. Paul. *Will Rogers*. New York: Twayne, 1974.

Anderson, Sherwood. *The Buck Fever Papers*. Edited by Welford Dunaway Taylor. Charlottesville: Univ. Press of Virginia, 1971.

Anthony, Edward. *O Rare Don Marquis: A Biography*. Garden City, N.Y.: Doubleday, 1962.

Austin, James C. *Bill Arp*. New York: Twayne, 1969.

Bier, Jesse. *The Rise and Fall of American Humor*. New York: Holt, 1968.

Bing, Phil C. *The Country Weekly: A Manual for the Rural Journalist and for Students of the Country Field*. New York: D. Appleton, 1917.

Blair, Walter. *Horse Sense in American Humor from Benjamin Franklin to Ogden Nash*. Chicago: Univ. of Chicago Press, 1942.

_____. *Native American Humor*. 1937. Reprint. San Francisco: Chandler, 1960.

Blair, Walter, and Hamlin Hill. *America's Humor: From Poor Richard to Doonesbury*. New York: Oxford, 1978.

Blair, Walter, and Raven I. McDavid, eds. *Mirth of a Nation: America's Great Dialect Humor*. Minneapolis: Univ. of Minnesota Press, 1983.

Bleyer, William Grosvenor. *Main Currents in the History of American Journalism*. Boston: Houghton Mifflin, 1927.

Bond, Richmond P. "Isaac Bickerstaff, Esq." In *Restoration and Eighteenth-Century Literature*, edited by Carroll Camden, 103–24. Chicago: Univ. of Chicago Press, 1963.

_____. *The Tatler: The Making of a Literary Periodical*. Cambridge, Mass.: Harvard Univ. Press, 1971.

_____, ed. *Studies in the Early English Periodical*. Chapel Hill: Univ. of North Carolina Press, 1957.

[Browne, Charles Farrar.] *Artemus Ward, His Book*. New York: Carleton, 1862.

[_____.] *Artemus Ward; His Travels*. New York: Carleton, 1865.

Buckingham, Joseph T. *Specimens of Newspaper Literature*. 2 vols. Boston: Charles C. Little and James Brown, 1850.

Cannon, Carl L. *Journalism: A Bibliography*. New York: N.Y. Public Library, 1924.

Capp, Bernard. *English Almanacs 1500–1800*. Ithaca: Cornell Univ. Press, 1979.

Clark, Thomas D. *The Rural Press and the New South*. Baton Rouge: Louisiana State Univ. Press, 1948.

_____. *The Southern Country Editor*. Indianapolis: Bobbs-Merrill, 1948.

Clark, William Bedford and W. Craig Turner, eds. *Critical Essays on American Humor*. Boston: G. K. Hall, 1984.

Clemens, Samuel L. *The Innocents Abroad*. Hartford: American Publishing, 1869.

Clemens, Will M. *Famous Funny Fellows.* London: W. Scott, 1893.

Cook, Elizabeth C. *Literary Influences in Colonial Newspapers, 1704–1750.* New York: Columbia Univ. Press, 1912.

Current-Garcia, Eugene. "Newspaper Humorists of the Old South." *Alabama Review* 2(April 1949): 102–21.

Cushing, William. *Anonyms; A Dictionary of Revealed Authorship.* Cambridge, Mass.: W. Cushing, 1889.

_____. *Initials & Pseudonyms; A Dictionary of Literary Disguises.* New York: Crowell, 1885.

Davis, Hallam Walker. *The Column.* New York: Alfred A. Knopf, 1926.

Demuth, James. *Small Town Chicago: The Comic Perspective of Finley Peter Dunne, George Ade, Ring Lardner.* Port Washington and London: Kennikat, 1980.

Dennie, Joseph. *The Lay Preacher.* New York: Scholars' Facsimiles and Reprints, 1943.

Dudden, Arthur P., ed. *The Assault of Laughter: A Treasury of American Political Humor.* New York: Yoseloff, 1962.

[Dunne, Finley Peter.] *Dissertations by Mr. Dooley.* London and New York: Harper, 1906.

[_____.] *Mr. Dooley in Peace and War.* Boston: Small, Maynard, 1898.

[_____.] *Mr. Dooley's Opinions.* New York: Russell, 1901.

[_____.] *Mr. Dooley's Philosophy.* New York: Russell, 1902.

Edson, C. L. *The Gentle Art of Columning.* New York: Brentano's, 1920.

Ellis, Elmer. *Mr. Dooley's America.* New York: Alfred A. Knopf, 1941.

Ferguson, DeLancey. *Mark Twain: Man and Legend.* Indianapolis and New York: Bobbs-Merrill, 1943.

_____. "On Humor as One of the Fine Arts." *South Atlantic Quarterly* 38(April 1939): 177–86.

Figh, Margaret Gillis. "Bartow Lloyd, Humorist and Philosopher of the Alabama Back Country." *Alabama Review* 5(April 1952): 83–99.

Forster, E. M. "Anonymity: An Enquiry." In *Two Cheers for Democracy,* 77–88. New York: Harcourt, Brace, 1951.

Franklin, Benjamin. *The Writings of Benjamin Franklin.* Edited by Albert Henry Smyth. Vol. 2. New York: Macmillan Company, 1907.

Freneau, Philip. *The Prose of Philip Freneau.* Edited by Philip M. Marsh. New Brunswick, N.J.: Scarecrow Press, 1955.

Gale, Steven H., ed. *Encyclopedia of American Humorists.* New York: Garland Publishing, 1988.

Gilot, Michel, Jean Sgard, et al. "Le Journaliste Masque: Personnages et Formes Personnelles." In *Le Journalisme d'Ancien Regime: Questions et Propositions,* 285–313. Lyon: Presses Universitaires de Lyon, 1982.

Gladden, Jack B. "M. Quad, A Lost American Humorist." *American Humor: An Interdisciplinary Newsletter* 3(Fall 1976): 5–7.

Hall, Wade H. *Reflections of the Civil War in Southern Humor.* Gainesville: Univ. of Florida Press, 1962.

_____. *The Smiling Phoenix: Southern Humor from 1865 to 1914.* Gainesville: Univ. of Florida Press, 1965.

Harris, George W. *Sut Lovingood. Yarns Spun by a Nat'ral Born Durn'd Fool. Warped and Wove for Public Wear.* New York: Dick & Fitzgerald, 1867.

Harris, Joel Chandler. *Uncle Remus and His Friends*. Boston and New York: Houghton, Mifflin, 1892.

Harrison, John M. *The Man Who Made Nasby, David Ross Locke*. Chapel Hill: Univ. of North Carolina Press, 1969.

Herzberg, Max J. *The Reader's Encyclopedia of American Literature*. New York: Crowell, 1962.

Hinkle, Olin, and John Henry. *How to Write Columns*. Ames, Iowa: Iowa State College Press, 1952.

Hubbard, Frank McKinney. *Abe Martin's Broadcast*. Indianapolis: Bobbs-Merrill, 1930.

_____. *Abe Martin's Primer*. Indianapolis: Abe Martin Publishing Company, 1914.

Hudson, Frederic. *Journalism in the United States*. New York: Harper, 1873.

Johnson, Philander Chase. *Sayings of Uncle Eben*. Washington, D.C.: Bauble, 1896.

_____. *Senator Sorghum's Primer of Politics*. Philadelphia: Henry Altemus, 1906.

Kesterson, David B. *Josh Billings (Henry Wheeler Shaw)*. New York: Twayne, 1973.

_____. "Those *Literary* Comedians." In *Critical Essays on American Humor*. Edited by William Bradford Clark and W. Craig Turner, 167–83. Boston: G. K. Hall, 1984.

Ketchum, Richard M. *Will Rogers, His Life and Times*. New York: American Heritage, 1973.

Kobre, Sidney. *Development of American Journalism*. Dubuque, Iowa: William C. Brown, 1969.

Landon, Melville D., ed. *Kings of the Platform and Pulpit*. Chicago: F. C. Smedley, 1891.

Lathem, Edward C., comp. *Chronological Tables of American Newspapers 1690–1820*. Barre, Mass.: American Antiquarian Society and Barre Publishers, 1972.

Lee, Lynn. *Don Marquis*. Boston: Twayne, 1981.

Lewis, Charles Bertrand [M. Quad and Brother Gardner, pseud.]. *Brother Gardner's Lime Kiln Club*. Chicago: Belford, Clark, 1882.

Lilly, Paul R., Jr. "Newspaper Humorists Look at Three American Wars." *Illinois Quarterly* 44(Summer 1982): 22–33.

Lindstrom, Carl E. *The Fading American Newspaper*. Garden City, N.Y.: Doubleday, 1960.

Linneman, William R. "Humorous Views of Yellow Journalism." *Studies in American Humor* 3(1976): 23–33.

_____. "Immigrant Stereotypes: 1880–1900." *Studies in American Humor* 1(1974): 28–39.

Lloyd, Francis Bartow. *Sketches of Country Life; Humor, Wisdom and Pathos from the 'Sage of Rocky Creek'*. Birmingham, Ala.: Roberts & Son, 1898.

Locke, David Ross. *The Struggles (Social, Financial and Political) of Petroleum Vesuvius Nasby*. Boston: Lee and Shepard, 1888.

Lowell, James Russell. *Writings*, 8 vols. Cambridge, Mass.: Houghton, Mifflin, 1893.

Lukens, Henry Clay. "American Literary Comedians." *Harper's Magazine* 80(April 1890): 1783-97.

Marquis, Don. *archy and mehitabel.* Garden City, N.Y.: Doubleday, Doran, 1927.

———. *archy s life of mehitabel.* Garden City, N.Y.: Doubleday, Doran, 1933.

———. *Hermione and Her Little Group of Serious Thinkers.* New York & London: Appleton, 1916.

———. *The Old Soak and Hail and Farewell.* Garden City, N.Y. and Toronto: Doubleday, Page, 1921.

———. *The Old Soak's History of the World.* Garden City, N.Y.: Doubleday, Page, 1924.

Matthews, Brander. "The Comic Periodical Literature of the United States." *American Bibliopolist* 7(August 1875): 199-201.

Meyer, Karl E. *Pundits, Poets, & Wits: An Omnibus of American Newspaper Columns.* New York and Oxford: Oxford, 1990.

Mott, Frank Luther. *American Journalism: A History of Newspapers in the United States through 250 Years, 1690-1940.* 1841. Reprint. New York: Macmillan, 1949.

Mott, George Fox, ed. *New Survey of Journalism.* New York: Barnes & Noble, 1950.

Nesbitt, W. D. "The Humor of Today." *Independent* 29 May 1902, 1300-4.

Newell, Robert Henry. *The Orpheus C. Kerr Papers.* New York: Blakemore & Mason, 1862.

Paneth, Donald. *The Encyclopedia of American Journalism.* New York: Facts on File, 1983.

Peck, George Wilbur. *Adventures of One Terence McGrant.* New York: Lambert, 1871.

Pickett, Calder. *Voices of the Past: Key Documents in the History of American Journalism.* Columbus, Ohio: Grid, 1977.

Pinsker, Sanford. "On or about December 1910: When Human Character—and American Humor—Changed." In *Critical Essays on American Humor.* Edited by William Bradford Clark and W. Craig Turner, 184-99. Boston: G. K. Hall, 1984.

Price, Warren C. *The Literature of Journalism: An Annotated Bibliography.* Minneapolis: Univ. of Minnesota Press, 1959.

Price, Warren C., and Calder M. Pickett. *An Annotated Journalism Bibliography: 1959-1968.* Minneapolis: Univ. of Minnesota Press, 1970.

Rickels, Milton. "The Grotesque Body of Southwestern Humor." In *Critical Essays on American Humor.* Edited by William Bradford Clark and W. Craig Turner, 155-66. Boston: G. K. Hall, 1984.

Rickels, Patricia, and Milton Rickels. *Seba Smith.* Boston: Twayne, 1977.

Rogers, Will. *Convention Articles of Will Rogers.* Vol. 2 of *The Writings of Will Rogers.* Edited by Joseph A. Stout, Jr., et al. Stillwater: Oklahoma State Univ. Press, 1976.

———. *Daily Telegrams.* Edited by James M. Smallwood et al. Ser. 3, vols. 1-3 of *The Writings of Will Rogers.* Stillwater: Oklahoma State Univ. Press, 1978-1979.

———. *The Illiterate Digest.* New York: Albert & Charles Boni, 1935.

———. *Will Rogers' Weekly Articles.* Edited by James M. Smallwood et al.

Ser. 4, vols. 1 and 3 of *The Writings of Will Rogers.* Stillwater: Oklahoma State Univ. Press, 1980.

Sappenfield, James A. *A Sweet Introduction: Franklin's Journalism as a Literary Apprenticeship.* Carbondale and Edwardsville: Southern Illinois Univ. Press, 1973.

Shaw, Henry Wheeler. *The Complete Works of Josh Billings.* Rev. ed. New York: Dillingham, 1899.

Shaw, J. Thomas. "The Problem of the Persona in Journalism: Pushkin's Feofilakt Kisickin." In *American Contributions to the Fifth International Congress of Slavists* [Sofia, September, 1963], 301–25. Hague: Mouton, 1963.

Sims, Norman, ed. *The Literary Journalists.* New York: Ballantine, 1986.

Sloane, David E. *Mark Twain As a Literary Comedian.* Baton Rouge: Louisiana State Univ. Press, 1979.

Sloane, David E., ed. *American Humor Magazines and Comic Periodicals.* In *Historical Guides to the World's Periodicals and Newspapers.* New York: Greenwood Press, 1987.

Small, Samuel W. *Old Si's Sayings.* Chicago: Revell, 1886.

[Smith, Charles H.] *Bill Arp, So Called.* New York: Metropolitan Record Office, 1866.

[_____.] *Bill Arp's Scrap Book, Humor and Philosophy.* Atlanta: Harrison, 1884.

[Smith, Seba.] *The Life and Writings of Major Jack Downing.* Boston: Lily, Wait, Colman, & Holden, 1834.

Stewart, Kenneth, and John Tebbel. *Makers of Modern Journalism.* New York: Prentice-Hall, 1929.

Streeter, Edward. *Dere Mable.* New York: Dodd, Mead, 1941.

_____. *That's Me All Over, Mable.* New York: Frederick A. Stokes, 1919.

Tandy, Jeanette. *Crackerbox Philosophers in American Humor and Satire.* New York: Columbia Univ. Press, 1925.

[Thompson, William T.] *Major Jones's Courtship and Travels.* Philadelphia: Peterson, [1848].

Tourtellot, Arthur Bernon. *Benjamin Franklin: The Shaping of a Genius: The Boston Years.* New York: Doubleday, 1977.

Townsend, Edward W. *Chimmie Fadden Explains, Major Max Expounds.* New York: U.S. Book Company, 1895.

Trachtenberg, Stanley, ed. *American Humorists, 1800–1950.* 2 vols. Detroit: Gale, 1982.

Van Doren, Carl. "Day In and Day Out." *Century* 107(December 1923): 308–15.

Visscher, William Lightfoot. *Ten Wise Men and Some More.* Chicago: Atwell, 1909.

Watson, Melvin R. *Magazine Serials and the Essay Tradition, 1746–1820.* Baton Rouge: Louisiana State Univ. Press, 1956.

Weisberger, Bernard A. *The American Newspaperman.* Chicago: Univ. of Chicago Press, 1961.

Wheeler, Otis. "William Tappan Thompson." In *Southern Writers: A Biographical Dictionary,* edited by Robert Bain, Joseph M. Flora, and Louis D. Rubin, 453–54. Baton Rouge: Louisiana State Univ. Press, 1979.

Whitcher, Frances M. *The Widow Bedott Papers.* New York: Hurst, 1883.
_____. *Widow Spriggins, Mary Elmer and Other Sketches.* New York: Carleton, 1867.
Williams, Kenny J., and Bernard Duffey, eds. *Chicago's Public Wits.* Baton Rouge: Louisiana State Univ. Press, 1983.
Wolseley, Roland E. *The Journalist's Bookshelf.* Philadelphia: Chilton, 1939.
Wroth, Lawrence C. *William Parks: Printer and Journalist of England and Colonial America.* Richmond: Appeals Press, 1926.
Wyman, Mary Alice. *Two American Pioneers: Seba Smith and Elizabeth Oakes Smith.* New York: Columbia Univ. Press, 1927.
Yates, Norris W. *William T. Porter and "The Spirit of the Times."* Baton Rouge: Louisiana State Univ. Press, 1957.

Index

All fictional names are stated Christian name first and are enclosed in quotation marks.